The Fox LSAT

LOGIC GAMES PLAYBOOK

Nathan Fox

Design by Eric Uhlich

Published by Avocado Books,
Los Angeles, California

ISBN: 978-1-5309-5629-6

WELCOME

Many new LSAT students do fine in reading comprehension and logical reasoning but get flummoxed by the logic games. Future lawyers of America are sometimes skittish about anything that seems remotely math or science-y. "I can handle the verbal stuff, but what the hell am I supposed to do with *this*?" Never fear. Your logic games skills are the easiest to improve, and you are absolutely not limited by your starting proficiency. Take a deep breath. We got this.

How To Use This Book

The purpose of this book is to give you a playbook for tackling the LSAT's Logic Games. The basic agenda is this:

1) Try each game on your own. Go ahead and write on the pages, like you'll do on the actual exam. (There's no scratch paper on the LSAT, so you have to write on the test itself.) I recommend using a real wooden pencil, like you'll do on test day. On your first attempt on each game, you might totally crash and burn. That's fine! We're here to learn, and making mistakes is a big part of that.

2) Watch me do it. Each game is accompanied by step-by-step instructions on how I would approach each game and build each diagram. Then, you'll find full explanations for how to solve each question with 100% certainty. This is your playbook. Study it!

3) Practice what you've learned. Playbooks don't help unless you practice the plays. So after you're pretty sure you understand my explanations, you'll have two opportunities to practice what you've learned. Immediately following the explanations you'll find two more copies of the same game. It doesn't matter whether you do the games again right away, or the next day, or next week. Just do them. I recommend writing directly on the games themselves, like you'll do on test day. You'll find the games much easier the second and third time around. Refer back to the explanations if you get stuck.

The Logic Games section is the place where you can improve your score the most, by far. It's not uncommon for a student to go from four or five correct on a Logic Games section on the first night of class to 19 or 20 correct a few weeks later. Right now you're probably intimidated. But early in this book you'll say, "Wow, Nathan makes it look easy." And by the end of the book you'll say, "Oh, that's because it really is easy." That's the most satisfying thing a teacher can hear.

A QUICK NOTE ABOUT TIMING: Frequently students ask how long it should take them on each game, or what the "average" time is for any given game. But I don't like to put specific numbers on it. In my experience, it's more fruitful to concentrate on accuracy, not speed. If you can get accurate, it's easy to get fast. But it doesn't work the other way around. If you try to go fast, the test will always seem hard to you, and you'll keep stumbling. So take however long it takes. Don't look at the questions until you're sure you understand the rules. Don't pick an answer until you're confident that it's correct. If you're just starting out, it might take 35 minutes to solve a single game. Doesn't matter. If you got them all right, that's a victory because the test is starting to make sense. Once you get in the habit of carefully figuring out the answers, with certainty, you'll start to realize how easy the games actually are. Then, without even trying, you'll start to go fast. That is how you make the giant improvements that I see so often in my classes.

This book is divided into groups, and I can't take credit for them. Here's a quick note from my Thinking LSAT Podcast co-host Ben Olson, who teaches very popular LSAT classes in Washington, D.C. He created the groups, so I'll let him explain them:

FOREWORD REGARDING GAME GROUPING: To get better at the games, it often helps to repeat games that you've done before until you master them. But doing the same game over and over again can get a little tedious. It helps to do a few other games in between.

So a few years ago, I started organizing the games into groups. I wanted to give my students a simple way to work on several games at once. And I've been happy with the results.

Instead of doing the same game back-to-back, students will often do all the games in the first group once or twice. At that point, they will then go back and repeat the games that were hard or that took too long. Granted, if one of the games seems unusually hard to you, you might decide to repeat it a few times right away. In short, be flexible.

As you work on mastering the games in the first group, you can start doing the games in the second group. But I wouldn't finish the second group until you've mastered the first. The groups are roughly organized by difficulty. The second group, for example, is slightly harder than the first; the third is slightly harder than the second; and so on.

By the way, you'll probably remember the correct answers for many of the games you repeat. That's okay. The goal here is not to simply choose the right answer, but to prove why it's correct. If you can do that the second or third time you tackle a game, you're doing it right.

So take your time and have fun.

Ben Olson

strategyprep.com

GROUP 1

GROUP 1, GAME 1

A closet contains exactly six hangers—1, 2, 3, 4, 5, and 6—hanging, in that order, from left to right. It also contains exactly six dresses—one gauze, one linen, one polyester, one rayon, one silk, and one wool—a different dress on each of the hangers, in an order satisfying the following conditions:

The gauze dress is on a lower-numbered hanger than the polyester dress.
The rayon dress is on hanger 1 or hanger 6.
Either the wool dress or the silk dress is on hanger 3.
The linen dress hangs immediately to the right of the silk dress.

1. Which one of the following could be an accurate matching of the hangers to the fabrics of the dresses that hang on them?

(A) 1: wool; 2: gauze; 3: silk; 4: linen; 5: polyester; 6: rayon
(B) 1: rayon; 2: wool; 3: gauze; 4: silk; 5: linen; 6: polyester
(C) 1: polyester; 2: gauze; 3: wool; 4: silk; 5: linen; 6: rayon
(D) 1: linen; 2: silk; 3: wool; 4: gauze; 5: polyester; 6: rayon
(E) 1: gauze; 2: rayon; 3: silk; 4: linen; 5: wool; 6: polyester

2. If both the silk dress and the gauze dress are on odd-numbered hangers, then which one of following could be true?

(A) The polyester dress is on hanger 1.
(B) The wool dress is on hanger 2.
(C) The polyester dress is on hanger 4.
(D) The linen dress is on hanger 5.
(E) The wool dress is on hanger 6.

3. If the silk dress is on an even-numbered hanger, which one of the following could be on the hanger immediately to its left?

(A) the gauze dress
(B) the linen dress
(C) the polyester dress
(D) the rayon dress
(E) the wool dress

4. If the polyester dress is on hanger 2, then which one of the following must be true?

(A) The silk dress is on hanger 1.
(B) The wool dress is on hanger 3.
(C) The linen dress is on hanger 4.
(D) The linen dress is on hanger 5.
(E) The rayon dress is on hanger 6.

5. Which one of the following CANNOT be true?

(A) The linen dress hangs immediately next to the gauze dress.
(B) The polyester dress hangs immediately to the right of the rayon dress.
(C) The rayon dress hangs immediately to the left of the wool dress.
(D) The silk dress is on a lower-numbered hanger than the gauze dress.
(E) The wool dress is on a higher-numbered hanger than the rayon dress.

6. Which one of the following CANNOT hang immediately next to the rayon dress?

(A) the gauze dress
(B) the linen dress
(C) the polyester dress
(D) the silk dress
(E) the wool dress

7. Assume that the original condition that the linen dress hangs immediately to the right of the silk dress is replaced by the condition that the wool dress hangs immediately to the right of the silk dress. If all the other initial conditions remain in effect, which one of the following must be false?

(A) The linen dress is on hanger 1.
(B) The gauze dress is on hanger 2.
(C) The wool dress is on hanger 4.
(D) The silk dress is on hanger 5.
(E) The polyester dress is on hanger 6.

GROUP 1, GAME 1 FROM PREPTEST 41, OCTOBER 2003

EXPLANATION

This game, from the October 2003 LSAT, is a great example of the type of game that absolutely everyone can master with enough practice. It's a *Linear* type and also the most common type of game. In fact, it's hard to find an LSAT that doesn't have at least one game like this, if not two or three. So if you're looking for a foothold, this is it.

As we walk through this game, step by step, follow along with us on a new sheet of paper. The best way to learn anything is to do it, not just read about it. Let's start with the rules:

A closet contains exactly six hangers—1, 2, 3, 4, 5, and 6—hanging, in that order, from left to right. It also contains exactly six dresses—one gauze, one linen, one polyester, one rayon, one silk, and one wool—a different dress on each of the hangers, in an order satisfying the following conditions:

- The gauze dress is on a lower-numbered hanger than the polyester dress.
- The rayon dress is on hanger 1 or hanger 6.
- Either the wool dress or the silk dress is on hanger 3.
- The linen dress hangs immediately to the right of the silk dress.

First, before you write anything, read the setup, which is just the first paragraph above, and all the rules. This will give you a 40,000-foot overview, and save you needless erasing. Measure twice, cut once. Reread everything, if necessary. Ask yourself: *What's going on here? What's our main task?* Most games require us to put things in order, put things in groups, or do both simultaneously. Here, we're only asked to put things in order. With practice, this type of game will become very familiar. Let's dive in.

To solve the games efficiently, we need to draw a picture. It's not that we *can't* do this in our heads; it's simply faster to write things down, freeing up our limited brain resources for other operations. So on the page, let's draw the following:

G L P R S W

All we've done so far is write down the list of variables, the six slots from left to right, and the four rules.

It's better to write things that we know for sure, so let's change "R must go first or last" into "R can't go second, third, fourth, or fifth." We'll write things that positively must be true on top of the lines (W or S must completely fill the third spot) and we'll write things that *can't* be true below the lines. (R can't go 2-5.)

With rules like "G is on a lower number than P," we'll represent them spatially. Because lower numbers go to the left, and higher numbers go to the right, the notation "G...P" means "G must go somewhere to the left of P," perhaps immediately to the left of P or perhaps several slots to the left of P.

With rules like "S one lower than L," we won't use the dots. The notation "SL" means that they're right next to each other, in that order.

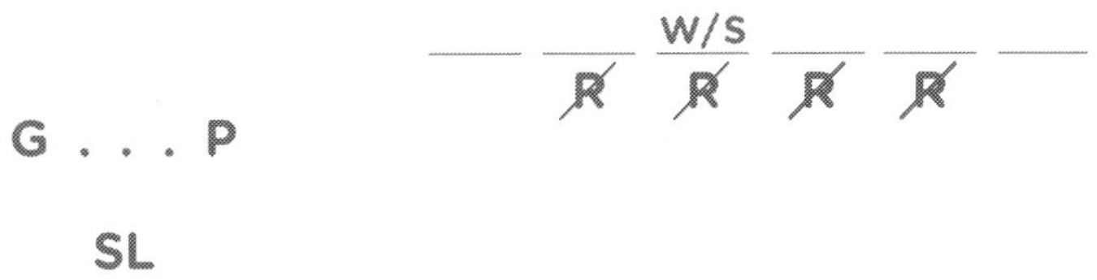

G . . . P

SL

_ _ W/S _ _
R̸ R̸ R̸ R̸

At this point, many students will dive straight into the questions. This is a mistake. Instead, first try to solve the system, at least partially. The rules don't exist in a vacuum; they intersect and interact with each other. These overlaps and connections allow you to figure certain things out, sometimes answering questions before those questions are even asked. This process is called "making inferences," but don't be fooled into thinking that this is some kind of mystical, magical process. It's really just common sense. Watch:

First-Order Inferences

A journey of a thousand miles begins with a single step, or some such sentimental bullshit. The point is, let's start with baby steps. The rule "G before P" has two immediate implications: P can't go first, and G can't go last. These might be obvious, but our goal is to document everything we can about the game. If we add stuff to our diagram, we don't have to hold it in our brain. If we don't have to hold it in our brain, our brain is freed up to work on the trickier stuff.

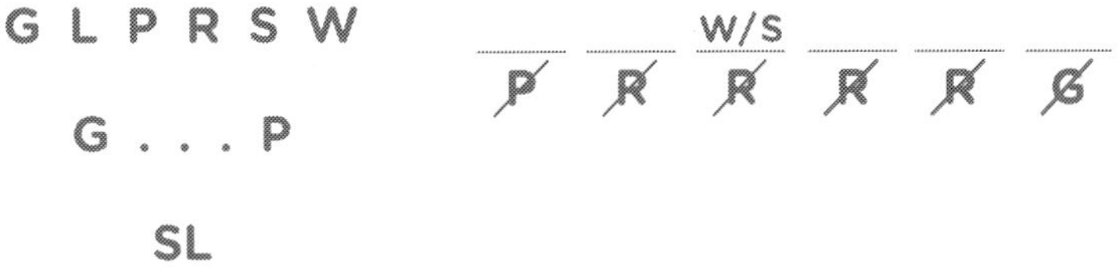

G L P R S W

G . . . P

SL

_ _ W/S _ _ _
P̸ R̸ R̸ R̸ R̸ G̸

Now, more baby steps. The rule "SL" has two immediate implications of its own: S can't go last, and L can't go first. Add these to the diagram as well.

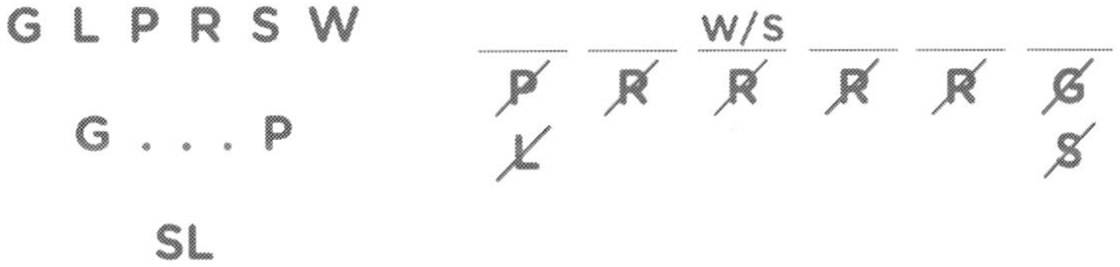

G L P R S W

G . . . P

SL

_ _ W/S _ _ _
P̸ R̸ R̸ R̸ R̸ G̸
L̸ S̸

For better or worse, we're going to call these *first-order inferences*.

Second-Order Inferences

After we've learned everything we can from looking at each rule, one at a time, we're going to move on to making bigger leaps. There's nothing earth-shattering here. The only difference is that, instead of looking each rule in isolation, we're going to look at what happens when two or more rules *interact with each other*.

Look at the "SL" rules and the "W or S must go third" rule, for example. The intersection of these two rules creates another rule: S can't go second. (If S were second, L would have to go third, but that's not possible because W or S must go third.) So let's add "S can't go second" to the diagram:

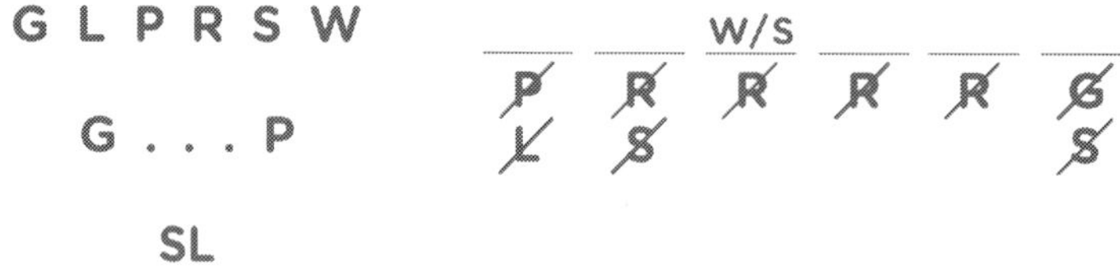

We'll refer to an inference like this one as a *second-order inference* because we needed to use at least two rules to make it.

Before we go to the questions, we want to stress something: All we're doing here is putting one foot in front of the other. Understand each rule, look at how the rules interact with each other, and write down everything that you know for sure. Good things will happen. It might not seem easy now, but it will soon.

QUESTION 1

Which one of the following could be an accurate matching of the hangers to the fabrics of the dresses that hang on them?

(A) 1: wool; 2: gauze; 3: silk; 4: linen; 5: polyester; 6: rayon
(B) 1: rayon; 2: wool; 3: gauze; 4: silk; 5: linen; 6: polyester
(C) 1: polyester; 2: gauze; 3: wool; 4: silk; 5: linen; 6: rayon
(D) 1: linen; 2: silk; 3: wool; 4: gauze; 5: polyester; 6: rayon
(E) 1: gauze; 2: rayon; 3: silk; 4: linen; 5: wool; 6: polyester

This type of question appears first in almost every game. Because it's so common, we need to answer it as efficiently as possible. The fastest, surest way is the process of elimination: Grab one rule and use it to eliminate any answer that violates it. Like this:

- **G before P.** That gets rid of C. Cross out C.
- **Rayon on 1 or 6.** A's okay, B's okay, we don't have to look at C because C's already dead, D's okay, but E breaks this rule. Cross out E.
- **Wool or silk on hanger 3.** A's okay, B's out because of this rule. D's okay.
- **S immediately before L.** A's okay, but D is out because of this rule.

Having systematically tested all the rules in the game, we've eliminated C, E, B, and then D.

Our answer, with 100% certainty, is A.

This is the level of certainty you should be shooting for in the games. The Logic Games don't involve guesswork. If you're not sure, then you're usually not doing it right.

QUESTION 2

If both the silk dress and the gauze dress are on odd-numbered hangers, then which one of the following could be true?

(A) The polyester dress is on hanger 1.
(B) The wool dress is on hanger 2.
(C) The polyester dress is on hanger 4.
(D) The linen dress is on hanger 5.
(E) The wool dress is on hanger 6.

When a question starts with the word "If," we make a new diagram. We started with G here, since there are only two odd hangers where G can go:

If G is first, then S will have to go third or fifth. Let's split the "G first" scenario into two:

G _ S L _ R

~~G _ W _ S L~~

Why the cross-out? Just as quickly as we created the "G first, S fifth" world, that world dies. If S is fifth, then L is sixth, but with G first and L last, R, which must go first or last, is screwed. So we cross this world out. Don't erase; crossing out is faster.

In the world where G is first and S is third, L goes fourth and R goes last. This leaves us with P and W, which can flip-flop between the second and fifth spots:

G W/P S L P/W R

In the world where G goes fifth, S must go third which means L must go fourth. Since G has to go before P, P has to go last, which forces R to go first, leaving only W for the second spot:

R W S L G P

So as it turns out, we've got two ways to put both G and S on odd hangers. Once again, here they are:

G W/P S L P/W R

R W S L G P

That took some time, but we got there taking nothing but baby steps. And now it will be trivial to answer the question.

A) Nope, P was never first in our two scenarios. This is out.
B) Well, yeah, this happens for sure in the second scenario. It's possible in the first scenario as well. This definitely looks like something that could be true. At this point in the test, given how clearly the two scenarios lay things out, we'd probably just pick this answer and move on. But for now, check the other answers to see why they're wrong.
C) Nope, L is fourth in both worlds.
D) Nope, L is fourth.
E) Nope, W wasn't last in either world.

Our answer is B.

It's the only one that could be true in either of the two scenarios (or "worlds") that we created for this question. It just so happens that it could be true in both scenarios, but it only had to be possible in one of them to be correct.

QUESTION 3

If the silk dress is on an even-numbered hanger, which one of the following could be on the hanger immediately to its left?

(A) the gauze dress
(B) the linen dress
(C) the polyester dress
(D) the rayon dress
(E) the wool dress

Look back at our initial diagram. This is where our "inferences" pay off. Our diagram says that S can't go second and sixth. (If you don't remember why, reread how we created the main diagram.) But *why* isn't so important here; we need to trust our diagram—which is why it's important to go slow and get them right. If S can't go second and it can't go sixth, then the only way to put it on an even hanger is to put it fourth, which would put L fifth. That would also put W third, since if S doesn't go third, W has to. Like this:

Because the question asked specifically about the spot immediately to the left of S, the answer must be W.

So our answer is E.

QUESTION 4

If the polyester dress is on hanger 2, then which one of the following must be true?

(A) The silk dress is on hanger 1.
(B) The wool dress is on hanger 3.
(C) The linen dress is on hanger 4.
(D) The linen dress is on hanger 5.
(E) The rayon dress is on hanger 6.

If P is second, then two things immediately happen: G goes first (G before P), and R goes last (R first or last).

G P __ __ __ R

There are two ways to go from here, which we'd quickly sketch:

G P W S L R

G P S L W R

From here, the answer is simple:

A) Not only does this not have to be true, it *can't be true.* Next contestant.
B) This *can* be true, but it doesn't have to be. We're looking for something that *must* be true whenever P is second.
C) Same thing. This *can* be true, but doesn't have to be .
D) Can be true, not must be true.
E) Yep. This has to be true in both of our scenarios.

Our answer is E.

At this point, students will often say something like "But Nathan, you overcomplicated this question with your two diagrams. You knew that R must go sixth right off the bat, why didn't you just pick it immediately?" That's a fair question, but the approach above is the best way to do it. When we're given a new condition, it's best to carry that new condition as far as it will take us *before* looking at the answer choices. Splitting the diagram into two worlds—GPWSLR and GPSLWR—was a trivial matter that took five seconds. As it happened, it was overkill. *But overkill is absolutely fine here.* Our goal isn't to shave off every single second. If we tried to do that, we'd frequently find ourselves going "Oh, let's check the answers. Did we get it? No, okay, let's do one more step and check the answers again. Did we get it *now?* No, let's go back to the diagram again then..." This is an obvious waste of time.

Instead, by taking the new rule as far as it will take us, we can answer the question confidently once we dive into the answer choices. The correct answer won't always be so simple. Instead of "W on hanger 3," the correct answer to this "must be true" question could easily have been something like "either L or W must go next to R." If we hadn't split our diagram in two, we wouldn't have been as confident. So what if we did a tad more work than was strictly necessary this time? It's a small investment to make, and it will pay off on harder questions. You want to get in the habit of having thorough diagrams you can depend on. Generally speaking (and this applies to the entire test, not just the games), *we are not looking for shortcuts.*

In my experience, there are two extremes: Some students read the new rule, blink, and then dive recklessly into the answers. Other students read the new rule, try to make inferences, and then never give up until they completely fill out their diagram for that question, which is often impossible. Both extremes usually take longer than the middle road that we're trying to advocate here: Try to make as many inferences as you can *until you hit a wall*. When you hit that wall, you can either split your diagram or dive into the answers. If there's an obvious split, take it. If not, dive into the answers.

QUESTION 5

Which one of the following CANNOT be true?

(A) The linen dress hangs immediately next to the gauze dress.
(B) The polyester dress hangs immediately to the right of the rayon dress.
(C) The rayon dress hangs immediately to the left of the wool dress.
(D) The silk dress is on a lower-numbered hanger than the gauze dress.
(E) The wool dress is on a higher-numbered hanger than the rayon dress.

Unlike questions 2, 3, and 4, this question doesn't give us anything new to work with. So, we're not going to make a new diagram. Instead, we're going to use our previous work to help eliminate answer choices. We're asked to identify something that CANNOT be true. So anything that's been true in any previous question can't possibly be the answer. Watch:

A) L was right next to G in one of the scenarios we created for question 2. As long as our scenarios for that question were valid, this can't be the answer for question 5. Note that we'll need to be very careful and methodical throughout the game in order for this approach to work. If we missed question 2, we might miss this one as well. Also, remember how we crossed out the world that didn't work in that question? We crossed it out so we wouldn't refer back to it later.
B) This hasn't happened in any of our previous scenarios. That doesn't instantly make this the answer, but it does make it a very a strong suspect. Let's leave this for now, and see if we can eliminate C, D, and E from the lineup. If we can, then B will be the guy we're looking for.
C) RW also happened in one of our scenarios for question 2. So this isn't the answer.
D) S...G *also* happened in one of our scenarios for question 2. This is out.
E) R...W *also* happened in one of our scenarios for question 2. (Thank you, question 2! The work we did for it just made question 5 much easier.)

Our answer is B because we were able to eliminate four answers that *can* be true. Note that we don't actually need to prove that B cannot be true as long as we see why answers A, C, D, and E are definitely wrong,

It has to be B.

QUESTION 6

Which one of the following CANNOT hang immediately next to the rayon dress?

(A) the gauze dress
(B) the linen dress
(C) the polyester dress
(D) the silk dress
(E) the wool dress

Again, we'll lean on our previous work here: *Who has been able to hang right next to R?* From the correct answer for question 1—WGSLPR—we know that P *can* go next to R, and therefore can't be the answer for question 6. Our scenarios for question 2 show W next to R, so that's out as well. And in question 4, we saw L next to R.

If the answer isn't P, W, or L, it must be G or S. So let's just test one of them. It's not immediately apparent why R G_ _ _ _ would cause a problem, so let's switch our attention to S.

R S L _ _ _ wouldn't work, since the third spot has to be W or S. And _ _ _ _ S R doesn't work either, since it leaves no room for L. So the one that can't go next to R is definitely S.

Our answer is D.

QUESTION 7

Assume that the original condition that the linen dress hangs immediately to the right of the silk dress is replaced by the condition that the wool dress hangs immediately to the right of the silk dress. If all the other initial conditions remain in effect, which one of the following must be false?

(A) The linen dress is on hanger 1.
(B) The gauze dress is on hanger 2.
(C) The wool dress is on hanger 4.
(D) The silk dress is on hanger 5.
(E) The polyester dress is on hanger 6.

Here, we're getting rid of one of the original rules, and replacing it with a different one. Instead of SL, we have SW. The rule that one of them must go third, however, still applies, along with all the other rules. That leaves us with two scenarios, which we should quickly sketch:

__ __ S W __ __

__ S W __ __ __

We're still not sure whether R goes first or last in either of these scenarios, so some flexibility remains. It looks tough to go any deeper into these sketches without creating four (or more) scenarios, so let's just dive into the answer choices.

A) It's hard to see why this would be a problem. Instead of testing it to make sure it works, though, let's just move on to the next answer. If all else fails, we'll eventually come back later. But what can't be true will often jump out at us when we see it, so there's no point in wasting more time testing this one until we've looked at all the answers.
B) Same thing here. Why wouldn't this work?
C) This can definitely happen.
D) Oh, yeah, this definitely *can't* happen. Our two scenarios are the only ways to have "SW" without violating the rule that either S or W must go third. Let's just glance at E, quickly.
E) Hard to see a problem with this.

Our answer is D.

Our scenarios for this question have proven that it can't happen.

This is an extremely common and easy-to-learn logic game. If you're really struggling with the games, this is the easiest place to start getting a grasp. If you're already getting pretty good at the games, this one is still worth mastering, since this is the game that you'll learn to crush in five minutes. And that will free up time to invest in harder games. No matter who you are, *you must master this game.*

GROUP 1, GAME 1

FROM PREPTEST 41, OCTOBER 2003

GROUP 1, GAME 1
EXTRA PRACTICE

A closet contains exactly six hangers—1, 2, 3, 4, 5, and 6—hanging, in that order, from left to right. It also contains exactly six dresses—one gauze, one linen, one polyester, one rayon, one silk, and one wool—a different dress on each of the hangers, in an order satisfying the following conditions:

The gauze dress is on a lower-numbered hanger than the polyester dress.
The rayon dress is on hanger 1 or hanger 6.
Either the wool dress or the silk dress is on hanger 3.
The linen dress hangs immediately to the right of the silk dress.

1. Which one of the following could be an accurate matching of the hangers to the fabrics of the dresses that hang on them?

(A) 1: wool; 2: gauze; 3: silk; 4: linen; 5: polyester; 6: rayon
(B) 1: rayon; 2: wool; 3: gauze; 4: silk; 5: linen; 6: polyester
(C) 1: polyester; 2: gauze; 3: wool; 4: silk; 5: linen; 6: rayon
(D) 1: linen; 2: silk; 3: wool; 4: gauze; 5: polyester; 6: rayon
(E) 1: gauze; 2: rayon; 3: silk; 4: linen; 5: wool; 6: polyester

2. If both the silk dress and the gauze dress are on odd-numbered hangers, then which one of following could be true?

   (A) The polyester dress is on hanger 1.
   (B) The wool dress is on hanger 2.
   (C) The polyester dress is on hanger 4.
   (D) The linen dress is on hanger 5.
   (E) The wool dress is on hanger 6.

3. If the silk dress is on an even-numbered hanger, which one of the following could be on the hanger immediately to its left?

   (A) the gauze dress
   (B) the linen dress
   (C) the polyester dress
   (D) the rayon dress
   (E) the wool dress

4. If the polyester dress is on hanger 2, then which one of the following must be true?

   (A) The silk dress is on hanger 1.
   (B) The wool dress is on hanger 3.
   (C) The linen dress is on hanger 4.
   (D) The linen dress is on hanger 5.
   (E) The rayon dress is on hanger 6.

5. Which one of the following CANNOT be true?

   (A) The linen dress hangs immediately next to the gauze dress.
   (B) The polyester dress hangs immediately to the right of the rayon dress.
   (C) The rayon dress hangs immediately to the left of the wool dress.
   (D) The silk dress is on a lower-numbered hanger than the gauze dress.
   (E) The wool dress is on a higher-numbered hanger than the rayon dress.

6. Which one of the following CANNOT hang immediately next to the rayon dress?

   (A) the gauze dress
   (B) the linen dress
   (C) the polyester dress
   (D) the silk dress
   (E) the wool dress

7. Assume that the original condition that the linen dress hangs immediately to the right of the silk dress is replaced by the condition that the wool dress hangs immediately to the right of the silk dress. If all the other initial conditions remain in effect, which one of the following must be false?

   (A) The linen dress is on hanger 1.
   (B) The gauze dress is on hanger 2.
   (C) The wool dress is on hanger 4.
   (D) The silk dress is on hanger 5.
   (E) The polyester dress is on hanger 6.

GROUP 1, GAME 1
EXTRA PRACTICE

A closet contains exactly six hangers—1, 2, 3, 4, 5, and 6—hanging, in that order, from left to right. It also contains exactly six dresses—one gauze, one linen, one polyester, one rayon, one silk, and one wool—a different dress on each of the hangers, in an order satisfying the following conditions:

The gauze dress is on a lower-numbered hanger than the polyester dress.
The rayon dress is on hanger 1 or hanger 6.
Either the wool dress or the silk dress is on hanger 3.
The linen dress hangs immediately to the right of the silk dress.

1. Which one of the following could be an accurate matching of the hangers to the fabrics of the dresses that hang on them?

(A) 1: wool; 2: gauze; 3: silk; 4: linen; 5: polyester; 6: rayon
(B) 1: rayon; 2: wool; 3: gauze; 4: silk; 5: linen; 6: polyester
(C) 1: polyester; 2: gauze; 3: wool; 4: silk; 5: linen; 6: rayon
(D) 1: linen; 2: silk; 3: wool; 4: gauze; 5: polyester; 6: rayon
(E) 1: gauze; 2: rayon; 3: silk; 4: linen; 5: wool; 6: polyester

2. If both the silk dress and the gauze dress are on odd-numbered hangers, then which one of following could be true?

   (A) The polyester dress is on hanger 1.
   (B) The wool dress is on hanger 2.
   (C) The polyester dress is on hanger 4.
   (D) The linen dress is on hanger 5.
   (E) The wool dress is on hanger 6.

3. If the silk dress is on an even-numbered hanger, which one of the following could be on the hanger immediately to its left?

   (A) the gauze dress
   (B) the linen dress
   (C) the polyester dress
   (D) the rayon dress
   (E) the wool dress

4. If the polyester dress is on hanger 2, then which one of the following must be true?

   (A) The silk dress is on hanger 1.
   (B) The wool dress is on hanger 3.
   (C) The linen dress is on hanger 4.
   (D) The linen dress is on hanger 5.
   (E) The rayon dress is on hanger 6.

5. Which one of the following CANNOT be true?

   (A) The linen dress hangs immediately next to the gauze dress.
   (B) The polyester dress hangs immediately to the right of the rayon dress.
   (C) The rayon dress hangs immediately to the left of the wool dress.
   (D) The silk dress is on a lower-numbered hanger than the gauze dress.
   (E) The wool dress is on a higher-numbered hanger than the rayon dress.

6. Which one of the following CANNOT hang immediately next to the rayon dress?

   (A) the gauze dress
   (B) the linen dress
   (C) the polyester dress
   (D) the silk dress
   (E) the wool dress

7. Assume that the original condition that the linen dress hangs immediately to the right of the silk dress is replaced by the condition that the wool dress hangs immediately to the right of the silk dress. If all the other initial conditions remain in effect, which one of the following must be false?

   (A) The linen dress is on hanger 1.
   (B) The gauze dress is on hanger 2.
   (C) The wool dress is on hanger 4.
   (D) The silk dress is on hanger 5.
   (E) The polyester dress is on hanger 6.

GROUP 1, GAME 2

A loading dock consists of exactly six bays numbered 1 through 6 consecutively from one side of the dock to the other. Each bay is holding a different one of exactly six types of cargo—fuel, grain, livestock, machinery, produce, or textiles. The following apply:

The bay holding grain has a higher number than the bay holding livestock.
The bay holding livestock has a higher number than the bay holding textiles.
The bay holding produce has a higher number than the bay holding fuel.
The bay holding textiles is next to the bay holding produce.

6. Which one of the following lists could accurately identify the cargo held in each of the loading dock's first three bays, listed in order from bay 1 to bay 3?

(A) fuel, machinery, textiles
(B) grain, machinery, fuel
(C) machinery, livestock, fuel
(D) machinery, textiles, fuel
(E) machinery, textiles, produce

7. Which one of the following CANNOT be the type of cargo held in bay 4?

(A) grain
(B) livestock
(C) machinery
(D) produce
(E) textiles

8. If there is exactly one bay between the bay holding machinery and the bay holding grain, then for exactly how many of the six bays is the type of cargo that bay is holding completely determined?

(A) two
(B) three
(C) four
(D) five
(E) six

9. Which one of the following could be the bay holding livestock?

(A) bay 1
(B) bay 2
(C) bay 3
(D) bay 5
(E) bay 6

10. Which one of the following must be false?

(A) The bay holding fuel is next to the bay holding machinery.
(B) The bay holding grain is next to the bay holding machinery.
(C) The bay holding livestock is next to the bay holding fuel.
(D) The bay holding produce is next to the bay holding livestock.
(E) The bay holding textiles is next to the bay holding fuel.

11. If the bay holding produce is next to the bay holding livestock, then each of the following could be true EXCEPT:

(A) Bay 2 is holding fuel.
(B) Bay 4 is holding produce.
(C) Bay 4 is holding textiles.
(D) Bay 5 is holding grain.
(E) Bay 5 is holding machinery.

12. If bay 4 is holding produce, then for exactly how many of the six bays is the type of cargo that bay is holding completely determined?

(A) two
(B) three
(C) four
(D) five
(E) six

EXPLANATION

If you mastered game 1, then this game shouldn't present a problem. *It's essentially the exact same thing.* The secret about the LSAT is that there is absolutely no secret; the patterns constantly repeat. As this book goes to print, there are roughly 80 official LSAT practice tests in distribution, each of which was the official test in its day. This game, which is from 2003, is *exactly* the type of thing you can expect to see on the day of the test. Keep practicing, and you're sure to improve.

Old tests repeating themselves is just like law school. In my 1L year, I was shocked to learn that I could go to the law library and check out, even photocopy, the final exams from my professors in previous years. In some classes, there were so many old finals available that it was possible, even advisable, to ignore the prof's reading assignments and exclusively study the old exams. Read the cases, and you'll sound smart in class. This counts for 0% of your grade. Read the exams, and you'll sound smart on the final, which determines 100% of your grade. You should read both, of course, but with limited time, there's no doubt which one you should emphasize. I read a little bit of both during my 1L year and got middling grades. I read neither during my 2L and 3L years, but still comfortably graduated. (Law schools want tuition money.)

Just like game 1, we're putting six things in order. Just like game 1, our attack will be:

1) Look at each rule individually.
2) Look at how the rules *interact.*
3) Attack the questions.

Let's go.

If you ever feel stuck, the first thing to do is simply write down your list of variables. We know for sure that our six players are FGLMPT, so we'll write them down. We'll then try to write down something else that we know for sure. There are six spots, so let's write that, too. So far, we've got:

F G L M P T ___ ___ ___ ___ ___ ___

G has a higher number than L. Because the higher numbers go to the right, G has to go somewhere to the right of L.

L ... G

L has a higher number than T. Interesting. L was also mentioned in the first rule. When we have two sequencing rules like we do here, we get to combine the rules together. Don't even bother writing T...L separately. Use L to weld the two rules together:

T ... L ... G

The next rule doesn't connect, so we have a choice: either write it separately or write *nothing*—for now—and then come back to it. Let's choose the second option here, since it looks like the fourth rule might help us tie in the third.

Sure enough, the fourth rule links to the second rule:

P T... L... G

New notation here: P and T go right next to each other—hence no dots between them—but they can go in either order—PT or TP. To show this flexibility, we'll draw a "handle" that connects them at the top. Imagine grabbing that handle and flipping them around; it shows that they can go back and forth.

We can now go back to the third rule and link it in via P. Adding that to our list, the final diagram looks like this:

F G L M P T ___ ___ ___ ___ ___ ___

F... P T... L ... G

M *

We've marked M with an asterisk because it's a "floater"—it's not explicitly constrained by any of the rules.

This chain is literally all we need on our page. Many students insist on writing each rule individually at first and *then* combining them together, but that's a bad habit. It wastes time and space. It also suggests that you're not thinking enough about the big picture. If we see connections, we leverage them *immediately.*

The rules, when linked together, become far more powerful than they are when they stand alone. Like Voltron. This tactic of combination is where the big inferences come from—and those big inferences will help increase your LSAT score.

I had completely forgotten about Voltron, so I figured some of you might need a refresher or, perhaps, an introduction. Wiki says it best, so I'll just give you the full quote: The first season, which aired in 1984, "featured a team of five young pilots commanding five robot lions [that] could be combined to form Voltron." Clearly applicable. Take note.

Check out F at the front of the diagram and G at the end. F and G are not directly related by any one rule, but the combined effect of *all* of the rules means that not only does F have to go before G, but F must go *far* before G because P, T, and L must be between them. Also, because only M can move around freely, there are only two places that F can go—first or second—and only two places that G can go—fifth or sixth.

This diagram is filled with all sorts of similar inferences. So many, in fact, that on a game like this one, we don't need to bother writing down all the baby steps like "G can't go first, second, third, or fourth." There are too many of them, and all of them are obvious with a quick glance at our chain of rules—once you get the hang of it, of course.

Generally, we *crush* this type of game. It's a simple matter of linking the rules together, which you can learn.

QUESTION 6

Which one of the following lists could accurately identify the cargo held in each of the loading dock's first three bays, listed in order from bay 1 to bay 3?

(A) fuel, machinery, textiles
(B) grain, machinery, fuel
(C) machinery, livestock, fuel
(D) machinery, textiles, fuel
(E) machinery, textiles, produce

Normally, we'd expect a full-list question here, since almost every game starts with one. Instead, this slight curveball is asking us for only the first three slots, in order. But that shouldn't be too much trouble. We know, from our diagram, that the correct answer cannot include L or G. Only F, P, T, and M are eligible to go in the first three spots. Let's scan for L and G to see if we can cross out some answers. Sure enough, that gets rid of both B and C.

Now let's check F before P. That gets rid of E.

P and T have to touch. That gets rid of D.

Having eliminated B, C, D, and E, our answer must be A. Next!

The questions for this game are a little different from the first one we covered, so we'll approach it differently as well. **From this point forward, we'll always do the list questions first and then do all the "if" questions before we do anything else.** So we'll skip question 7, and come back to it in a minute. The list questions generally only require applying the rules of the game, but we do the "if" questions before the others because they almost always give us a new mini-diagram that might help us answer the non-if questions. You'll get the hang of it, just watch.

Note: To avoid misbubbling your answer sheet, especially when you're skipping around like this, bubble in all the answers when you're done with a game. When we answer a question, we'll *circle* its letter—A, B, C, D, or E—on the page. And then, when we're about to turn the page, we'll stop and bubble in all the answers for that page. While we're at it, we'll double-check that we're bubbling in answers for the right numbers. In this case, that'd be questions 6 to 12. It's worth checking twice to avoid a mistake.

There's another, not-so-obvious reason to circle your answers for the entire game and *then* go to your bubble sheet. Many test centers, if not most, will put you in a auditorium chair with a small, fold-down desk. And by small, I mean smaller than 8.5" x 11" sheet of paper. Yes, smaller than your test. That means you'll probably slide your bubble sheet under your test while you're working on the questions. You don't want to slide out that sheet every time you answer a question.

DO THE "IF..." QUESTIONS FIRST

All credit for this technique goes to my Thinking LSAT Podcast co-host Ben Olson. (You met him in the foreword.) Ben taught me this tip after I'd already been teaching the LSAT for years; as an LSAT teacher, I never stop learning about this test. The awesome thing about this technique is that when it helps, it helps a lot. You'll see me employ it throughout the book. Here goes:

After doing the list question (usually the first question in every game), you'll notice that I then do all the questions that start with "If..." before circling back and doing everything else. I do this because 1) the "if" questions are often easier and 2) sometimes you can use the work you do on the "if" questions to eliminate wrong answers on other questions. Quick example. Let's say there's a rule that Clown X must get out of the clown car immediately before Clown Y. And let's say there's a question that starts out "if X gets out fifth, blah blah blah." In that case, Y obviously gets out sixth, right? Too easy. Of course, that doesn't mean that Y always goes sixth, because the "if" rule is only active for that one question. (The "if" rules do not accumulate, or apply to any other questions.) However, it does mean that in some cases, Y does go sixth. Y cannot be prohibited from going sixth, otherwise, the question itself would be invalid. So if another question asks something like "which of the following cannot go sixth," we would know right away, based on the "if" question we did earlier, that Y cannot be the answer for this question. Sometimes you can eliminate two, or three, or even all four wrong answers on a question like this by using the work you've already done on the list and "if" questions.

If that example doesn't make it immediately clear, don't panic. You'll see plenty of examples later in the book. For now, just notice that I'm doing the list question first (if there is one), then the "if" questions, then all the rest. This will make heaps more sense with lots and lots of practice. If it doesn't, blame Ben. ;)

QUESTION 8

If there is exactly one bay between the bay holding machinery and the bay holding grain, then for exactly how many of the six bays is the type of cargo that bay is holding completely determined?

(A) two
(B) three
(C) four
(D) five
(E) six

At first, it may seem like there are two ways to arrange the cargo so that M and G have exactly one bay between them— one where M is in a higher numbered bay than G and one where it's in a lower numbered bay. Let's try to create these two scenarios, starting with "M is higher than G":

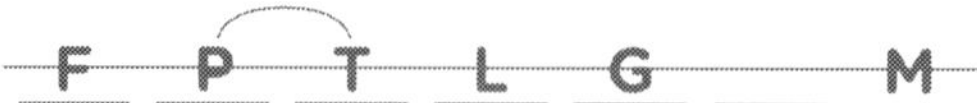

Whoops. M gets pushed off our game board by the force of our Voltron chain. The absolute lowest numbered bay G can go in is 5, and even that isn't enough to get M onto the board because it would require a seventh bay. There's just no way this scenario can happen, so we'll cross it out.

So now we know that for M and G to be exactly one bay apart, M must be in a lower numbered bay than G. In that case, G has to be in Bay 6, and our "M is lower than G" diagram looks like this:

Using this diagram, we can completely determine where each type of cargo goes except for P and T (they can switch freely between Bay 2 and 3).

Sure enough, the answer is four, or C.

QUESTION 11

If the bay holding produce is next to the bay holding livestock, then each of the following could be true EXCEPT:

(A) Bay 2 is holding fuel.
(B) Bay 4 is holding produce.
(C) Bay 4 is holding textiles.
(D) Bay 5 is holding grain.
(E) Bay 5 is holding machinery.

To create a scenario where P and L are touching, we'll need T to go immediately before P. F will have to go somewhere before that chunk, and G will have to go somewhere after that chunk. Like this:

F ... T P L ... G

M *

Note that M is still a floater in this scenario, although it won't be able to go third or fourth, since that would split up TPL. "Could be true EXCEPT" is saying the same thing as "which one must be false." So four of the answers could be true, and the one correct answer could *not* be true—that is, it must be false.

A) This would be fine if M were first. Next.
B) This would be fine if M were first or second.
C) Yeah, this can never happen. Even if M goes first or second, the latest that T is going to go in this scenario is third. This is our answer.
D) Possible, if M goes last.
E) Possible, if G goes last.

Our answer is C because it's the only one that won't work.

QUESTION 12

If bay 4 is holding produce, then for exactly how many of the six bays is the type of cargo that bay is holding completely determined?

(A) two
(B) three
(C) four
(D) five
(E) six

At first it looked like there might be two ways to do this—one with PT in bays 4 and 5 and one with TP in bays 3 and 4. Here's a quick diagram:

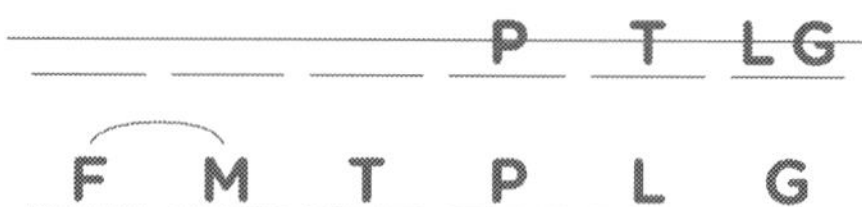

We've crossed out the first scenario, though, because there wasn't room in the sixth spot for both L and G. It's critical that we cross out this dead scenario, because we're going to use these mini-diagrams when we go back to the non-if questions. Note that they asked here "for exactly how many of the six bays can the type of cargo be completely determined and NOT "for exactly how many of the other bays" can the type of cargo be completely determined. For those that read through this question or the answer choices fast, they may have incorrectly identified the answer as three (B). However, we're better than that and we know that we have bays 3, 4, 5, and 6 all locked up here, while 1 and 2 still have some flexibility.

So the answer is four, or C.

Okay, back to the questions we skipped. The diagrams we just made for questions 8, 11, and 12 might help us now. Let's see.

QUESTION 7

Which one of the following CANNOT be the type of cargo held in bay 4?

(A) grain
(B) livestock
(C) machinery
(D) produce
(E) textiles

Actually, this one's easy even without looking at the mini-diagrams. Our main diagram shows us instantly that F can't go fourth, because there are four other players that have to follow it. Similarly G can't be fourth, because there are four other players that have to precede it. So the answer here could be either F or G. Scanning the answers, we see that only G is listed.

So our answer is A.

Mimic this approach as much as you can. It's a wonderful confidence booster and time saver when you can tell *them* what the answer has to be, even before you look at the answer choices.

QUESTION 9

Which one of the following could be the bay holding livestock?

(A) bay 1
(B) bay 2
(C) bay 3
(D) bay 5
(E) bay 6

Here we can quickly glance at all our mini-diagrams, looking for L. In question 8, L was fourth. In question 11, L could have gone fourth or fifth. In question 12, L was fifth. If one of the answers says fourth or fifth, that's our answer.

Yep, sure enough, the answer is D.

QUESTION 10

Which one of the following must be false?

(A) The bay holding fuel is next to the bay holding machinery.
(B) The bay holding grain is next to the bay holding machinery.
(C) The bay holding livestock is next to the bay holding fuel.
(D) The bay holding produce is next to the bay holding livestock.
(E) The bay holding textiles is next to the bay holding fuel.

Again, let's use the mini-diagrams on this one. But instead of using them to *find* the correct answer, as we did for question 9, let's use them to *eliminate* the wrong answers for this "must be false" question. Basically, anything that we've seen happen (or possibly happen) in a previous scenario must be eliminated because if something "must be false," then it must *always* be false and can *never* be true in any scenario. Let's see.

A) FM or MF could have happened in our diagrams for questions 11 and 12. This is out.
B) This could have happened in question 11. Out.
C) Oh, this is definitely the answer; our main diagram predicted this. The PT pair has to be between F and L, so F and L can't ever touch. This is the answer, but let's quickly scan D and E just to be 100% sure.
D) This had to happen in questions 11 and 12. No way.
E) Could have happened in questions 8 and 11. This is out.

Our answer is C, because it was proven false by our main diagram.

At this point, all the correct answers would be circled on the page. The next step is simply bubbling them all in on the score sheet—where we actually get credit—and moving on to the next game.

GROUP 1, GAME 2
EXTRA PRACTICE

A loading dock consists of exactly six bays numbered 1 through 6 consecutively from one side of the dock to the other. Each bay is holding a different one of exactly six types of cargo—fuel, grain, livestock, machinery, produce, or textiles. The following apply:

The bay holding grain has a higher number than the bay holding livestock.
The bay holding livestock has a higher number than the bay holding textiles.
The bay holding produce has a higher number than the bay holding fuel.
The bay holding textiles is next to the bay holding produce.

6. Which one of the following lists could accurately identify the cargo held in each of the loading dock's first three bays, listed in order from bay 1 to bay 3?

(A) fuel, machinery, textiles
(B) grain, machinery, fuel
(C) machinery, livestock, fuel
(D) machinery, textiles, fuel
(E) machinery, textiles, produce

7. Which one of the following CANNOT be the type of cargo held in bay 4?

(A) grain
(B) livestock
(C) machinery
(D) produce
(E) textiles

8. If there is exactly one bay between the bay holding machinery and the bay holding grain, then for exactly how many of the six bays is the type of cargo that bay is holding completely determined?

(A) two
(B) three
(C) four
(D) five
(E) six

9. Which one of the following could be the bay holding livestock?

(A) bay 1
(B) bay 2
(C) bay 3
(D) bay 5
(E) bay 6

10. Which one of the following must be false?

(A) The bay holding fuel is next to the bay holding machinery.
(B) The bay holding grain is next to the bay holding machinery.
(C) The bay holding livestock is next to the bay holding fuel.
(D) The bay holding produce is next to the bay holding livestock.
(E) The bay holding textiles is next to the bay holding fuel.

11. If the bay holding produce is next to the bay holding livestock, then each of the following could be true EXCEPT:

(A) Bay 2 is holding fuel.
(B) Bay 4 is holding produce.
(C) Bay 4 is holding textiles.
(D) Bay 5 is holding grain.
(E) Bay 5 is holding machinery.

12. If bay 4 is holding produce, then for exactly how many of the six bays is the type of cargo that bay is holding completely determined?

(A) two
(B) three
(C) four
(D) five
(E) six

GROUP 1, GAME 2
EXTRA PRACTICE

A loading dock consists of exactly six bays numbered 1 through 6 consecutively from one side of the dock to the other. Each bay is holding a different one of exactly six types of cargo—fuel, grain, livestock, machinery, produce, or textiles. The following apply:

The bay holding grain has a higher number than the bay holding livestock.
The bay holding livestock has a higher number than the bay holding textiles.
The bay holding produce has a higher number than the bay holding fuel.
The bay holding textiles is next to the bay holding produce.

6. Which one of the following lists could accurately identify the cargo held in each of the loading dock's first three bays, listed in order from bay 1 to bay 3?

(A) fuel, machinery, textiles
(B) grain, machinery, fuel
(C) machinery, livestock, fuel
(D) machinery, textiles, fuel
(E) machinery, textiles, produce

7. Which one of the following CANNOT be the type of cargo held in bay 4?

   (A) grain
   (B) livestock
   (C) machinery
   (D) produce
   (E) textiles

8. If there is exactly one bay between the bay holding machinery and the bay holding grain, then for exactly how many of the six bays is the type of cargo that bay is holding completely determined?

   (A) two
   (B) three
   (C) four
   (D) five
   (E) six

9. Which one of the following could be the bay holding livestock?

   (A) bay 1
   (B) bay 2
   (C) bay 3
   (D) bay 5
   (E) bay 6

10. Which one of the following must be false?

    (A) The bay holding fuel is next to the bay holding machinery.
    (B) The bay holding grain is next to the bay holding machinery.
    (C) The bay holding livestock is next to the bay holding fuel.
    (D) The bay holding produce is next to the bay holding livestock.
    (E) The bay holding textiles is next to the bay holding fuel.

11. If the bay holding produce is next to the bay holding livestock, then each of the following could be true EXCEPT:

    (A) Bay 2 is holding fuel.
    (B) Bay 4 is holding produce.
    (C) Bay 4 is holding textiles.
    (D) Bay 5 is holding grain.
    (E) Bay 5 is holding machinery.

12. If bay 4 is holding produce, then for exactly how many of the six bays is the type of cargo that bay is holding completely determined?

    (A) two
    (B) three
    (C) four
    (D) five
    (E) six

GROUP 1, GAME 3

One afternoon, a single thunderstorm passes over exactly five towns—Jackson, Lofton, Nordique, Oceana, and Plattesville—dropping some form of precipitation on each. The storm is the only source of precipitation in the towns that afternoon. On some towns, it drops both hail and rain; on the remaining towns, it drops only rain. It passes over each town exactly once and does not pass over any two towns at the same time. The following must obtain:

The third town the storm passes over is Plattesville.
The storm drops hail and rain on the second town it passes over.
The storm drops only rain on both Lofton and Oceana.
The storm passes over Jackson at some time after it passes over Lofton and at some time after it passes over Nordique.

12. Which one of the following could be the order, from first to fifth, in which the storm passes over the towns?

(A) Lofton, Nordique, Plattesville, Oceana, Jackson
(B) Lofton, Oceana, Plattesville, Nordique, Jackson
(C) Nordique, Jackson, Plattesville, Oceana, Lofton
(D) Nordique, Lofton, Plattesville, Jackson, Oceana
(E) Nordique, Plattesville, Lofton, Oceana, Jackson

13. If the storm passes over Oceana at some time before it passes over Jackson, then each of the following could be true EXCEPT:

(A) The first town the storm passes over is Oceana.
(B) The fourth town the storm passes over is Lofton.
(C) The fourth town the storm passes over receives hail and rain.
(D) The fifth town the storm passes over is Jackson.
(E) The fifth town the storm passes over receives only rain.

14. If the storm drops only rain on each town it passes over after passing over Lofton, then which one of the following could be false?

(A) The first town the storm passes over is Oceana.
(B) The fourth town the storm passes over receives only rain.
(C) The fifth town the storm passes over is Jackson.
(D) Jackson receives only rain.
(E) Plattesville receives only rain.

15. If the storm passes over Jackson at some time before it passes over Oceana, then which one of the following could be false?

(A) The storm passes over Lofton at some time before it passes over Jackson.
(B) The storm passes over Lofton at some time before it passes over Oceana.
(C) The storm passes over Nordique at some time before it passes over Oceana.
(D) The fourth town the storm passes over receives only rain.
(E) The fifth town the storm passes over receives only rain.

16. If the storm passes over Oceana at some time before it passes over Lofton, then which one of the following must be true?

(A) The third town the storm passes over receives only rain.
(B) The fourth town the storm passes over receives only rain.
(C) The fourth town the storm passes over receives hail and rain.
(D) The fifth town the storm passes over receives only rain.
(E) The fifth town the storm passes over receives hail and rain.

EXPLANATION

Don't panic, we're going from 2D to 3D. It's way easier than you think.

In our previous two games, we simply arranged six things in order. Here, we're only arranging *five* things—in this case, towns—in order. (Five is easier than six.) But we're also asked to figure out one more piece of information for each of those five towns—hail or no hail. This twist *seems* more difficult on the surface. More dimensions is harder, right? Not necessarily. In this game, the added dimension turns out to provide more certainty, and thus makes the game easier. Maybe you don't believe me yet, but just watch.

J L N O P ___ ___ ___ ___ ___

H / H̸ ___ ___ ___ ___ ___

As always, the first step is to write out the players and the slots. Because we have another dimension, we're including *two* lines for each position. On the top line, we'll write the name of the town. On the bottom line, we can write H and not H. Choosing H and not H is arbitrary. You could use R for "rain only" and H for "hail and rain." Or R and HR. Whatever, there are lots of ways to do it. Point is, we're going to write the name of the town on the top line, and the kind of precipitation on the bottom.

Next, let's deal with the rules. The first rule couldn't be easier—we simply write P into the third slot, like this:

Many students would insist on writing something like "P3" in the margin, but this is a waste of time and space. As much as possible, we're going to include the rules in our picture and let our brains solve this thing visually. There's no point in shorthanding a rule like this if we can completely capture it in our diagram visually.

Same thing with the second rule:

For the third and fourth rules, we'll need to write something in the margin. Like this:

Now we're going to make a really big inference. You ready? It's not that hard. Look at the second spot. We know it has to get hail. We also know that (1) neither L nor O can get hail, so they can't go second; (2) J has to go after both L and N, which means it can't go second; and (3) P has to go third, so obviously it can't go second either. Drumroll, please: If L, O, J, and P all can't go second, then the only remaining player, N, must go second. Let's go ahead and write that in.

Believe it or not, that last step is about as complicated as it's ever going to get in the logic games. We used every rule in the game to reach this inference. Many of your fellow test-takers will *not* make this leap. This is the difference between people who dominate the games and people who don't.

Stepping back, what prompted this leap? Whenever you see a negative rule—a rule that says something *can't* happen—look to see if there are any other negative rules affecting that spot. Here, the first clues were the negative rules that L and O can't go second. Negative rules are great by themselves, but several negative rules almost always leads to a positive rule—telling us what *must* happen.

With that behind us, we can go even further. Since J has to go later than N, it's forced into one of the last two spots. Let's write that in, with brackets and a comma. Like this:

___ N P (J , ___)

___ H ___ ___ ___

That leaves L and O for the first spot. And since neither of them can get hail, the first spot can't get hail either. Like this:

L/O N P (J , O/L)

~~H~~ H ___ ___ ___

We can put another O/L placeholder in the last two spots, where it will flip-flop with J. Remember here that though L can go first or fourth, L always has to go before J, and can never be last. O, however, can go in the first, fourth, or fifth spots. We don't get to make the inference about no hail, though, because we don't know exactly what spot the L/O will fall into. Our completed diagram:

J L N O P

H / ~~H~~

[L ~~H~~] [O ~~H~~]

[L ~~H~~] ··· J

N ··· J

L/O N P (J , O/L)

~~L~~ (under the last spot)

~~H~~ H ___ ___ ___

At this point, the game is basically over. Let's tackle the questions.

QUESTION 12

Which one of the following could be the order, from first to fifth, in which the storm passes over the towns?

(A) Lofton, Nordique, Plattesville, Oceana, Jackson
(B) Lofton, Oceana, Plattesville, Nordique, Jackson
(C) Nordique, Jackson, Plattesville, Oceana, Lofton
(D) Nordique, Lofton, Plattesville, Jackson, Oceana
(E) Nordique, Plattesville, Lofton, Oceana, Jackson

Our big inference crushes this question. (This game is, after all, ours.) Since N must go second, and since A is the only choice that has N in the second spot, the answer must be A. But let's go step-by-step here just to be sure. It's good practice, especially when you're just starting out, to go ahead and test all of the rules on a list question like this. Sometimes, we might discover that we've misunderstood something about the game. If we did, we'd want to learn that now instead of figuring it out after wasting a bunch of time.

P must be third. That gets rid of E.
Second town gets hail / L and O don't get hail. That gets rid of both B and D.
L and N before J. That gets rid of C.

That only took a second, and it double-confirms that the correct answer for this question is A. Let's move on.

QUESTION 13

If the storm passes over Oceana at some time before it passes over Jackson, then each of the following could be true EXCEPT:

(A) The first town the storm passes over is Oceana.
(B) The fourth town the storm passes over is Lofton.
(C) The fourth town the storm passes over receives hail and rain.
(D) The fifth town the storm passes over is Jackson.
(E) The fifth town the storm passes over receives only rain.

There are two ways to put O before J, which we can quickly sketch. The obvious one is to put O first (which would put L fourth and J fifth, since L always goes before J, like this:

But we could also put O fourth while J is fifth. Like this:

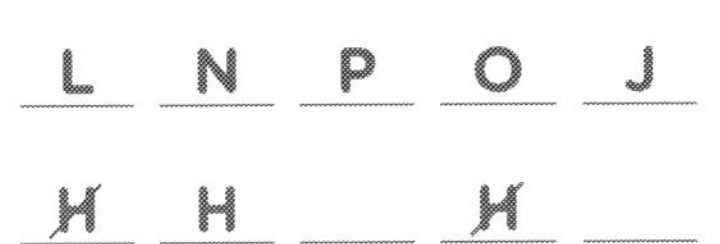

In both cases, J is fifth. Let's see, which one of these answers can't be true?

A) This can definitely work, we sketched this one out.
B) Yep, we've also got this on the page.
C) Nope. The fourth town can't get hail in either scenario, because L and O can't get hail.
D) Not only could this be true, but it *must* be true.
E) This could be true; we have no rule about whether J gets hail or not.

Our answer is C, because it can't be true in either scenario.

QUESTION 14

If the storm drops only rain on each town it passes over after passing over Lofton, then which one of the following could be false?

(A) The first town the storm passes over is Oceana.
(B) The fourth town the storm passes over receives only rain.
(C) The fifth town the storm passes over is Jackson.
(D) Jackson receives only rain.
(E) Plattesville receives only rain.

Since the second town gets hail, the only way to do this would be to put O first. L always goes before J, so L is fourth and J is fifth. That means for this question J can't get hail. Like this:

So the only thing we *don't* know, in this scenario, is whether or not P gets hail. Since the question is asking which one could be false, we might have an inkling that P is going to be involved. Let's scan the answer choices. Sure enough, one of them (E) is about P. Since P could get only rain, but could also get hail, we can be 99.99% sure that this is the correct answer. But let's get 100% certainty:

A) Yep, must be true.
B) Yep, must be true.
C) Yep, must be true.
D) Yep, must be true.

It really only takes 10 seconds to get rid of A-D. We're not in the business of trying to shave off 10 seconds, we're in the business of accurately answering all the questions.

Our answer is E.

QUESTION 15

If the storm passes over Jackson at some time before it passes over Oceana, then which one of the following could be false?

(A) The storm passes over Lofton at some time before it passes over Jackson.
(B) The storm passes over Lofton at some time before it passes over Oceana.
(C) The storm passes over Nordique at some time before it passes over Oceana.
(D) The fourth town the storm passes over receives only rain.
(E) The fifth town the storm passes over receives only rain.

The only way to put J before O is to put L first, J fourth, and O fifth. Like this:

It's another "could be false" question. Let's just go through all five answer choices in order this time.

A) Nope, this must be true.
B) Also must be true.
C) Also must be true.
D) This could be true or could be false, so it's probably the answer.
E) Must be true.

Our answer is D, because it's the only one of the five answer choices that could be false while J is before O.

QUESTION 16

If the storm passes over Oceana at some time before it passes over Lofton, then which one of the following must be true?

(A) The third town the storm passes over receives only rain.
(B) The fourth town the storm passes over receives only rain.
(C) The fourth town the storm passes over receives hail and rain.
(D) The fifth town the storm passes over receives only rain.
(E) The fifth town the storm passes over receives hail and rain.

To put O before L, O has to be first, L has to be fourth, and J has to be fifth. It's almost the same diagram as the one we made for #14, but be careful! In #14, J had to get only rain, no hail. There's no such restriction for this question. Look:

The question's a Must Be True. Let's see:

A) No, the third spot can get either type of weather.
B) This definitely has to be true. It's gotta be the answer.
C) Not only does this not have to be true, but it has to be false. Next.
D) No, the fifth spot can get either type of weather.
E) Like we just said, the fifth spot can get either type of weather.

Our answer is B, because it must be true and all the other choices could be false.

Adding the extra dimension wasn't so bad, was it? Not at all. If your instinct was to panic, just keep this question in mind. These are totally doable.

GROUP 1, GAME 3 FROM PREPTEST 46, JUNE 2005

GROUP 1, GAME 3
EXTRA PRACTICE

One afternoon, a single thunderstorm passes over exactly five towns—Jackson, Lofton, Nordique, Oceana, and Plattesville—dropping some form of precipitation on each. The storm is the only source of precipitation in the towns that afternoon. On some towns, it drops both hail and rain; on the remaining towns, it drops only rain. It passes over each town exactly once and does not pass over any two towns at the same time. The following must obtain:

The third town the storm passes over is Plattesville.
The storm drops hail and rain on the second town it passes over.
The storm drops only rain on both Lofton and Oceana.
The storm passes over Jackson at some time after it passes over Lofton and at some time after it passes over Nordique.

12. Which one of the following could be the order, from first to fifth, in which the storm passes over the towns?

(A) Lofton, Nordique, Plattesville, Oceana, Jackson
(B) Lofton, Oceana, Plattesville, Nordique, Jackson
(C) Nordique, Jackson, Plattesville, Oceana, Lofton
(D) Nordique, Lofton, Plattesville, Jackson, Oceana
(E) Nordique, Plattesville, Lofton, Oceana, Jackson

13. If the storm passes over Oceana at some time before it passes over Jackson, then each of the following could be true EXCEPT:

(A) The first town the storm passes over is Oceana.
(B) The fourth town the storm passes over is Lofton.
(C) The fourth town the storm passes over receives hail and rain.
(D) The fifth town the storm passes over is Jackson.
(E) The fifth town the storm passes over receives only rain.

14. If the storm drops only rain on each town it passes over after passing over Lofton, then which one of the following could be false?

(A) The first town the storm passes over is Oceana.
(B) The fourth town the storm passes over receives only rain.
(C) The fifth town the storm passes over is Jackson.
(D) Jackson receives only rain.
(E) Plattesville receives only rain.

15. If the storm passes over Jackson at some time before it passes over Oceana, then which one of the following could be false?

(A) The storm passes over Lofton at some time before it passes over Jackson.
(B) The storm passes over Lofton at some time before it passes over Oceana.
(C) The storm passes over Nordique at some time before it passes over Oceana.
(D) The fourth town the storm passes over receives only rain.
(E) The fifth town the storm passes over receives only rain.

16. If the storm passes over Oceana at some time before it passes over Lofton, then which one of the following must be true?

(A) The third town the storm passes over receives only rain.
(B) The fourth town the storm passes over receives only rain.
(C) The fourth town the storm passes over receives hail and rain.
(D) The fifth town the storm passes over receives only rain.
(E) The fifth town the storm passes over receives hail and rain.

GROUP 1, GAME 3
EXTRA PRACTICE

One afternoon, a single thunderstorm passes over exactly five towns—Jackson, Lofton, Nordique, Oceana, and Plattesville—dropping some form of precipitation on each. The storm is the only source of precipitation in the towns that afternoon. On some towns, it drops both hail and rain; on the remaining towns, it drops only rain. It passes over each town exactly once and does not pass over any two towns at the same time. The following must obtain:

The third town the storm passes over is Plattesville.
The storm drops hail and rain on the second town it passes over.
The storm drops only rain on both Lofton and Oceana.
The storm passes over Jackson at some time after it passes over Lofton and at some time after it passes over Nordique.

12. Which one of the following could be the order, from first to fifth, in which the storm passes over the towns?

(A) Lofton, Nordique, Plattesville, Oceana, Jackson
(B) Lofton, Oceana, Plattesville, Nordique, Jackson
(C) Nordique, Jackson, Plattesville, Oceana, Lofton
(D) Nordique, Lofton, Plattesville, Jackson, Oceana
(E) Nordique, Plattesville, Lofton, Oceana, Jackson

13. If the storm passes over Oceana at some time before it passes over Jackson, then each of the following could be true EXCEPT:

(A) The first town the storm passes over is Oceana.
(B) The fourth town the storm passes over is Lofton.
(C) The fourth town the storm passes over receives hail and rain.
(D) The fifth town the storm passes over is Jackson.
(E) The fifth town the storm passes over receives only rain.

14. If the storm drops only rain on each town it passes over after passing over Lofton, then which one of the following could be false?

(A) The first town the storm passes over is Oceana.
(B) The fourth town the storm passes over receives only rain.
(C) The fifth town the storm passes over is Jackson.
(D) Jackson receives only rain.
(E) Plattesville receives only rain.

15. If the storm passes over Jackson at some time before it passes over Oceana, then which one of the following could be false?

(A) The storm passes over Lofton at some time before it passes over Jackson.
(B) The storm passes over Lofton at some time before it passes over Oceana.
(C) The storm passes over Nordique at some time before it passes over Oceana.
(D) The fourth town the storm passes over receives only rain.
(E) The fifth town the storm passes over receives only rain.

16. If the storm passes over Oceana at some time before it passes over Lofton, then which one of the following must be true?

(A) The third town the storm passes over receives only rain.
(B) The fourth town the storm passes over receives only rain.
(C) The fourth town the storm passes over receives hail and rain.
(D) The fifth town the storm passes over receives only rain.
(E) The fifth town the storm passes over receives hail and rain.

GROUP 1, GAME 4

A company employee generates a series of five-digit product codes in accordance with the following rules:

The codes use the digits 0, 1, 2, 3, and 4, and no others.
Each digit occurs exactly once in any code.
The second digit has a value exactly twice that of the first digit.
The value of the third digit is less than the value of the fifth digit.

1. If the last digit of an acceptable product code is 1, it must be true that the

(A) first digit is 2
(B) second digit is 0
(C) third digit is 3
(D) fourth digit is 4
(E) fourth digit is 0

2. Which one of the following must be true about any acceptable product code?

(A) The digit 1 appears in some position before the digit 2.
(B) The digit 1 appears in some position before the digit 3.
(C) The digit 2 appears in some position before the digit 3.
(D) The digit 3 appears in some position before the digit 0.
(E) The digit 4 appears in some position before the digit 3.

3. If the third digit of an acceptable product code is not 0, which one of the following must be true?

(A) The second digit of the product code is 2.
(B) The third digit of the product code is 3.
(C) The fourth digit of the product code is 0.
(D) The fifth digit of the product code is 3.
(E) The fifth digit of the product code is 1.

4. Any of the following pairs could be the third and fourth digits, respectively, of an acceptable product code, EXCEPT:

(A) 0, 1
(B) 0, 3
(C) 1, 0
(D) 3, 0
(E) 3, 4

5. Which one of the following must be true about any acceptable product code?

(A) There is exactly one digit between the digit 0 and the digit 1.
(B) There is exactly one digit between the digit 1 and the digit 2.
(C) There are at most two digits between the digit 1 and the digit 3.
(D) There are at most two digits between the digit 2 and the digit 3.
(E) There are at most two digits between the digit 2 and the digit 4.

EXPLANATION

Some games, including this one, can be split into two templates or "worlds." You don't have to split it, but the best gamers will do so from time to time. Experts aggressively look for opportunities to execute an attack like the one you're about to see. When it works, it can bring a game to its knees. This game, which happens to be the first game in the June 2007 LSAT, isn't really all that challenging. But two worlds make it even easier, giving us more time for the harder games that come after it.

A company employee generates a series of five-digit product codes in accordance with the following rules:

- The codes use the digits 0, 1, 2, 3, and 4, and no others.
- Each digit occurs exactly once in any code.
- The second digit has a value exactly twice that of the first digit.
- The value of the third digit is less than the value of the fifth digit.

The rule that allows for this "two worlds" approach is the third one: "The second digit has a value exactly twice that of the first digit." Because our digits are only 0, 1, 2, 3, and 4, there are only two ways to have the second digit be twice the first:

1 2 __ __ __

2 4 __ __ __

That realization alone is enough to crush this game, but we can go further. To deal with the last rule--that the third spot is less than the fifth--we can draw arrows connecting the third and fifth spots, with little "less than" signs between them:

0 1 2 3 4

1 2 __ __ __ (third < fifth)

2 4 __ __ __ (third < fifth)

In our first world, the three remaining digits are 0, 3, and 4. The "less than" rule prevents 4 from going in the third spot and 0 from going in the fifth spot. That means the third spot must be 0 or 3, and the fifth spot must be 3 or 4.

0 1 2 3 4

1 2 0/3 __ 3/4 (third < fifth)

In our second world, on the other hand, the three remaining digits are 0, 1, and 3, which are also constrained by the "less than" rule. Because 3 can't go third and 0 can't go fifth, 0 or 1 must be third and 1 or 3 must be fifth:

2 4 0/1 __ 1/3 (third < fifth)

As it turns out, this game has very little flexibility. All conceivable scenarios are captured by our two worlds; there are no other possibilities. It's time to attack the questions.

QUESTION 1

If the last digit of an acceptable product code is 1, it must be true that the

(A) first digit is 2
(B) second digit is 0
(C) third digit is 3
(D) fourth digit is 4
(E) fourth digit is 0

The only way to make the last digit 1 would be in our second world. So let's use that world and incorporate the new rule:

2 4 ___ ___ 1

By the way, we do *not*—under any circumstances—write this new sketch on top of our original diagram. We need to keep our original diagram pristine to answer the other questions. The new condition "fifth digit is 1" applies to only question 1, so we're making a *new* mini-diagram to solve this question.

And now that we have this diagram, we can go further. Given that the third digit must be less than the fifth, 0 must go third, which forces 3 into the fourth spot:

2 4 0 3 1

It shouldn't be too tough to answer the question from here. We're asked to find what must be true.

A) Yes, the first digit is two. We went a couple steps further than necessary to solve this question, but that's going to happen sometimes. And it's not a wasted effort; we might return to this diagram when solving a later question. Let's just skim through B-E before we pick A.
B) No, the second digit is 4.
C) No, the third digit is 0.
D) No, the fourth digit is 3.
E) No, the fourth digit is 3.

Our answer is A.

QUESTION 3

If the third digit of an acceptable product code is not 0, which one of the following must be true?

(A) The second digit of the product code is 2.
(B) The third digit of the product code is 3.
(C) The fourth digit of the product code is 0.
(D) The fifth digit of the product code is 3.
(E) The fifth digit of the product code is 1.

Doing the "if" questions first, we'll skip question 2 for now. For question 3, we look at our two original worlds and realize that the third digit doesn't have to be 0 in either one. So we'll sketch two mini-diagrams for this question:

1 2 3 __ __

2 4 1 __ __

Because the fifth digit has to be greater than the third, that forces 4 into the last spot for our first scenario and 3 into the last spot for our second scenario. We can then fill in the only remaining number in both worlds, which happens to be 0:

1 2 3 0 4

2 4 1 0 3

Because we're asked to find a must be true, the correct answer must be true in *both* worlds.

Looking at our two scenarios, the only spot that's the same in both is the fourth one, which is 0. To save time, we scan the answers for 0 and quickly notice that answer C is the only one. That doesn't mean it's correct, of course. We have to read the entire answer. But doing so does confirm that it is correct.

As you get better at the games, you can move on. But for now, let's scan the rest of these answers to be sure we didn't miss anything:

A) No, this is only true in our first scenario.
B) No, this is only true in our first scenario.
C) Yes, this is true in both scenarios.
D) No, this is only true in our second scenario.
E) No, this isn't true in either scenario.

Our answer is C, after all.

QUESTION 2

Which one of the following must be true about any acceptable product code?

(A) The digit 1 appears in some position before the digit 2.
(B) The digit 1 appears in some position before the digit 3.
(C) The digit 2 appears in some position before the digit 3.
(D) The digit 3 appears in some position before the digit 0.
(E) The digit 4 appears in some position before the digit 3.

Having exhausted the "if" questions, we return to question 2. We're asked to find something that must be true, and this means must be true in *every* valid scenario, which now includes not only our two original worlds, but also the diagrams we drew for questions 1 and 3. Let's see.

A) No, this doesn't have to be true in the world that starts 2 4 _ _ _.
B) No, this didn't happen in our diagram for question 1.
C) Yep, our two templates start with 1 2 and 2 4. In both scenarios, digit 2 is in either the first or second spot and digit 3 has yet to appear. To be 100% sure, let's scan D and E.
D) No, this didn't happen in question 1.
E) This didn't happen in our first diagram for question 3.

Our answer is C, because it's *always* true in every scenario.

QUESTION 4

Any of the following pairs could be the third and fourth digits, respectively, of an acceptable product code, EXCEPT:

(A) 0, 1
(B) 0, 3
(C) 1, 0
(D) 3, 0
(E) 3, 4

We're looking for something that *won't* work in the third and fourth spots. So anything that *will* work in the third and fourth spots, in any of our existing scenarios, is out.

A) Haven't seen this happen yet. Let's leave it for now, and see if we can eliminate everything else. If we can, then we can choose this answer without even testing it.
B) This happened in our diagram for question 1. So this is out.
C) This happened in our second diagram for question 3. Also out.
D) This happened in our first diagram for question 3. Out.
E) Haven't seen this happen yet either. Let's quickly test A and E, and see which one won't work.

For answer A (_ _ 0 1 _) to work, we have to use the scenario that starts with 2 4:

2 4 0 1 3

That seems to work, so I bet the answer is E. Let's prove it.

For answer E (_ _ 3 4 _) to work, we have to use the scenario that starts with 1 2. Like this:

1 2 3 4 0

But in that scenario, we're breaking the rule that says the fifth digit has to be greater than the third. So 3, 4 isn't an acceptable scenario. We'll cross that scenario out, so we don't mistakenly assume that it's valid later.

Our answer is E.

2 4 1 0 3 ✓

~~1 2 3 4 0~~ X

QUESTION 5

Which one of the following must be true about any acceptable product code?

(A) There is exactly one digit between the digit 0 and the digit 1.
(B) There is exactly one digit between the digit 1 and the digit 2.
(C) There are at most two digits between the digit 1 and the digit 3.
(D) There are at most two digits between the digit 2 and the digit 3.
(E) There are at most two digits between the digit 2 and the digit 4.

Again, we're asked to identify something that must be true, and again this means something that is true *in all scenarios.* So we should be able to do a process of elimination here, knocking out any answer choices that were *not* true in any valid scenario.

A) This wasn't true in our first diagram for question 3.
B) This wasn't true in our diagram for question 1.
C) This is true in all of our special diagrams, but in our original first world—the one that starts with 1 & 2—it looks like 3 could have been last, which would violate this condition.
D) This wasn't true in our first scenario for question 4.
E) This is true in all of our mini-diagrams, and looking at our two worlds, it's always going to be true. In the first world, 2 is second, so even if 4 is last, there are still only two digits separating them. In the second world, 2 and 4 are right next to each other, so 2 and 4 are never going to be separated by more than two digits. This is our answer.

Our answer is E.

This game tends to throw some LSAT students for a loop simply because it has numbers and the "twice than" rule, which makes students' math-phobia kick in. But you couldn't have graduated from *third grade,* much less high school, and much less college, without this level of mathematical proficiency. Don't let it get in your head—it's an easy game as long as you don't panic.

We can say the same thing about many, many logic games. As professional LSAT teachers, we frequently hear our students say, "You make it look so easy!" By the time we're done with you, our hope is to convince you that the reason we make it look so easy is that it actually *is* easy.

GROUP 1, GAME 4
EXTRA PRACTICE

A company employee generates a series of five-digit product codes in accordance with the following rules:

The codes use the digits 0, 1, 2, 3, and 4, and no others.
Each digit occurs exactly once in any code.
The second digit has a value exactly twice that of the first digit.
The value of the third digit is less than the value of the fifth digit.

1. If the last digit of an acceptable product code is 1, it must be true that the

(A) first digit is 2
(B) second digit is 0
(C) third digit is 3
(D) fourth digit is 4
(E) fourth digit is 0

2. Which one of the following must be true about any acceptable product code?

(A) The digit 1 appears in some position before the digit 2.
(B) The digit 1 appears in some position before the digit 3.
(C) The digit 2 appears in some position before the digit 3.
(D) The digit 3 appears in some position before the digit 0.
(E) The digit 4 appears in some position before the digit 3.

3. If the third digit of an acceptable product code is not 0, which one of the following must be true?

(A) The second digit of the product code is 2.
(B) The third digit of the product code is 3.
(C) The fourth digit of the product code is 0.
(D) The fifth digit of the product code is 3.
(E) The fifth digit of the product code is 1.

4. Any of the following pairs could be the third and fourth digits, respectively, of an acceptable product code, EXCEPT:

(A) 0, 1
(B) 0, 3
(C) 1, 0
(D) 3, 0
(E) 3, 4

5. Which one of the following must be true about any acceptable product code?

(A) There is exactly one digit between the digit 0 and the digit 1.
(B) There is exactly one digit between the digit 1 and the digit 2.
(C) There are at most two digits between the digit 1 and the digit 3.
(D) There are at most two digits between the digit 2 and the digit 3.
(E) There are at most two digits between the digit 2 and the digit 4.

GROUP 1, GAME 4
EXTRA PRACTICE

A company employee generates a series of five-digit product codes in accordance with the following rules:

The codes use the digits 0, 1, 2, 3, and 4, and no others.
Each digit occurs exactly once in any code.
The second digit has a value exactly twice that of the first digit.
The value of the third digit is less than the value of the fifth digit.

1. If the last digit of an acceptable product code is 1, it must be true that the

(A) first digit is 2
(B) second digit is 0
(C) third digit is 3
(D) fourth digit is 4
(E) fourth digit is 0

2. Which one of the following must be true about any acceptable product code?

(A) The digit 1 appears in some position before the digit 2.
(B) The digit 1 appears in some position before the digit 3.
(C) The digit 2 appears in some position before the digit 3.
(D) The digit 3 appears in some position before the digit 0.
(E) The digit 4 appears in some position before the digit 3.

3. If the third digit of an acceptable product code is not 0, which one of the following must be true?

(A) The second digit of the product code is 2.
(B) The third digit of the product code is 3.
(C) The fourth digit of the product code is 0.
(D) The fifth digit of the product code is 3.
(E) The fifth digit of the product code is 1.

4. Any of the following pairs could be the third and fourth digits, respectively, of an acceptable product code, EXCEPT:

(A) 0, 1
(B) 0, 3
(C) 1, 0
(D) 3, 0
(E) 3, 4

5. Which one of the following must be true about any acceptable product code?

(A) There is exactly one digit between the digit 0 and the digit 1.
(B) There is exactly one digit between the digit 1 and the digit 2.
(C) There are at most two digits between the digit 1 and the digit 3.
(D) There are at most two digits between the digit 2 and the digit 3.
(E) There are at most two digits between the digit 2 and the digit 4.

GROUP 1, GAME 5

The Export Alliance consists of exactly three nations: Nation X, Nation Y, and Nation Z. Each nation in the Alliance exports exactly two of the following five crops: oranges, rice, soybeans, tea, and wheat. Each of these crops is exported by at least one of the nations in the Alliance. The following conditions hold:

None of the nations exports both wheat and oranges.
Nation X exports soybeans if, but only if, Nation Y does also.
If Nation Y exports rice, then Nations X and Z both export tea.
Nation Y does not export any crop that Nation Z exports.

18. Which one of the following could be an accurate list, for each of the nations, of the crops it exports?

(A) Nation X: oranges, rice; Nation Y: oranges, tea; Nation Z: soybeans, wheat
(B) Nation X: oranges, tea; Nation Y: oranges, rice; Nation Z: soybeans, wheat
(C) Nation X: oranges, wheat; Nation Y: oranges, tea; Nation Z: rice, soybeans
(D) Nation X: rice, wheat; Nation Y: oranges, tea; Nation Z: oranges, soybeans
(E) Nation X: soybeans, rice; Nation Y: oranges, tea; Nation Z: soybeans, wheat

19. If Nation X exports soybeans and tea, then which one of the following could be true?

    (A) Nation Y exports oranges.
    (B) Nation Y exports rice.
    (C) Nation Y exports tea.
    (D) Nation Z exports soybeans.
    (E) Nation Z exports tea.

20. If Nation Z exports tea and wheat, then which one of the following must be true?

    (A) Nation X exports oranges.
    (B) Nation X exports tea.
    (C) Nation X exports wheat.
    (D) Nation Y exports rice.
    (E) Nation Y exports soybeans.

21. It CANNOT be the case that both Nation X and Nation Z export which one of the following crops?

    (A) oranges
    (B) rice
    (C) soybeans
    (D) tea
    (E) wheat

22. Which one of the following pairs CANNOT be the two crops that Nation Y exports?

    (A) oranges and rice
    (B) oranges and soybeans
    (C) rice and tea
    (D) rice and wheat
    (E) soybeans and wheat

EXPLANATION

Just like our previous game, we're going to solve this one using two worlds. The key here is the second rule, which contains an "if and only if." (Actually, it says "if *but* only if," which nobody would ever say in real life, but it appears frequently on the LSAT, and it means the exact same thing.) We might not always dive into a two-world setup every time we see "if and only if," but since we're aggressively looking for opportunities to do so, we'll try when it looks like it might work. Here, it's going to work.

First, let's settle on the general setup for the game. We have three countries and five crops. It's usually better to use the smaller set for the "base" of the diagram, so the starting picture is going to look like this:

Next, let's attack the "if and only if" rule. The beauty of making two worlds based on this rule is that it *kills the rule*. Instead of having to remember the rule, and repeatedly apply it, we'll be left with one world in which both sides of the rule are true, and another world in which both sides are false. Your head might be spinning now, but you'll get the hang of it. Baby steps. Let's start with the two templates:

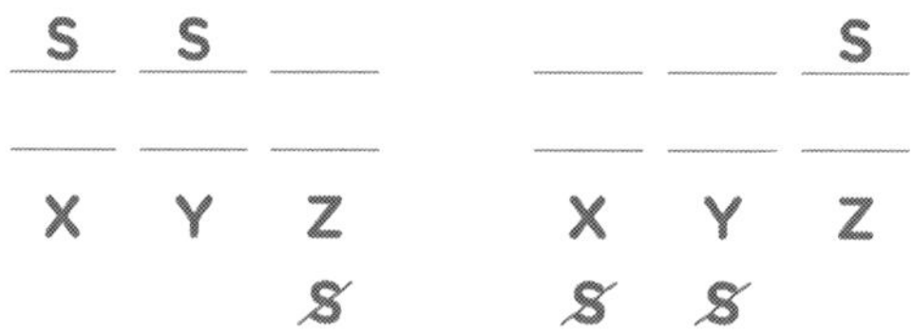

As you can see, in the left world we have affirmatively applied the rule—both X and Y export soybeans. Because we have five crops that have to be distributed and only six spots, we know that exactly one of the crops will go exactly twice (and not three times). So in our first world, nation Z can't have soybeans. Note that Nation Z couldn't have soybeans anyway because Y ≠ Z.

In our second world, neither X nor Y have soybeans; if either nation did, they would *both* need to have soybeans. But soybeans does have to go somewhere, so in this world, nation Z has to have soybeans.

Now let's deal with the other rules. The first rule is easy. O and W can't ever go together:

We're drawing this rule vertically, since it would be a vertical WO block if the two were grouped together under the same nation.

Next, we'll draw a conditional (if-then) notation for the third rule:

$Y^R \rightarrow X^T$, $Y^R \rightarrow Z^T$ ~~X^T~~ → ~~Y^R~~, ~~Z^T~~ → ~~Y^R~~

Three notes here, since this is our first look at conditional rules:

First, the notation → means "IF → THEN"

Second, it's a good habit to write the contrapositive every time we see an if-then rule. An expert might not do this every time, and we might not do it on every single game in this book, but if you're a novice or intermediate on the logic games, you need to do this.

Third, we're *splitting* the arrows here. The correct notation is *not* this:

$$Y^R \longrightarrow X^T Z^T$$

Change first sentence to read: That's a bad habit to get into, because later rules might involve only X^T or only Z^T, and if they did, we'd really like to be able to link those rules to this first rule. It doesn't happen in this game, but we'll see this happen soon. And when we do, we'll revisit this principle, since it's a common bad habit.

The final rule, Y and Z have nothing in common, can be denoted by an internal "not" arrow placed between the Y and Z, like this:

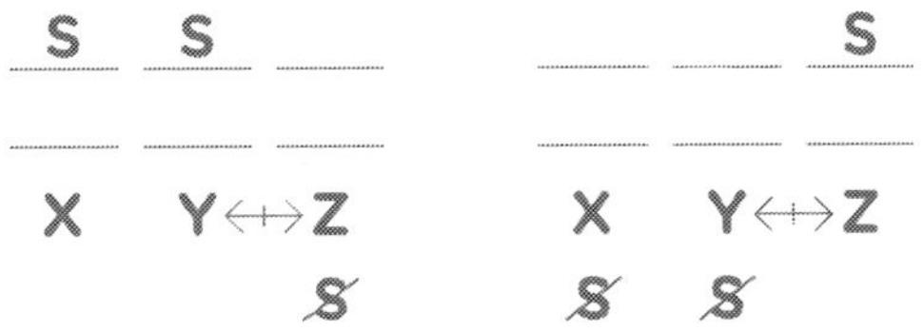

S S __   __ __ S

X Y↔Z   X Y↔Z

~~S~~   ~~S~~ ~~S~~

Finally, one big inference based on the third rule. If Y^R triggers T in two groups, then Y^R can't happen in our first world. This world is already exporting S twice, so R can't go in the Y group:

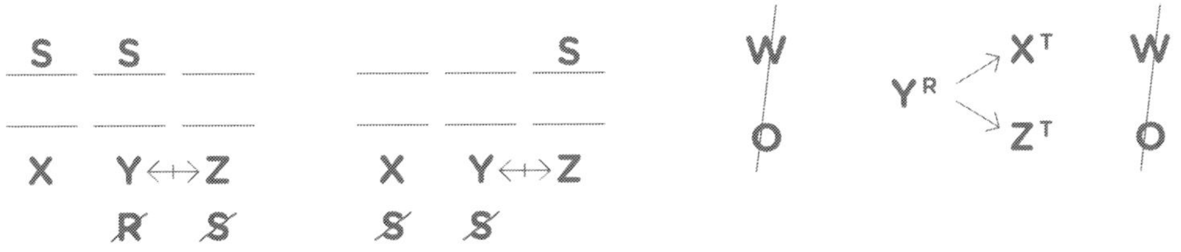

S S __   __ __ S   W/O $Y^R \rightarrow X^T$, $Y^R \rightarrow Z^T$ W/O

X Y↔Z   X Y↔Z

~~R~~ ~~S~~   ~~S~~ ~~S~~

That admittedly took several steps, and many students might think we've made the game more complicated. We've made it less complicated, however, in two ways: First, the "if and only if" rule has been eliminated by using two worlds. Second, the Y^R rule has been eliminated in the first world; we'll have to consider it only in the second world. Let's tackle the questions.

QUESTION 18

Which one of the following could be an accurate list, for each of the nations, of the crops it exports?

(A) Nation X: oranges, rice; Nation Y: oranges, tea; Nation Z: soybeans, wheat
(B) Nation X: oranges, tea; Nation Y: oranges, rice; Nation Z: soybeans, wheat
(C) Nation X: oranges, wheat; Nation Y: oranges, tea; Nation Z: rice, soybeans
(D) Nation X: rice, wheat; Nation Y: oranges, tea; Nation Z: oranges, soybeans
(E) Nation X: soybeans, rice; Nation Y: oranges, tea; Nation Z: soybeans, wheat

Process of elimination, as always. Grab a rule, eliminate as many answers as you can, and then move on to the next rule. Like this:

O and W are never together. This gets rid of C.
S in both X and Y, or neither X nor Y. This gets rid of E.
If Y^R, then X^T and Z^T. This gets rid of B.
Y and Z have nothing in common. This gets rid of D.

Our answer is A.

QUESTION 19

If Nation X exports soybeans and tea, then which one of the following could be true?

(A) Nation Y exports oranges.
(B) Nation Y exports rice.
(C) Nation Y exports tea.
(D) Nation Z exports soybeans.
(E) Nation Z exports tea.

If X has soybeans, that puts us squarely in our first world, where Y has soybeans as well. So our first step toward solving this question is this:

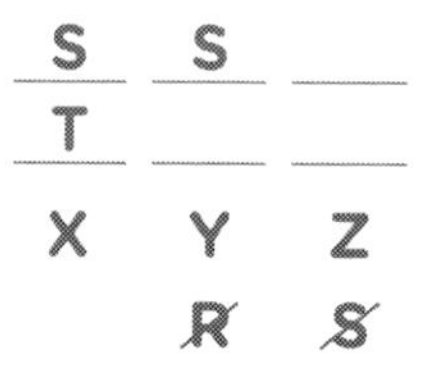

X	Y	Z
S	S	___
T	___	___
	~~R~~	~~S~~

The next step is an important little trick; you'll see it several times throughout the book. We'll call it "Seat the Assholes First." Here, the assholes are O and W. They're assholes because they don't like each other. Because S and T fill up the X group, we have only two groups left. O and W have to go somewhere, and they can't go together because, well, they're assholes. So we can go ahead and reserve one spot in each of the two remaining groups with a W/O. We don't know which one goes where, but one of them has to go in each spot. This leaves only one remaining spot for R:

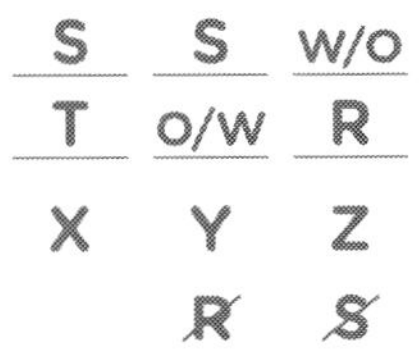

X	Y	Z
S	S	W/O
T	O/W	R
	~~R~~	~~S~~

Seat the assholes first! It's an extremely valuable technique in grouping games like this one. When you have only two open groups, look for two people who hate each other and then sit their asses down. This pattern has appeared on the LSAT for decades, and it continues to appear. It's a great example of how practicing old games *will* improve your score. Anyway, let's answer the question.

We're asked to identify something that could be true. So four answers will be conclusively false. Let's see.

A) O can go in either the Y group or the Z group, so this looks good. Let's eliminate answers B through E just to be 100% sure.
B) Nope, not if we're going to separate O and W.
C) No, having two players that go twice (both S and T) wouldn't leave enough room for everybody to appear at least once.
D) No, that would be three soybeans, which again wouldn't leave enough room for everybody to appear at least once.
E) Same explanation as C.

Our answer is A, because it's the only one of the five answers that could be true without breaking any of the rules.

QUESTION 20

If Nation Z exports tea and wheat, then which one of the following must be true?

(A) Nation X exports oranges.
(B) Nation X exports tea.
(C) Nation X exports wheat.
(D) Nation Y exports rice.
(E) Nation Y exports soybeans.

Oh boy, our two-worlds approach on this game kicks *so much ass.* Check out our two starting templates. Here they are again for convenience:

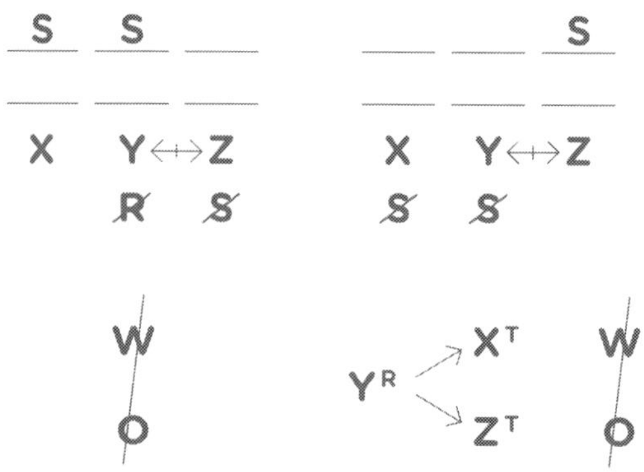

S	S	
X	Y↔Z	
	~~R~~	~~S~~

		S
X	Y↔Z	
~~S~~	~~S~~	

~~W~~ / ~~O~~

$Y^R \rightarrow X^T$, $Y^R \rightarrow Z^T$ ~~W~~ / ~~O~~

It's clear from our two worlds that in order for Z to have both T and W, we have to be in the first world. So we can immediately draw this sketch:

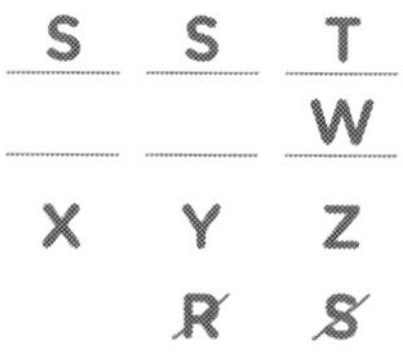

S	S	T
		W
X	Y	Z
	~~R~~	~~S~~

Next, we can place R in the X group, because it would be impossible to place R in the Y group due to the funky rule about Y^R. Putting R in the X group leaves only one place for O:

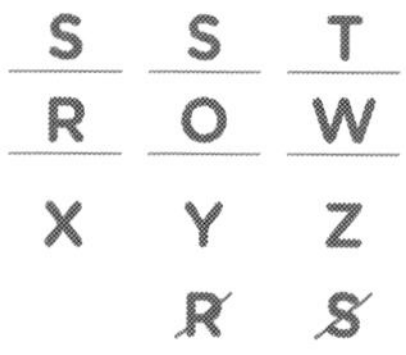

S	S	T
R	O	W
X	Y	Z
	~~R~~	~~S~~

So basically, we know everything. It's nice when that happens. The question asks for a Must Be True. Let's see...

A) No, this must be false.
B) No, this also must be false.
C) Again, must be false.
D) Also must be false.
E) Yep. Notice that, once again, we went a step or two further than necessary to answer the question. So what? It took five seconds, and helped us answer the question with 100% certainty.

Our answer is E.

QUESTION 21

It CANNOT be the case that both Nation X and Nation Z export which one of the following crops?

(A) oranges
(B) rice
(C) soybeans
(D) tea
(E) wheat

They're not giving us a new condition, so we're not making a mini-diagram. That sometimes indicates that the question is going to be hard. In this case, the question is relatively easy—if, of course, you understand the game. We're asked for a crop that can't be exported by both nation X and Z. The answer, which some readers might predict immediately, is soybeans.

Why? Well, if soybeans is exported by country X, then it also has to be exported by country Y. And if it were also exported by country Z, then there would be only three remaining slots, with four crops yet to be exported (and each crop has to go at least once). If soybeans is one of the answers, then it's *the* answer.

Sure enough, our answer is C.

QUESTION 22

Which one of the following pairs CANNOT be the two crops that Nation Y exports?

(A) oranges and rice
(B) oranges and soybeans
(C) rice and tea
(D) rice and wheat
(E) soybeans and wheat

This question's slightly tougher; most students will probably have to test some answer choices to figure this one out. But the one that *won't* work here is C, and it really boils down to just one rule. If nation Y has R, then nations X and Z have to have T. So nation Y can't have both R and T, because that would be three T's, and as we've seen, we can't ever have three of anything. Feel free to test the other answers; they all work.

Our answer is C, because it's the one that won't.

GROUP 1, GAME 5
EXTRA PRACTICE

The Export Alliance consists of exactly three nations: Nation X, Nation Y, and Nation Z. Each nation in the Alliance exports exactly two of the following five crops: oranges, rice, soybeans, tea, and wheat. Each of these crops is exported by at least one of the nations in the Alliance. The following conditions hold:

None of the nations exports both wheat and oranges.
Nation X exports soybeans if, but only if, Nation Y does also.
If Nation Y exports rice, then Nations X and Z both export tea.
Nation Y does not export any crop that Nation Z exports.

18. Which one of the following could be an accurate list, for each of the nations, of the crops it exports?

(A) Nation X: oranges, rice; Nation Y: oranges, tea; Nation Z: soybeans, wheat
(B) Nation X: oranges, tea; Nation Y: oranges, rice; Nation Z: soybeans, wheat
(C) Nation X: oranges, wheat; Nation Y: oranges, tea; Nation Z: rice, soybeans
(D) Nation X: rice, wheat; Nation Y: oranges, tea; Nation Z: oranges, soybeans
(E) Nation X: soybeans, rice; Nation Y: oranges, tea; Nation Z: soybeans, wheat

19. If Nation X exports soybeans and tea, then which one of the following could be true?

(A) Nation Y exports oranges.
(B) Nation Y exports rice.
(C) Nation Y exports tea.
(D) Nation Z exports soybeans.
(E) Nation Z exports tea.

20. If Nation Z exports tea and wheat, then which one of the following must be true?

(A) Nation X exports oranges.
(B) Nation X exports tea.
(C) Nation X exports wheat.
(D) Nation Y exports rice.
(E) Nation Y exports soybeans.

21. It CANNOT be the case that both Nation X and Nation Z export which one of the following crops?

(A) oranges
(B) rice
(C) soybeans
(D) tea
(E) wheat

22. Which one of the following pairs CANNOT be the two crops that Nation Y exports?

(A) oranges and rice
(B) oranges and soybeans
(C) rice and tea
(D) rice and wheat
(E) soybeans and wheat

GROUP 1, GAME 5
EXTRA PRACTICE

The Export Alliance consists of exactly three nations: Nation X, Nation Y, and Nation Z. Each nation in the Alliance exports exactly two of the following five crops: oranges, rice, soybeans, tea, and wheat. Each of these crops is exported by at least one of the nations in the Alliance. The following conditions hold:

None of the nations exports both wheat and oranges.
Nation X exports soybeans if, but only if, Nation Y does also.
If Nation Y exports rice, then Nations X and Z both export tea.
Nation Y does not export any crop that Nation Z exports.

18. Which one of the following could be an accurate list, for each of the nations, of the crops it exports?

(A) Nation X: oranges, rice; Nation Y: oranges, tea; Nation Z: soybeans, wheat
(B) Nation X: oranges, tea; Nation Y: oranges, rice; Nation Z: soybeans, wheat
(C) Nation X: oranges, wheat; Nation Y: oranges, tea; Nation Z: rice, soybeans
(D) Nation X: rice, wheat; Nation Y: oranges, tea; Nation Z: oranges, soybeans
(E) Nation X: soybeans, rice; Nation Y: oranges, tea; Nation Z: soybeans, wheat

19. If Nation X exports soybeans and tea, then which one of the following could be true?

(A) Nation Y exports oranges.
(B) Nation Y exports rice.
(C) Nation Y exports tea.
(D) Nation Z exports soybeans.
(E) Nation Z exports tea.

20. If Nation Z exports tea and wheat, then which one of the following must be true?

(A) Nation X exports oranges.
(B) Nation X exports tea.
(C) Nation X exports wheat.
(D) Nation Y exports rice.
(E) Nation Y exports soybeans.

21. It CANNOT be the case that both Nation X and Nation Z export which one of the following crops?

(A) oranges
(B) rice
(C) soybeans
(D) tea
(E) wheat

22. Which one of the following pairs CANNOT be the two crops that Nation Y exports?

(A) oranges and rice
(B) oranges and soybeans
(C) rice and tea
(D) rice and wheat
(E) soybeans and wheat

GROUP 1, GAME 6

Henri has exactly five electrical appliances in his dormitory room: a hairdryer, a microwave oven, a razor, a television, and a vacuum. As a consequence of fire department regulations, Henri can use these appliances only in accordance with the following conditions:

Henri cannot use both the hairdryer and the razor simultaneously.
Henri cannot use both the hairdryer and the television simultaneously.
When Henri uses the vacuum, he cannot at the same time use any of the following: the hairdryer, the razor, and the television.

1. Which one of the following is a pair of appliances Henri could be using simultaneously?

(A) the hairdryer and the razor
(B) the hairdryer and the television
(C) the razor and the television
(D) the razor and the vacuum
(E) the television and the vacuum

2. Assume that Henri is using exactly two appliances and is not using the microwave oven. Which one of the following is a list of all the appliances, other than the microwave oven, that Henri CANNOT be using?

(A) hairdryer
(B) razor
(C) vacuum
(D) hairdryer, razor
(E) hairdryer, vacuum

3. Which one of the following CANNOT be true?

(A) Henri uses the hairdryer while using the microwave oven.
(B) Henri uses the microwave oven while using the razor.
(C) Henri uses the microwave oven while using two other appliances.
(D) Henri uses the television while using two other appliances.
(E) Henri uses the vacuum while using two other appliances.

4. If Henri were to use exactly three appliances, then what is the total number of different groups of three appliances any one of which could be the group of appliances he is using?

(A) one
(B) two
(C) three
(D) four
(E) five

5. Which one of the following statements, if true, guarantees that Henri is using no more than one of the following: the hairdryer, the razor, the television?

(A) Henri is using the hairdryer.
(B) Henri is using the television.
(C) Henri is not using the hairdryer.
(D) Henri is not using the microwave oven.
(E) Henri is not using the vacuum.

6. Which one of the following must be true?

(A) Henri uses at most three appliances simultaneously.
(B) Henri uses at most four appliances simultaneously.
(C) Henri uses at most one other appliance while using the microwave oven.
(D) Henri uses at most one other appliance while using the razor.
(E) Henri uses at least two other appliances while using the hairdryer.

EXPLANATION

We end Group One with *possibly* the easiest game of all time. But there are probably a dozen other games of which we'd be tempted to say the exact same thing, so perhaps we should save the superlatives. This one is easy, though; we can say that much for sure.

It's the rare game that we can solve, completely, before we even glance at the first question. There's an extraordinary lack of flexibility in the game, with only 11 possible outcomes. It's a great example of how an aggressive approach can make you the boss of the game, rather than letting the game be the boss of you.

The rules provide a bunch of pairs of appliances that can't be on simultaneously. In fact, they are the *only* rules. They look like this:

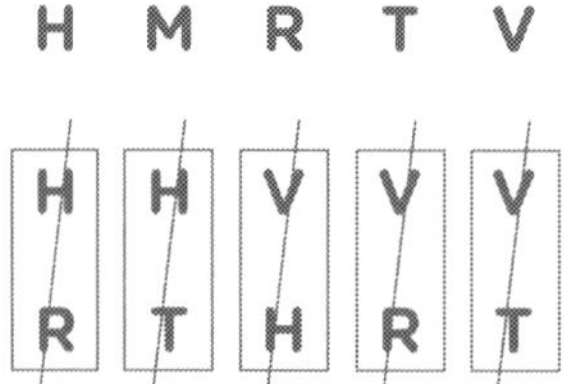

There are two major assholes here, two minor assholes, and one nice guy. The major assholes are H and V; they each have *three* other appliances they don't get along with. The minor assholes are R and T, who each hate H and V. The only nice guy is M, who gets along with everybody.

Let's start with the basics. There are no minimum conditions in this game; it's okay if Henri decides to conserve power and turn everything off simultaneously. It's also okay if Henri turns on any single appliance by itself, giving us five possible scenarios:

H
M
R
T
V

We've got one nice guy, M, who gets along with everybody. So there are four pairs that will obviously work (M with everybody else):

HM
RM
TM
VM

Beyond that, it starts getting really sticky. Our two major assholes, H and V, both hate everyone except M. So they're either on solo or on with M, and we've already dealt with those scenarios. We turn our attention to our two minor assholes, R and T, who, unlike H and V, at least get along with *each other.* So that gives us one more pair:

RT

For the grand finale, if Henri wants to have a global warming fiesta in his crappy, under-electrified dorm room, he can turn on three appliances at once:

RTM

But that's the *only* way to turn on three appliances at once. Knock yourself out Henri; you can shave, watch Oprah, and microwave a hot pocket all at once. But you'd better use the razor to shave your head, because the hairdryer is a problem. And you'd better do the shaving on the fire escape, because the vacuum's a problem as well.

Stupid jokes aside, we're left with the following 11 scenarios:

H, M, R, T, V, HM, VM, RT, RM, TM, RTM

Those are all the combos that will work.

We're not saying this exhaustive solution is the *only* solution to the game. But it's certainly a *possible* solution, and it's also one of the best. Many students can figure all this out in less than two or three minutes. The questions, from here, will also take just a couple minutes. Onward!

QUESTION 1

Which one of the following is a pair of appliances Henri could be using simultaneously?

(A) the hairdryer and the razor
(B) the hairdryer and the television
(C) the razor and the television
(D) the razor and the vacuum
(E) the television and the vacuum

Which pair could be on simultaneously? Well, the answer has to be M with anybody (HM, RM, TM, or VM) or the only other possible pair, RT. We can scan the answers for M, which isn't here, so the answer must be RT.

Yep, our answer is C.

QUESTION 4

If Henri were to use exactly three appliances, then what is the total number of different groups of three appliances any one of which could be the group of appliances he is using?

(A) one
(B) two
(C) three
(D) four
(E) five

Skipping ahead to question 4 (to do the "if" questions first), we're asked about what would happen if we turned on as many appliances as we could simultaneously. This question is way too easy. There's only one group of three appliances Henri can use at once: RTM, the global warming party.

Sure enough, our answer is A.

QUESTION 2

Assume that Henri is using exactly two appliances and is not using the microwave oven. Which one of the following is a list of all the appliances, other than the microwave oven, that Henri CANNOT be using?

(A) hairdryer
(B) razor
(C) vacuum
(D) hairdryer, razor
(E) hairdryer, vacuum

This question is a hidden "if" question. We didn't see it the first time through when we were looking for "if" questions. No matter. If we're not using the microwave, and we have exactly two appliances on, then those appliances, as we've already seen, must be RT. So H and V, the major assholes, are both off. Since we're asked to identify "all the appliances" we're looking for an answer choice with both H and V.

And yes, once again, we have predicted the correct answer, which is E.

QUESTION 3

Which one of the following CANNOT be true?

(A) Henri uses the hairdryer while using the microwave oven.
(B) Henri uses the microwave oven while using the razor.
(C) Henri uses the microwave oven while using two other appliances.
(D) Henri uses the television while using two other appliances.
(E) Henri uses the vacuum while using two other appliances.

We have no choice but to evaluate the answer choices here, looking for a must be false. Let's see:

A) No, this is fine; the microwave loves everyone.
B) Again, this is fine, because the microwave is a lover, not a fighter.
C) This is possible: RTM.
D) Still possible: RTM.
E) Nope, the vacuum is a major asshole who hates everyone, except M.

Our answer is E.

QUESTION 5

Which one of the following statements, if true, guarantees that Henri is using no more than one of the following: the hairdryer, the razor, the television?

(A) Henri is using the hairdryer.
(B) Henri is using the television.
(C) Henri is not using the hairdryer.
(D) Henri is not using the microwave oven.
(E) Henri is not using the vacuum.

Take a deep breath; this question wields some complicated wording, but it's simply not that tough. We're asked to find a condition that would guarantee that at least two out of H, R, and T are off. The simplest answers would be "H is on" and "V is on," since H and V are major assholes who hate both R and T.

OMG, yes, it's the *very first answer.*

Our answer is A, because if Henri turns on his hairdryer, he has to turn off both the razor and the television.

QUESTION 6

Which one of the following must be true?

(A) Henri uses at most three appliances simultaneously.
(B) Henri uses at most four appliances simultaneously.
(C) Henri uses at most one other appliance while using the microwave oven.
(D) Henri uses at most one other appliance while using the razor.
(E) Henri uses at least two other appliances while using the hairdryer.

Let's look at all five answer choices, hunting down something that must always be true. (The four incorrect answers, of course, are the ones that don't have to be true—that is, they could be false.)

A) Well, yeah. RTM is the only way to turn on three appliances, and it's impossible to turn on four. We answered this question before we even attempted question 1.
B) No, Henri must turn on at most three appliances simultaneously.
C) No, RTM is a Could Be True.
D) No, RTM is a Could Be True.
E) Definitely not. This is a Must Be False, not a Must Be True.

Our answer is A.

In retrospect, maybe this is the easiest game of all time. But there are plenty more easy games to come. Never forget: This shit just ain't that hard.

GROUP 1, GAME 6
EXTRA PRACTICE

Henri has exactly five electrical appliances in his dormitory room: a hairdryer, a microwave oven, a razor, a television, and a vacuum. As a consequence of fire department regulations, Henri can use these appliances only in accordance with the following conditions:

Henri cannot use both the hairdryer and the razor simultaneously.
Henri cannot use both the hairdryer and the television simultaneously.
When Henri uses the vacuum, he cannot at the same time use any of the following: the hairdryer, the razor, and the television.

1. Which one of the following is a pair of appliances Henri could be using simultaneously?

(A) the hairdryer and the razor
(B) the hairdryer and the television
(C) the razor and the television
(D) the razor and the vacuum
(E) the television and the vacuum

2. Assume that Henri is using exactly two appliances and is not using the microwave oven. Which one of the following is a list of all the appliances, other than the microwave oven, that Henri CANNOT be using?

(A) hairdryer
(B) razor
(C) vacuum
(D) hairdryer, razor
(E) hairdryer, vacuum

3. Which one of the following CANNOT be true?

(A) Henri uses the hairdryer while using the microwave oven.
(B) Henri uses the microwave oven while using the razor.
(C) Henri uses the microwave oven while using two other appliances.
(D) Henri uses the television while using two other appliances.
(E) Henri uses the vacuum while using two other appliances.

4. If Henri were to use exactly three appliances, then what is the total number of different groups of three appliances any one of which could be the group of appliances he is using?

(A) one
(B) two
(C) three
(D) four
(E) five

5. Which one of the following statements, if true, guarantees that Henri is using no more than one of the following: the hairdryer, the razor, the television?

(A) Henri is using the hairdryer.
(B) Henri is using the television.
(C) Henri is not using the hairdryer.
(D) Henri is not using the microwave oven.
(E) Henri is not using the vacuum.

6. Which one of the following must be true?

(A) Henri uses at most three appliances simultaneously.
(B) Henri uses at most four appliances simultaneously.
(C) Henri uses at most one other appliance while using the microwave oven.
(D) Henri uses at most one other appliance while using the razor.
(E) Henri uses at least two other appliances while using the hairdryer.

GROUP 1, GAME 6
EXTRA PRACTICE

Henri has exactly five electrical appliances in his dormitory room: a hairdryer, a microwave oven, a razor, a television, and a vacuum. As a consequence of fire department regulations, Henri can use these appliances only in accordance with the following conditions:

Henri cannot use both the hairdryer and the razor simultaneously.
Henri cannot use both the hairdryer and the television simultaneously.
When Henri uses the vacuum, he cannot at the same time use any of the following: the hairdryer, the razor, and the television.

1. Which one of the following is a pair of appliances Henri could be using simultaneously?

(A) the hairdryer and the razor
(B) the hairdryer and the television
(C) the razor and the television
(D) the razor and the vacuum
(E) the television and the vacuum

2. Assume that Henri is using exactly two appliances and is not using the microwave oven. Which one of the following is a list of all the appliances, other than the microwave oven, that Henri CANNOT be using?

(A) hairdryer
(B) razor
(C) vacuum
(D) hairdryer, razor
(E) hairdryer, vacuum

3. Which one of the following CANNOT be true?

(A) Henri uses the hairdryer while using the microwave oven.
(B) Henri uses the microwave oven while using the razor.
(C) Henri uses the microwave oven while using two other appliances.
(D) Henri uses the television while using two other appliances.
(E) Henri uses the vacuum while using two other appliances.

4. If Henri were to use exactly three appliances, then what is the total number of different groups of three appliances any one of which could be the group of appliances he is using?

(A) one
(B) two
(C) three
(D) four
(E) five

5. Which one of the following statements, if true, guarantees that Henri is using no more than one of the following: the hairdryer, the razor, the television?

(A) Henri is using the hairdryer.
(B) Henri is using the television.
(C) Henri is not using the hairdryer.
(D) Henri is not using the microwave oven.
(E) Henri is not using the vacuum.

6. Which one of the following must be true?

(A) Henri uses at most three appliances simultaneously.
(B) Henri uses at most four appliances simultaneously.
(C) Henri uses at most one other appliance while using the microwave oven.
(D) Henri uses at most one other appliance while using the razor.
(E) Henri uses at least two other appliances while using the hairdryer.

GROUP **2**

GROUP 2, GAME 1

On one afternoon, Patterson meets individually with each of exactly five clients—Reilly, Sanchez, Tang, Upton, and Yansky—and also goes to the gym by herself for a workout. Patterson's workout and her five meetings each start at either 1:00, 2:00, 3:00, 4:00, 5:00, or 6:00. The following conditions must apply:

Patterson meets with Sanchez at some time before her workout.
Patterson meets with Tang at some time after her workout.
Patterson meets with Yansky either immediately before or immediately after her workout.
Patterson meets with Upton at some time before she meets with Reilly.

1. Which one of the following could be an acceptable schedule of Patterson's workout and meetings, in order from 1:00 to 6:00?

(A) Yansky, workout, Upton, Reilly, Sanchez, Tang
(B) Upton, Tang, Sanchez, Yansky, workout, Reilly
(C) Upton, Reilly, Sanchez, workout, Tang, Yansky
(D) Sanchez, Yansky, workout, Reilly, Tang, Upton
(E) Sanchez, Upton, workout, Yansky, Tang, Reilly

2. How many of the clients are there, any one of whom could meet with Patterson at 1:00?

(A) one
(B) two
(C) three
(D) four
(E) five

3. Patterson CANNOT meet with Upton at which one of the following times?

(A) 1:00
(B) 2:00
(C) 3:00
(D) 4:00
(E) 5:00

4. If Patterson meets with Sanchez the hour before she meets with Yansky, then each of the following could be true EXCEPT:

(A) Patterson meets with Reilly at 2:00.
(B) Patterson meets with Yansky at 3:00.
(C) Patterson meets with Tang at 4:00.
(D) Patterson meets with Yansky at 5:00.
(E) Patterson meets with Tang at 6:00.

5. If Patterson meets with Tang at 4:00, then which one of the following must be true?

(A) Patterson meets with Reilly at 5:00.
(B) Patterson meets with Upton at 5:00.
(C) Patterson meets with Yansky at 2:00.
(D) Patterson meets with Yansky at 3:00.
(E) Patterson's workout is at 2:00.

6. Which one of the following could be the order of Patterson's meetings, from earliest to latest?

(A) Upton, Yansky, Sanchez, Reilly, Tang
(B) Upton, Reilly, Sanchez, Tang, Yansky
(C) Sanchez, Yansky, Reilly, Tang, Upton
(D) Sanchez, Upton, Tang, Yansky, Reilly
(E) Sanchez, Upton, Reilly, Yansky, Tang

EXPLANATION

We saw a couple games just like this one in Group One. It's the easiest, most common type of logic game. If you're still struggling to wrap your head around the games, this is the kind of game that will likely start to make sense first. It'll click, don't worry.

There's one curveball here, but it's strictly minor-league. Consider the workout for a second. The game lists the workout separate from Patterson's five meetings. But is there really any difference? Nope, there's not. This game is really just six things for six spots, like this:

RSTUYW ____ ____ ____ ____ ____ ____

We'll deal with the rules next. Remember, the rules are far more powerful in combination than they are on their own. So let's immediately combine the first and second rules together, like this:

S ... W ... T

We've said it before, and we'll say it again: There's no point in writing these rules out separately, when they combine in such an obvious way. Don't spastically write down everything immediately; *think* before you write.

The third rule also links into these two rules. Notice that "workout" was mentioned in each of the first three rules. By itself, the rule "W immediately before or after Y" would look like this:

WY (with arc over WY)

But when you're really good at the games you'll skip writing that rule by itself as well, and go directly here:

S ... WY ... T (with arc over WY)

The last rule doesn't link in, so this one gets written on its own:

U ... R

Finally, before tackling the questions, let's think about the first and last spots. Quite frequently, on games that follow this pattern, these end spots get severely restricted. And that's happening here: only S and U are eligible to go first, and only T and R are eligible to go last. It's a good idea to note that before moving forward. So our final diagram looks like this:

RSTUYW S/U ___ ___ ___ ___ T/R

S...WY...T
U...R

Okay, now it's question time.

QUESTION 1

Which one of the following could be an acceptable schedule of Patterson's workout and meetings, in order from 1:00 to 6:00?

(A) Yansky, workout, Upton, Reilly, Sanchez, Tang
(B) Upton, Tang, Sanchez, Yansky, workout, Reilly
(C) Upton, Reilly, Sanchez, workout, Tang, Yansky
(D) Sanchez, Yansky, workout, Reilly, Tang, Upton
(E) Sanchez, Upton, workout, Yansky, Tang, Reilly

Process of elimination:

S...W This gets rid of A.
W...T This gets rid of B.
W and Y have to touch. This gets rid of C.
U...R This gets rid of D.

We've tested all the rules, and E is the only answer that survived. It satisfies the rules...

So our answer is E.

QUESTION 4

If Patterson meets with Sanchez the hour before she meets with Yansky, then each of the following could be true EXCEPT:

(A) Patterson meets with Reilly at 2:00.
(B) Patterson meets with Yansky at 3:00.
(C) Patterson meets with Tang at 4:00.
(D) Patterson meets with Yansky at 5:00.
(E) Patterson meets with Tang at 6:00.

Remember, we want to hunt down the "if" questions first, so we're skipping questions 2 and 3 for now. On this one, if S goes immediately before Y, then Y has to go immediately before W to keep Y and W touching:

RSTUYW S/U ____ ____ ____ ____ T/R

SYW...T
U...R

We're asked to find something that must be false. Let's see.

A) This would work: URSYWT
B) This would work: USYW(R,T)
C) No problem: SYWTUR
D) This won't work. If we put Y in the fifth spot, there wouldn't be room for W and T to follow it.
E) This would work in a variety of ways, no point in listing them all.

Our answer is D, because it's the one that won't work when S is immediately before Y.

QUESTION 5

If Patterson meets with Tang at 4:00, then which one of the following must be true?

(A) Patterson meets with Reilly at 5:00.
(B) Patterson meets with Upton at 5:00.
(C) Patterson meets with Yansky at 2:00.
(D) Patterson meets with Yansky at 3:00.
(E) Patterson's workout is at 2:00.

If T goes fourth, then S has to go first while W and Y have to share the second and third spots:

That setup leaves only the fifth and sixth spots for U...R, which have to go in that order:

S (W, Y) T U R

We're looking for something that must be true.

A) No, this must be false.
B) Yes, this looks like the one.
C) This could be true, but it doesn't *have* to be true.
D) This also could be true, but doesn't *have* to be.
E) Same thing, this doesn't have to be true, even though it could be.

Our answer is B, because it's the only one that has to be true when T is fourth.

QUESTION 2

How many of the clients are there, any one of whom could meet with Patterson at 1:00?

(A) one
(B) two
(C) three
(D) four
(E) five

Back to the non-if questions, and we actually anticipated this one a while back. Our main diagram says S and U are the only players who can go first. We knew this limitation before we even started, because every other variable has at least one other thing that must come before it and therefore is pushed out of first place.

So our answer is two, or B.

QUESTION 3

Patterson CANNOT meet with Upton at which one of the following times?

(A) 1:00
(B) 2:00
(C) 3:00
(D) 4:00
(E) 5:00

We know that U can't go at 6:00 p.m., because it has to go before R, but unfortunately 6:00 p.m. isn't one of the answers. Let's start by eliminating anything we've seen happen in our previous diagrams.

The correct answer for question 1 was E. In that scenario, U went at 2:00 p.m. So that can't be the answer here—B is out.

When we did question 4, we jotted down some quick scenarios. If those scenarios are valid (which they'd better be, or we're in trouble) we see that U can also go at 1:00 p.m. and 5:00 p.m. So answers A and E are out as well.

Apparently, based on the remaining answer choices, U can't meet at either 3:00 p.m. or 4:00 p.m. Let's test them:

The problem with U at 3:00 pm is probably easier to see than to explain in words: Look at the first and second spots. Who would go there? S, obviously, but nobody else will fit in those two spots without splitting up W and Y. U at 4:00 p.m., however, works in a couple of ways.

So our answer is C.

QUESTION 6

Which one of the following could be the order of Patterson's meetings, from earliest to latest?

(A) Upton, Yansky, Sanchez, Reilly, Tang
(B) Upton, Reilly, Sanchez, Tang, Yansky
(C) Sanchez, Yansky, Reilly, Tang, Upton
(D) Sanchez, Upton, Tang, Yansky, Reilly
(E) Sanchez, Upton, Reilly, Yansky, Tang

Process of elimination. We're only given a partial list here (meetings, no workout) but all the other rules and relationships stay the same:

S...WY...T This gets rid of A, B, and D.
U...R This gets rid of C.

Our answer is E, because it's the only one left.

GROUP 2, GAME 1
EXTRA PRACTICE

On one afternoon, Patterson meets individually with each of exactly five clients—Reilly, Sanchez, Tang, Upton, and Yansky—and also goes to the gym by herself for a workout. Patterson's workout and her five meetings each start at either 1:00, 2:00, 3:00, 4:00, 5:00, or 6:00. The following conditions must apply:

Patterson meets with Sanchez at some time before her workout.
Patterson meets with Tang at some time after her workout.
Patterson meets with Yansky either immediately before or immediately after her workout.
Patterson meets with Upton at some time before she meets with Reilly.

1. Which one of the following could be an acceptable schedule of Patterson's workout and meetings, in order from 1:00 to 6:00?

(A) Yansky, workout, Upton, Reilly, Sanchez, Tang
(B) Upton, Tang, Sanchez, Yansky, workout, Reilly
(C) Upton, Reilly, Sanchez, workout, Tang, Yansky
(D) Sanchez, Yansky, workout, Reilly, Tang, Upton
(E) Sanchez, Upton, workout, Yansky, Tang, Reilly

2. How many of the clients are there, any one of whom could meet with Patterson at 1:00?

(A) one
(B) two
(C) three
(D) four
(E) five

3. Patterson CANNOT meet with Upton at which one of the following times?

(A) 1:00
(B) 2:00
(C) 3:00
(D) 4:00
(E) 5:00

4. If Patterson meets with Sanchez the hour before she meets with Yansky, then each of the following could be true EXCEPT:

(A) Patterson meets with Reilly at 2:00.
(B) Patterson meets with Yansky at 3:00.
(C) Patterson meets with Tang at 4:00.
(D) Patterson meets with Yansky at 5:00.
(E) Patterson meets with Tang at 6:00.

5. If Patterson meets with Tang at 4:00, then which one of the following must be true?

(A) Patterson meets with Reilly at 5:00.
(B) Patterson meets with Upton at 5:00.
(C) Patterson meets with Yansky at 2:00.
(D) Patterson meets with Yansky at 3:00.
(E) Patterson's workout is at 2:00.

6. Which one of the following could be the order of Patterson's meetings, from earliest to latest?

(A) Upton, Yansky, Sanchez, Reilly, Tang
(B) Upton, Reilly, Sanchez, Tang, Yansky
(C) Sanchez, Yansky, Reilly, Tang, Upton
(D) Sanchez, Upton, Tang, Yansky, Reilly
(E) Sanchez, Upton, Reilly, Yansky, Tang

GROUP 2, GAME 1
EXTRA PRACTICE

On one afternoon, Patterson meets individually with each of exactly five clients—Reilly, Sanchez, Tang, Upton, and Yansky—and also goes to the gym by herself for a workout. Patterson's workout and her five meetings each start at either 1:00, 2:00, 3:00, 4:00, 5:00, or 6:00. The following conditions must apply:

Patterson meets with Sanchez at some time before her workout.
Patterson meets with Tang at some time after her workout.
Patterson meets with Yansky either immediately before or immediately after her workout.
Patterson meets with Upton at some time before she meets with Reilly.

1. Which one of the following could be an acceptable schedule of Patterson's workout and meetings, in order from 1:00 to 6:00?

(A) Yansky, workout, Upton, Reilly, Sanchez, Tang
(B) Upton, Tang, Sanchez, Yansky, workout, Reilly
(C) Upton, Reilly, Sanchez, workout, Tang, Yansky
(D) Sanchez, Yansky, workout, Reilly, Tang, Upton
(E) Sanchez, Upton, workout, Yansky, Tang, Reilly

2. How many of the clients are there, any one of whom could meet with Patterson at 1:00?

(A) one
(B) two
(C) three
(D) four
(E) five

3. Patterson CANNOT meet with Upton at which one of the following times?

(A) 1:00
(B) 2:00
(C) 3:00
(D) 4:00
(E) 5:00

4. If Patterson meets with Sanchez the hour before she meets with Yansky, then each of the following could be true EXCEPT:

(A) Patterson meets with Reilly at 2:00.
(B) Patterson meets with Yansky at 3:00.
(C) Patterson meets with Tang at 4:00.
(D) Patterson meets with Yansky at 5:00.
(E) Patterson meets with Tang at 6:00.

5. If Patterson meets with Tang at 4:00, then which one of the following must be true?

(A) Patterson meets with Reilly at 5:00.
(B) Patterson meets with Upton at 5:00.
(C) Patterson meets with Yansky at 2:00.
(D) Patterson meets with Yansky at 3:00.
(E) Patterson's workout is at 2:00.

6. Which one of the following could be the order of Patterson's meetings, from earliest to latest?

(A) Upton, Yansky, Sanchez, Reilly, Tang
(B) Upton, Reilly, Sanchez, Tang, Yansky
(C) Sanchez, Yansky, Reilly, Tang, Upton
(D) Sanchez, Upton, Tang, Yansky, Reilly
(E) Sanchez, Upton, Reilly, Yansky, Tang

GROUP 2, GAME 2

In Crescentville there are exactly five record stores, whose names are abbreviated S, T, V, X, and Z. Each of the five stores carries at least one of four distinct types of music: folk, jazz, opera, and rock. None of the stores carries any other type of music. The following conditions must hold:

Exactly two of the five stores carry jazz.
T carries rock and opera but no other type of music.
S carries more types of music than T carries.
X carries more types of music than any other store in Crescentville carries.
Jazz is among the types of music S carries.
V does not carry any type of music that Z carries.

12. Which one of the following could be true?

(A) S carries folk and rock but neither jazz nor opera.
(B) T carries jazz but neither opera nor rock.
(C) V carries folk, rock, and opera, but not jazz.
(D) X carries folk, rock, and jazz, but not opera.
(E) Z carries folk and opera but neither rock nor jazz.

13. Which one of the following could be true?

(A) S, V, and Z all carry folk.
(B) S, X, and Z all carry jazz.
(C) Of the five stores, only S and V carry jazz.
(D) Of the five stores, only T and X carry rock.
(E) Of the five stores, only S, T, and V carry opera.

14. If exactly one of the stores carries folk, then which one of the following could be true?

(A) S and V carry exactly two types of music in common.
(B) T and S carry exactly two types of music in common.
(C) T and V carry exactly two types of music in common.
(D) V and X carry exactly two types of music in common.
(E) X and Z carry exactly two types of music in common.

15. Which one of the following must be true?

(A) T carries exactly the same number of types of music as V carries.
(B) V carries exactly the same number of types of music as Z carries.
(C) S carries at least one more type of music than Z carries.
(D) Z carries at least one more type of music than T carries.
(E) X carries exactly two more types of music than S carries.

16. If V is one of exactly three stores that carry rock, then which one of the following must be true?

(A) S and Z carry no types of music in common.
(B) S and V carry at least one type of music in common.
(C) S and Z carry at least one type of music in common.
(D) T and Z carry at least one type of music in common.
(E) T and V carry at least two types of music in common.

17. If S and V both carry folk, then which one of the following could be true?

(A) S and T carry no types of music in common.
(B) S and Z carry no types of music in common.
(C) T and Z carry no types of music in common.
(D) S and Z carry two types of music in common.
(E) T and V carry two types of music in common.

EXPLANATION

This is a very satisfying game because there's so much we can figure out before we dive into the questions. Specifically, rules 2, 3, and 4 combine. Did you make the connections? If not, you might want to go back and look at the rules again before I spoil the surprise for you. Rules 2, 3, and 4. Think about it for a minute. Give it a few minutes if you need them, but figure that shit out! I know you can do it, and it's worth it to practice making those big connections.

First, a note about the general structure: Since every store has to sell at least one type of music (but each type of music does not necessarily have to be sold at all) we'd tend to start the game this way:

The blank spot above each store means that we must put at least one type of music in each of these spots. This is a good starting point. Note, however, that it's not the *only* starting point. As frequently happens, if you organized this game the other way, with F J O R as the foundation, you could still pull it off. I recommend that you try it both ways, if you have the time.

We'll just present it one way, using the stores as our foundation, and we'll lean heavily on rules 2, 3, and 4 to solve much of the game. Here come the spoilers:

- Rule 2 says T has R and O, exactly two types of music. (There are four, total.)
- Rule 3 says S has more types than T, so it must have at least three. We also know from Rule 5 that S has to have J and so we'll have two open spots to fill.
- Rule 4 says X has more types than anyone else (including S).

Add all that up, and X must have all four types of music, and S must have exactly three types. Like this:

F J O R

			F	
___			J	
___	R		O	
J	O	___	R	___
S^3	T^2	V	X^4	Z

It's impossible to oversell this point: The designers of the test *want* you to make these inferences. I'm not bullshitting here. The testmakers are carefully dropping the breadcrumbs, and they're hoping that you'll follow the trail. Lawyers need to be clever and well prepared. If you're very clever, you might have picked up the scent fairly quickly.

But even if you didn't sniff it right away, you can still train yourself to do so. (Which is why this book exists!) We can't all be Saul Goodman; some of us are going to have to actually work for it. Fortunately, we *can* all do a zillion logic games, and doing so will ensure that we're prepared when the patterns repeat themselves. As they always do.

That's it for the sermon, for now anyway. Let's go get the questions.

QUESTION 14

If exactly one of the stores carries folk, then which one of the following could be true?

(A) S and V carry exactly two types of music in common.
(B) T and S carry exactly two types of music in common.
(C) T and V carry exactly two types of music in common.
(D) V and X carry exactly two types of music in common.
(E) X and Z carry exactly two types of music in common.

Skipping ahead to the "if" questions, we tackle #14 first. If exactly one of the stores carries folk, that has to be store X, since store X has all four types of music. This forces S to have both O and R, since it has to have three types of music. It also means that both V and Z have to have either O or R, not both. (One will have O, one will have R.) Like this:

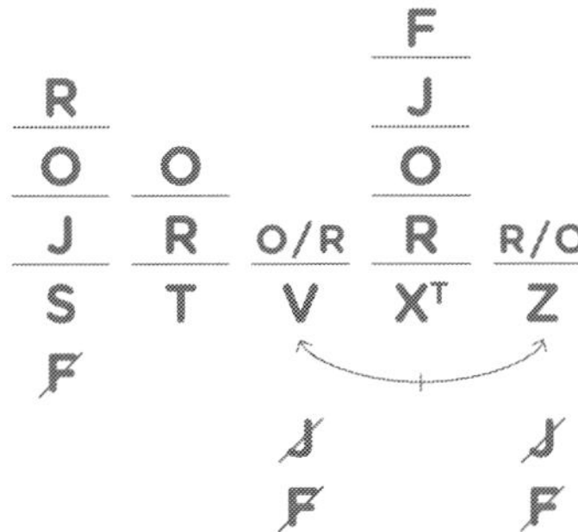

We're hunting for a Could Be True. Let's go.

A) No way, since V can only have one type of music.
B) Not only could this be true, but it must be true. This has got to be the answer.
C) No, since V has only one type of music.
D) No, since V has only one type of music.
E) No, since Z has only one type of music.

Our answer is B, since it's the only one that's possible.

QUESTION 16

If V is one of exactly three stores that carry rock, then which one of the following must be true?

(A) S and Z carry no types of music in common.
(B) S and V carry at least one type of music in common.
(C) S and Z carry at least one type of music in common.
(D) T and Z carry at least one type of music in common.
(E) T and V carry at least two types of music in common.

Since T and X already have rock, if V is one of exactly three stores with rock, then S and Z can't have rock. So S, which has to have three types of music, has F, O, and J. Like this:

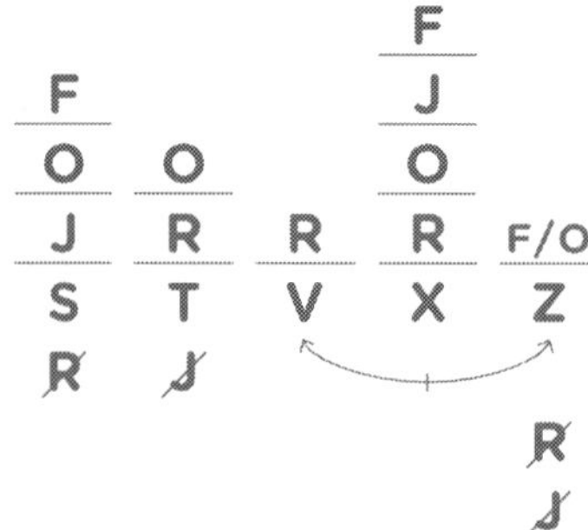

Let's see if that gets it done. We're looking for a Must Be True.

A) Nope. Matter of fact, S and Z *must* have something in common; either F or O.
B) No, this doesn't have to be true.
C) Yep. Z has to have something, and it can't have either R or J. So it has to have either F or O (and it could even have both). S has to have both of those, so no matter what Z has, S will match it. This is gonna be our answer.
D) Nope. If Z has F, this doesn't have to be true.
E) Nope. This could be true, but doesn't have to be true.

Our answer is C, because it's the only one that has to be true.

QUESTION 17

If S and V both carry folk, then which one of the following could be true?

(A) S and T carry no types of music in common.
(B) S and Z carry no types of music in common.
(C) T and Z carry no types of music in common.
(D) S and Z carry two types of music in common.
(E) T and V carry two types of music in common.

S and V both carrying folk doesn't add a lot to our diagram. It's only this:

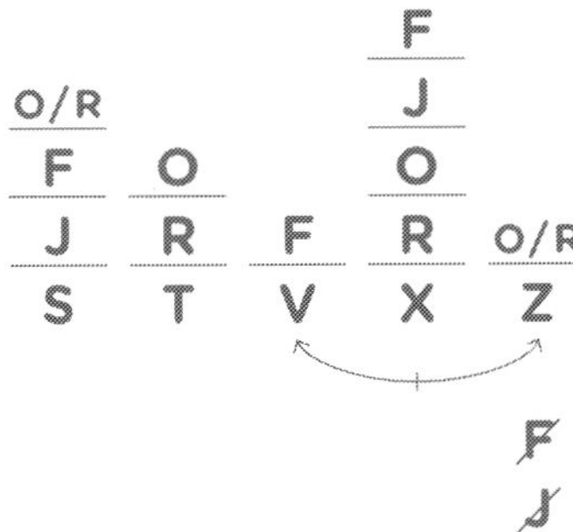

We're looking for a Could Be True. Let's see.

A) No, S will have to have either O or R, and T already has both of those.
B) There's no reason why this couldn't be true.
C) Nope. Z will have one of these, and T has both.
D) Nope. Z can't have either F or J, so Z and S aren't going to have two types in common.
E) No. V might have either O or R, but it can't have both.

Our answer is B, because it's the only one that can be true.

QUESTION 12

Which one of the following could be true?

(A) S carries folk and rock but neither jazz nor opera.
(B) T carries jazz but neither opera nor rock.
(C) V carries folk, rock, and opera, but not jazz.
(D) X carries folk, rock, and jazz, but not opera.
(E) Z carries folk and opera but neither rock nor jazz.

Circling back to the non-if questions, we find a Could Be True. Let's see:

A) S always has J and two other types of music, so this is out.
B) T always has both O and R, so this is out.
C) V can't have F, R, and O simultaneously, because if it did, then Z wouldn't have anything at all.
D) Nope. X has to have all four types of music.
E) Sure, this will work.

Our answer is E, because A-D won't work.

QUESTION 13

Which one of the following could be true?

(A) S, V, and Z all carry folk.
(B) S, X, and Z all carry jazz.
(C) Of the five stores, only S and V carry jazz.
(D) Of the five stores, only T and X carry rock.
(E) Of the five stores, only S, T, and V carry opera.

Another Could Be True question. Let's narrow it down:

A) No, because V and Z can't have anything in common.
B) No, because there can only be two jazz.
C) No, because X has to have jazz.
D) Sure, why not?
E) No, because X has to have opera.

Our answer is D.

QUESTION 15

Which one of the following must be true?

(A) T carries exactly the same number of types of music as V carries.
(B) V carries exactly the same number of types of music as Z carries.
(C) S carries at least one more type of music than Z carries.
(D) Z carries at least one more type of music than T carries.
(E) X carries exactly two more types of music than S carries.

Looking for something that must always be true. Let's do it.

A) No, because T always has two types and V can have either one or two types.
B) No, because both V and Z can have one or two types.
C) Yes. Z can't ever have more than two types (because it can't have anything in common with V) and S always has three types. This is the one.
D) Nope, it's fine for Z to have only one type and T always has two.
E) No. X has four types, and S has three.

Our answer is C, because it's the only one that must be true.

Very instructive grouping game here. Master this one! This pattern is repeated several times in the recent history of the LSAT.

GROUP 2, GAME 2
EXTRA PRACTICE

In Crescentville there are exactly five record stores, whose names are abbreviated S, T, V, X, and Z. Each of the five stores carries at least one of four distinct types of music: folk, jazz, opera, and rock. None of the stores carries any other type of music. The following conditions must hold:

Exactly two of the five stores carry jazz.
T carries rock and opera but no other type of music.
S carries more types of music than T carries.
X carries more types of music than any other store in Crescentville carries.
Jazz is among the types of music S carries.
V does not carry any type of music that Z carries.

12. Which one of the following could be true?

(A) S carries folk and rock but neither jazz nor opera.
(B) T carries jazz but neither opera nor rock.
(C) V carries folk, rock, and opera, but not jazz.
(D) X carries folk, rock, and jazz, but not opera.
(E) Z carries folk and opera but neither rock nor jazz.

13. Which one of the following could be true?

(A) S, V, and Z all carry folk.
(B) S, X, and Z all carry jazz.
(C) Of the five stores, only S and V carry jazz.
(D) Of the five stores, only T and X carry rock.
(E) Of the five stores, only S, T, and V carry opera.

14. If exactly one of the stores carries folk, then which one of the following could be true?

(A) S and V carry exactly two types of music in common.
(B) T and S carry exactly two types of music in common.
(C) T and V carry exactly two types of music in common.
(D) V and X carry exactly two types of music in common.
(E) X and Z carry exactly two types of music in common.

15. Which one of the following must be true?

(A) T carries exactly the same number of types of music as V carries.
(B) V carries exactly the same number of types of music as Z carries.
(C) S carries at least one more type of music than Z carries.
(D) Z carries at least one more type of music than T carries.
(E) X carries exactly two more types of music than S carries.

16. If V is one of exactly three stores that carry rock, then which one of the following must be true?

(A) S and Z carry no types of music in common.
(B) S and V carry at least one type of music in common.
(C) S and Z carry at least one type of music in common.
(D) T and Z carry at least one type of music in common.
(E) T and V carry at least two types of music in common.

17. If S and V both carry folk, then which one of the following could be true?

(A) S and T carry no types of music in common.
(B) S and Z carry no types of music in common.
(C) T and Z carry no types of music in common.
(D) S and Z carry two types of music in common.
(E) T and V carry two types of music in common.

GROUP 2, GAME 2
EXTRA PRACTICE

In Crescentville there are exactly five record stores, whose names are abbreviated S, T, V, X, and Z. Each of the five stores carries at least one of four distinct types of music: folk, jazz, opera, and rock. None of the stores carries any other type of music. The following conditions must hold:

Exactly two of the five stores carry jazz.
T carries rock and opera but no other type of music.
S carries more types of music than T carries.
X carries more types of music than any other store in Crescentville carries.
Jazz is among the types of music S carries.
V does not carry any type of music that Z carries.

12. Which one of the following could be true?

(A) S carries folk and rock but neither jazz nor opera.
(B) T carries jazz but neither opera nor rock.
(C) V carries folk, rock, and opera, but not jazz.
(D) X carries folk, rock, and jazz, but not opera.
(E) Z carries folk and opera but neither rock nor jazz.

13. Which one of the following could be true?

(A) S, V, and Z all carry folk.
(B) S, X, and Z all carry jazz.
(C) Of the five stores, only S and V carry jazz.
(D) Of the five stores, only T and X carry rock.
(E) Of the five stores, only S, T, and V carry opera.

14. If exactly one of the stores carries folk, then which one of the following could be true?

(A) S and V carry exactly two types of music in common.
(B) T and S carry exactly two types of music in common.
(C) T and V carry exactly two types of music in common.
(D) V and X carry exactly two types of music in common.
(E) X and Z carry exactly two types of music in common.

15. Which one of the following must be true?

(A) T carries exactly the same number of types of music as V carries.
(B) V carries exactly the same number of types of music as Z carries.
(C) S carries at least one more type of music than Z carries.
(D) Z carries at least one more type of music than T carries.
(E) X carries exactly two more types of music than S carries.

16. If V is one of exactly three stores that carry rock, then which one of the following must be true?

(A) S and Z carry no types of music in common.
(B) S and V carry at least one type of music in common.
(C) S and Z carry at least one type of music in common.
(D) T and Z carry at least one type of music in common.
(E) T and V carry at least two types of music in common.

17. If S and V both carry folk, then which one of the following could be true?

(A) S and T carry no types of music in common.
(B) S and Z carry no types of music in common.
(C) T and Z carry no types of music in common.
(D) S and Z carry two types of music in common.
(E) T and V carry two types of music in common.

GROUP 2, GAME 3

Exactly seven products—P, Q, R, S, T, W, and X—are each to be advertised exactly once in a section of a catalog. The order in which they will be displayed is governed by the following conditions:

> Q must be displayed in some position before W.
> R must be displayed immediately before X.
> T cannot be displayed immediately before or immediately after W.
> S must be displayed either first or seventh.
> Either Q or T must be displayed fourth.

1. Which one of the following CANNOT be the product that is displayed first?

(A) P
(B) Q
(C) R
(D) T
(E) X

2. If X is displayed immediately before Q, then which one of the following could be true?

(A) T is displayed first.
(B) R is displayed fifth.
(C) Q is displayed last.
(D) Q is displayed second.
(E) P is displayed second.

3. If P is displayed second, then which one of the following could be displayed third?

(A) R
(B) S
(C) T
(D) W
(E) X

4. Which one of the following could be true?

(A) Q is displayed fifth.
(B) Q is displayed seventh.
(C) R is displayed third.
(D) W is displayed third.
(E) X is displayed fifth.

5. If R is displayed sixth, then which one of the following must be displayed fifth?

(A) P
(B) Q
(C) T
(D) W
(E) X

EXPLANATION

By now, you're probably getting familiar with the basic setup for an ordering game like this one. Seven players for seven spots, like this:

P Q R S T W X ___ ___ ___ ___ ___ ___ ___

We'll draw the first three rules in the margin:

Q ... W

R X

~~T W~~

The last two rules don't need to go in the margin, since we can directly incorporate them into our diagram:

Before we get into the questions, let's try to learn a bit more about the way this game works. We prefer to play offense, not defense. We don't always write "not" inferences, especially when we have sequencing rules that link together well, as they did in Game 7, Patterson's meetings. But the sequencing rules in this game don't link together neatly, and there are a few "not" inferences worth noting.

The basics are super-basic: Q and R can't go last, because they each have at least one product that must go after them; and W and X can't go first, because they each have at least one product that must go before them. Let's go ahead and add these super-simple inferences:

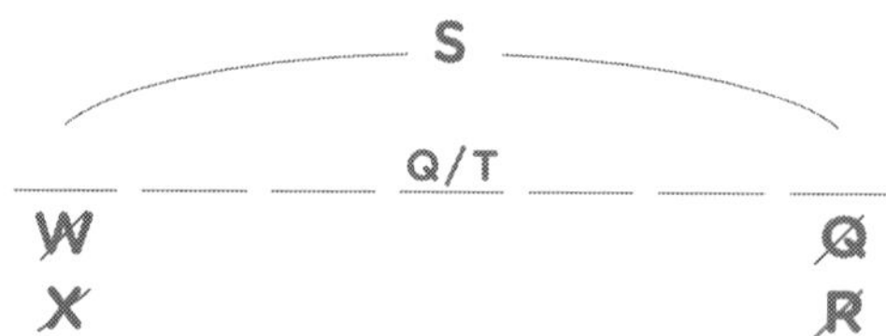

Here's where it gets more interesting. Think about the *combination* of the RX rule and the rule that says either Q or T must go fourth. Based on this connection, we know that R can't go third and X can't go fifth.

These inferences are kind of a big deal; they are the type of inferences that answer questions before they've been asked. As we've mentioned, the vast majority of test takers won't make these inferences, so if you can train yourself you notice these connections, you'll put yourself at a major advantage. The trick is simply to think about each rule, then think about how the rules connect.

As you look for these connections, here's something else to keep in mind: The more constrained the variables are, the more likely they are to lead to inferences. Here, R and X are more constrained than Q...W, because R and X have to come right next to each other. And they're even more constrained than T and W, both of which can go anywhere, just not next to each other. So when you're looking for more inferences, start with blocks like RX, the ones that are the most constrained.

In the end, here's our final diagram:

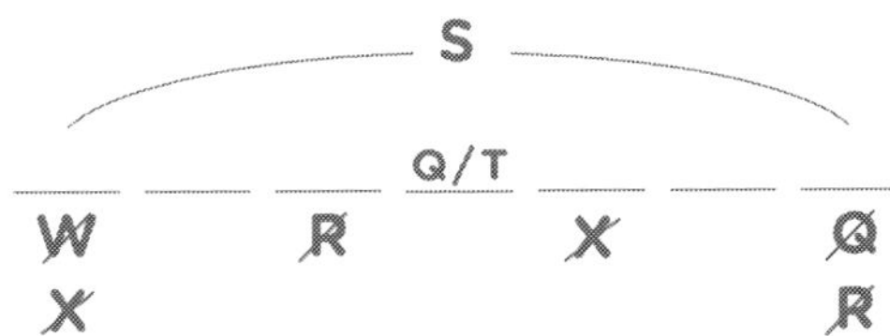

Having made a pair of nice inferences, we can now tackle the questions. Since there's no "list" question at the top of the game, we'll dive straight into the "if" questions.

QUESTION 2

If X is displayed immediately before Q, then which one of the following could be true?

(A) T is displayed first.
(B) R is displayed fifth.
(C) Q is displayed last.
(D) Q is displayed second.
(E) P is displayed second.

The new rule here, XQ, pastes the first and second rules together like this:

It's possible that that's enough to answer the question, but it looks like there are just going to be two ways to accommodate this new rule chain, given that either Q or T must be fourth. One approach (and it's a strong one) is to go ahead and pencil out those two scenarios:

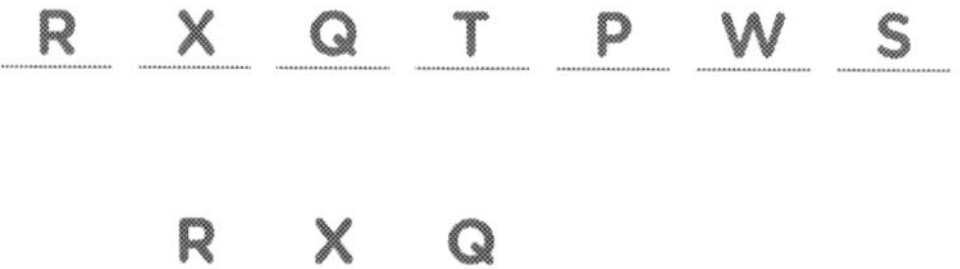

Now let's answer the question. We're looking for a Could Be True.

A) This seems possible, in our first scenario. Rather than test it, let's just see if answers B-E can be easily eliminated.
B) No, R is either first or second in our two scenarios.
C) No, Q is either third or fourth.
D) No, Q is either third or fourth.
E) No, R and X are our two possibilities for the second spot in these two scenarios.

Our answer is A, because we were able to eliminate B, C, D, and E.

QUESTION 3

If P is displayed second, then which one of the following could be displayed third?

(A) R
(B) S
(C) T
(D) W
(E) X

P is our floater, so it wouldn't seem like this new condition should force anything to happen. But it does! Given that either Q or T always goes fourth, if P is second, our RX block gets kicked to the back of the line. One way of notating this situation would be this:

We're asked about who could go in the third spot. Let's see:

A) No, R can't go third because there's no room for RX.
B) No, S always goes first or last.
C) Perhaps. Let's get through all five answers before we bother testing this.
D) No, because putting W into third would force Q into first, which would force T into fourth, right next to W. That violates the third rule, so this is out.
E) No, the RX block is going to have to go near the end.

Our answer is C, because it's the only one that will conceivably work.

QUESTION 5

If R is displayed sixth, then which one of the following must be displayed fifth?

(A) P
(B) Q
(C) T
(D) W
(E) X

If R is sixth, then X is seventh. This, in turn, puts S in the first spot:

S ___ ___ Q/T ___ R X

From there, let's split the diagram into two worlds based on who falls in the fourth spot. If Q is fourth, we get this:

S (P, T) Q W R X

If T is fourth... well, that actually doesn't work. There would be only one spot left for W without putting it next to T, and that's the second spot, which would put W before Q. So this world dies:

It's important to cross this world out, as we've noted before, so that we don't think it's valid when we're answering a later question.

We're asked to identify the product in the fifth spot, and since W is fifth in our only remaining scenario, that has to be our answer.

Our answer is D.

QUESTION 1

Which one of the following CANNOT be the product that is displayed first?

(A) P
(B) Q
(C) R
(D) T
(E) X

Circling back to pick up the non-"if" questions, we find perhaps the easiest question of all time. (Have we said that before?) We're asked who can't go first, and we've already got the answer in our diagram. Neither W nor X can go first, for reasons discussed above. One of them, X, is listed.

So our answer is E.

QUESTION 4

Which one of the following could be true?

(A) Q is displayed fifth.
(B) Q is displayed seventh.
(C) R is displayed third.
(D) W is displayed third.
(E) X is displayed fifth.

We're looking for a Could Be True, and we have two ways to arrive at the correct answer. We can either find something that already happened in one of our sketches or eliminate four answers that we know won't work. Let's see.

A) Q hasn't been fifth in any of our previous sketches, but it's not immediately apparent why this wouldn't work. Let's see if we can eliminate answers B-E.
B) No, Q can't ever be seventh; this was one of our cursory inferences.
C) No, R can't ever be third; this was one of our bigger inferences. (Told you it would come in handy.)
D) This won't work either. If W were third, then who would go fourth?
E) Nope, this is the other big inference we made.

Our answer is A, because it can't be B, C, D, or E.

GROUP 2, GAME 3
EXTRA PRACTICE

Exactly seven products—P, Q, R, S, T, W, and X—are each to be advertised exactly once in a section of a catalog. The order in which they will be displayed is governed by the following conditions:

Q must be displayed in some position before W.
R must be displayed immediately before X.
T cannot be displayed immediately before or immediately after W.
S must be displayed either first or seventh.
Either Q or T must be displayed fourth.

1. Which one of the following CANNOT be the product that is displayed first?

(A) P
(B) Q
(C) R
(D) T
(E) X

2. If X is displayed immediately before Q, then which one of the following could be true?

   (A) T is displayed first.
   (B) R is displayed fifth.
   (C) Q is displayed last.
   (D) Q is displayed second.
   (E) P is displayed second.

3. If P is displayed second, then which one of the following could be displayed third?

   (A) R
   (B) S
   (C) T
   (D) W
   (E) X

4. Which one of the following could be true?

   (A) Q is displayed fifth.
   (B) Q is displayed seventh.
   (C) R is displayed third.
   (D) W is displayed third.
   (E) X is displayed fifth.

5. If R is displayed sixth, then which one of the following must be displayed fifth?

   (A) P
   (B) Q
   (C) T
   (D) W
   (E) X

GROUP 2, GAME 3
EXTRA PRACTICE

Exactly seven products—P, Q, R, S, T, W, and X—are each to be advertised exactly once in a section of a catalog. The order in which they will be displayed is governed by the following conditions:

Q must be displayed in some position before W.
R must be displayed immediately before X.
T cannot be displayed immediately before or immediately after W.
S must be displayed either first or seventh.
Either Q or T must be displayed fourth.

1. Which one of the following CANNOT be the product that is displayed first?

(A) P
(B) Q
(C) R
(D) T
(E) X

2. If X is displayed immediately before Q, then which one of the following could be true?

(A) T is displayed first.
(B) R is displayed fifth.
(C) Q is displayed last.
(D) Q is displayed second.
(E) P is displayed second.

3. If P is displayed second, then which one of the following could be displayed third?

(A) R
(B) S
(C) T
(D) W
(E) X

4. Which one of the following could be true?

(A) Q is displayed fifth.
(B) Q is displayed seventh.
(C) R is displayed third.
(D) W is displayed third.
(E) X is displayed fifth.

5. If R is displayed sixth, then which one of the following must be displayed fifth?

(A) P
(B) Q
(C) T
(D) W
(E) X

GROUP 2, GAME 4

Exactly three films—*Greed, Harvest*, and *Limelight*—are shown during a film club's festival held on Thursday, Friday, and Saturday. Each film is shown at least once during the festival but never more than once on a given day. On each day at least one film is shown. Films are shown one at a time. The following conditions apply:

On Thursday *Harvest* is shown, and no film is shown after it on that day.

On Friday either Greed or Limelight, but not both, is shown, and no film is shown after it on that day.

On Saturday either Greed or Harvest, but not both, is shown, and no film is shown after it on that day.

6. Which one of the following could be a complete and accurate description of the order in which the films are shown at the festival?

(A) Thursday: *Limelight*, then *Harvest*; Friday: *Limelight*; Saturday: *Harvest*

(B) Thursday: *Harvest*; Friday: *Greed*, then *Limelight*; Saturday: *Limelight*, then *Greed*

(C) Thursday: *Harvest*; Friday: *Limelight*; Saturday: *Limelight*, then *Greed*

(D) Thursday: *Greed*, then *Harvest*, then *Limelight*; Friday: *Limelight*; Saturday: *Greed*

(E) Thursday: *Greed*, then *Harvest*; Friday: *Limelight*, then *Harvest*; Saturday: *Harvest*

7. Which one of the following CANNOT be true?

(A) *Harvest* is the last film shown on each day of the festival.
(B) *Limelight* is shown on each day of the festival.
(C) *Greed* is shown second on each day of the festival.
(D) A different film is shown first on each day of the festival.
(E) A different film is shown last on each day of the festival.

8. If *Limelight* is never shown again during the festival once *Greed* is shown, then which one of the following is the maximum number of film showings that could occur during the festival?

(A) three
(B) four
(C) five
(D) six
(E) seven

9. If *Greed* is shown exactly three times, *Harvest* is shown exactly twice, and *Limelight* is shown exactly once, then which one of the following must be true?

(A) All three films are shown on Thursday.
(B) Exactly two films are shown on Saturday.
(C) *Limelight* and *Harvest* are both shown on Thursday.
(D) *Greed* is the only film shown on Saturday.
(E) *Harvest* and *Greed* are both shown on Friday.

10. If *Limelight* is shown exactly three times, *Harvest* is shown exactly twice, and *Greed* is shown exactly once, then which one of the following is a complete and accurate list of the films that could be the first film shown on Thursday?

(A) *Harvest*
(B) *Limelight*
(C) *Greed, Harvest*
(D) *Greed, Limelight*
(E) *Greed, Harvest, Limelight*

EXPLANATION

Setup matters here, and it matters a *lot*. This game can be difficult if you don't come up with a sensible way of organizing yourself and *visualizing* the system. That's not to say that there's only one correct way of doing it; it's possible to do the game in many different ways. We'll present the strongest approach we can here, but it's worth noting that this diagram would be exactly the same from a logical standpoint if we rotated it by 90 degrees. There's usually not a single best way; our constant advice as professional LSAT teachers is to practice a ton and come up with solutions that work for *you.*

The way we've organized it here, we're sequencing from early shows to late shows on the vertical axis, and grouping by Thursday, Friday, Saturday on the horizontal axis. This allows us to incorporate something like "H must go last on Thursday" in an easy visual manner. We'll do the same thing with the second and third rules. Check it out:

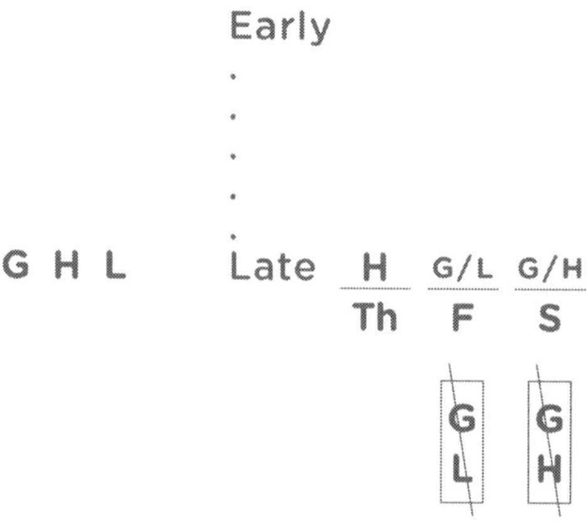

Makes sense, doesn't it? H is the midnight show on Thursday. G or L is the midnight show on Friday, and Friday can't have both movies. G or H is the midnight show on Saturday, and Saturday can't have both movies.

The rules "every film has to be shown at least once" and "no film is shown more than once on a single day" we can hold in our heads. There's nothing to do here; there's no super-awesome way to combine the rules together, nothing much else that we can learn. We've hit the wall. Sometimes that happens later, here it happened sooner. Let's attack the questions.

WE GOT TO THE DIAGRAM fairly quickly here, without a lot of exposition. If you don't get it, send me an email (nathan@foxlsat.com) and I'll put up an explanatory video on my blog, www.foxlsat.com/blog. (Test me, I'm not bullshitting! I love to hear from readers.)

QUESTION 6

Which one of the following could be a complete and accurate description of the order in which the films are shown at the festival?

(A) Thursday: *Limelight*, then *Harvest*; Friday: *Limelight*; Saturday: *Harvest*
(B) Thursday: *Harvest*; Friday: *Greed*, then *Limelight*; Saturday: *Limelight*, then *Greed*
(C) Thursday: *Harvest*; Friday: *Limelight*; Saturday: *Limelight*, then *Greed*
(D) Thursday: *Greed*, then *Harvest*, then *Limelight*; Friday: *Limelight*; Saturday: *Greed*
(E) Thursday: *Greed*, then *Harvest*; Friday: *Limelight*, then *Harvest*; Saturday: *Harvest*

A list question—let's crush it. Process of elimination, one rule at a time, like always.

H is last on Thursday. This gets rid of D.
G or L is last on Friday, and they can't both be shown that day. This gets rid of B and E.
G or H is last on Saturday, and they can't both be shown that day. This gets rid of nothing.
Every film must be shown at least once. This gets rid of A.

Our answer is C, because A, B, D, and E each violate at least one rule.

QUESTION 8

If *Limelight* is never shown again during the festival once *Greed* is shown, then which one of the following is the maximum number of film showings that could occur during the festival?

(A) three
(B) four
(C) five
(D) six
(E) seven

(Skipping #7 to do the "if" questions first.) This is a pretty tricky question; we want to maximize the total number of shows, but we can't show L any more after we show G. So there are two ways to do it; either put the first G late, or put the last L early. Like this:

Th	F	S
L		
G	H	
H	G	G/H

Early G

Th	F	S
L	H	L
H	L	G

Late G

Either way, the most films we're gonna show is six. So that's our answer, D.

QUESTION 9

If *Greed* is shown exactly three times, *Harvest* is shown exactly twice, and *Limelight* is shown exactly once, then which one of the following must be true?

(A) All three films are shown on Thursday.
(B) Exactly two films are shown on Saturday.
(C) Limelight and Harvest are both shown on Thursday.
(D) Greed is the only film shown on Saturday.
(E) Harvest and Greed are both shown on Friday.

If G is shown three times, then that's once per day. This means L can't be Friday and H can't be shown on Saturday. If H is shown twice, but not Saturday, then it has to go on Friday. There are three places where the lone L can go, denoted here by brackets / question marks.

```
(L?)
 G
(L?)   H   (L?)
 H     G    G
----  ---  ----
 Th    F    S
      ~~L~~ ~~H~~
```

On to the answer choices, looking for a Must Be True in our new diagram:

A) Nope. This could be true, but it doesn't have to be.
B) Nope. Could be two, could be one.
C) Nope. There are a couple ways where this *could* be true, but there's one where it doesn't have to be. So this doesn't have to be true.
D) Nope. L can also be shown on Saturday.
E) Yes. This must be true, because G has to go all three days and H must go two, but can't go Saturday.

Our answer is E.

QUESTION 10

If *Limelight* is shown exactly three times, *Harvest* is shown exactly twice, and *Greed* is shown exactly once, then which one of the following is a complete and accurate list of the films that could be the first film shown on Thursday?

(A) *Harvest*
(B) Limelight
(C) Greed, Harvest
(D) Greed, Limelight
(E) Greed, Harvest, *Limelight*

If L goes three times, then G can't go Friday. There are two places where the lone G *can* go, like this:

```
(G?)
 L
(G?)         L     |     L    H    L
 H     L     H     |     H    L    G
---   ---   ---    |    ---  ---  ---
 Th    F     S     |          G̸
       G̸     G̸     |
```

Note that you could also have split your diagram based on where the second H is; you'd have ended up at the exact same solution.

We're asked for *all* the films that can possibly be shown first on Thursday, and glancing at our diagrams the answer must be "L and G."

Sure enough, our answer is D.

QUESTION 7

Which one of the following CANNOT be true?

(A) *Harvest* is the last film shown on each day of the festival.
(B) *Limelight* is shown on each day of the festival.
(C) *Greed* is shown second on each day of the festival.
(D) A different film is shown first on each day of the festival.
(E) A different film is shown last on each day of the festival.

Circling back to pick up the non-if questions, we are asked to identify a Must Be False. We've got several scenarios on the board, so we can start here with a process of elimination and hope that gets us down to one answer. Let's see.

A) Whoa, wait a minute. This is the answer. The reason this is the answer is that either G or L has to be the last film shown on Friday. That's a rule. Putting H last every day would violate that rule, so it must be false. We got here quick, so let's scan through B-E and see if there's any reason to think we're wrong.
B) We've got L on all three days in a couple of our existing scenarios. No problem.
C) We've never seen this happen before, but it could happen. Like this:

Th	F	S
L		
G	H	L
H	G	G

D) This could have happened in our first scenario for #8, and could also have happened in our scenario for #9. No problem.
E) This happened in our second scenario for both #8 and #10.

Our answer is A, because it directly violates one of the game's rules.

GROUP 2, GAME 4
EXTRA PRACTICE

Exactly three films—*Greed, Harvest*, and *Limelight*—are shown during a film club's festival held on Thursday, Friday, and Saturday. Each film is shown at least once during the festival but never more than once on a given day. On each day at least one film is shown. Films are shown one at a time. The following conditions apply:

On Thursday *Harvest* is shown, and no film is shown after it on that day.

On Friday either Greed or Limelight, but not both, is shown, and no film is shown after it on that day.

On Saturday either Greed or Harvest, but not both, is shown, and no film is shown after it on that day.

6. Which one of the following could be a complete and accurate description of the order in which the films are shown at the festival?

(A) Thursday: *Limelight*, then *Harvest*; Friday: *Limelight*; Saturday: *Harvest*
(B) Thursday: *Harvest*; Friday: *Greed*, then *Limelight*; Saturday: *Limelight*, then *Greed*
(C) Thursday: *Harvest*; Friday: *Limelight*; Saturday: *Limelight*, then *Greed*
(D) Thursday: *Greed*, then *Harvest*, then *Limelight*; Friday: *Limelight*; Saturday: *Greed*
(E) Thursday: *Greed*, then *Harvest*; Friday: *Limelight*, then *Harvest*; Saturday: *Harvest*

7. Which one of the following CANNOT be true?

(A) *Harvest* is the last film shown on each day of the festival.
(B) *Limelight* is shown on each day of the festival.
(C) *Greed* is shown second on each day of the festival.
(D) A different film is shown first on each day of the festival.
(E) A different film is shown last on each day of the festival.

8. If *Limelight* is never shown again during the festival once *Greed* is shown, then which one of the following is the maximum number of film showings that could occur during the festival?

(A) three
(B) four
(C) five
(D) six
(E) seven

9. If *Greed* is shown exactly three times, *Harvest* is shown exactly twice, and *Limelight* is shown exactly once, then which one of the following must be true?

(A) All three films are shown on Thursday.
(B) Exactly two films are shown on Saturday.
(C) *Limelight* and *Harvest* are both shown on Thursday.
(D) *Greed* is the only film shown on Saturday.
(E) *Harvest* and *Greed* are both shown on Friday.

10. If *Limelight* is shown exactly three times, *Harvest* is shown exactly twice, and *Greed* is shown exactly once, then which one of the following is a complete and accurate list of the films that could be the first film shown on Thursday?

(A) *Harvest*
(B) *Limelight*
(C) *Greed, Harvest*
(D) *Greed, Limelight*
(E) *Greed, Harvest, Limelight*

GROUP 2, GAME 4
EXTRA PRACTICE

Exactly three films—*Greed, Harvest*, and *Limelight*—are shown during a film club's festival held on Thursday, Friday, and Saturday. Each film is shown at least once during the festival but never more than once on a given day. On each day at least one film is shown. Films are shown one at a time. The following conditions apply:

On Thursday *Harvest* is shown, and no film is shown after it on that day.
On Friday either Greed or Limelight, but not both, is shown, and no film is shown after it on that day.
On Saturday either Greed or Harvest, but not both, is shown, and no film is shown after it on that day.

6. Which one of the following could be a complete and accurate description of the order in which the films are shown at the festival?

(A) Thursday: *Limelight*, then *Harvest*; Friday: *Limelight*; Saturday: *Harvest*
(B) Thursday: *Harvest*; Friday: *Greed*, then *Limelight*; Saturday: *Limelight*, then *Greed*
(C) Thursday: *Harvest*; Friday: *Limelight*; Saturday: *Limelight*, then *Greed*
(D) Thursday: *Greed*, then *Harvest*, then *Limelight*; Friday: *Limelight*; Saturday: *Greed*
(E) Thursday: *Greed*, then *Harvest*; Friday: *Limelight*, then *Harvest*; Saturday: *Harvest*

7. Which one of the following CANNOT be true?

(A) *Harvest* is the last film shown on each day of the festival.
(B) *Limelight* is shown on each day of the festival.
(C) *Greed* is shown second on each day of the festival.
(D) A different film is shown first on each day of the festival.
(E) A different film is shown last on each day of the festival.

8. If *Limelight* is never shown again during the festival once *Greed* is shown, then which one of the following is the maximum number of film showings that could occur during the festival?

(A) three
(B) four
(C) five
(D) six
(E) seven

9. If *Greed* is shown exactly three times, *Harvest* is shown exactly twice, and *Limelight* is shown exactly once, then which one of the following must be true?

(A) All three films are shown on Thursday.
(B) Exactly two films are shown on Saturday.
(C) *Limelight* and *Harvest* are both shown on Thursday.
(D) *Greed* is the only film shown on Saturday.
(E) *Harvest* and *Greed* are both shown on Friday.

10. If *Limelight* is shown exactly three times, *Harvest* is shown exactly twice, and *Greed* is shown exactly once, then which one of the following is a complete and accurate list of the films that could be the first film shown on Thursday?

(A) *Harvest*
(B) *Limelight*
(C) *Greed*, *Harvest*
(D) *Greed*, *Limelight*
(E) *Greed*, *Harvest*, *Limelight*

GROUP 2, GAME 5

An album contains photographs picturing seven friends: Raimundo, Selma, Ty, Umiko, Wendy, Yakira, Zack. The friends appear either alone or in groups with one another, in accordance with the following:

Wendy appears in every photograph that Selma appears in.
Selma appears in every photograph that Umiko appears in.
Raimundo appears in every photograph that Yakira does not appear in.
Neither Ty nor Raimundo appears in any photograph that Wendy appears in.

13. Which one of the following could be a complete and accurate list of the friends who appear together in a photograph?

(A) Raimundo, Selma, Ty, Wendy
(B) Raimundo, Ty, Yakira, Zack
(C) Raimundo, Wendy, Yakira, Zack
(D) Selma, Ty, Umiko, Yakira
(E) Selma, Ty, Umiko, Zack

14. If Ty and Zack appear together in a photograph, then which one of the following must be true?

(A) Selma also appears in the photograph.
(B) Yakira also appears in the photograph.
(C) Wendy also appears in the photograph.
(D) Raimundo does not appear in the photograph.
(E) Umiko does not appear in the photograph.

15. What is the maximum number of friends who could appear in a photograph that Yakira does not appear in?

(A) six
(B) five
(C) four
(D) three
(E) two

16. If Umiko and Zack appear together in a photograph, then exactly how many of the other friends must also appear in that photograph?

(A) four
(B) three
(C) two
(D) one
(E) zero

17. If exactly three friends appear together in a photograph, then each of the following could be true EXCEPT:

(A) Selma and Zack both appear in the photograph.
(B) Ty and Yakira both appear in the photograph.
(C) Wendy and Selma both appear in the photograph.
(D) Yakira and Zack both appear in the photograph.
(E) Zack and Raimundo both appear in the photograph.

EXPLANATION

Two tricks here: First, understand the rules. Second, link the rules together. If you can do that, this game is a piece of cake.

First rule: The sufficient condition, the trigger, the thing that makes something happen, is S. Not W, even though W appeared first in the rule. W has to appear every time S appears; that's what the rule says. The rule does not say that S gets triggered by W. The proper diagram here is this:

$$S \rightarrow W$$

The second rule follows the exact same form. U is the trigger here, not S. The rule, by itself, looks like this:

$$U \rightarrow S$$

But we'd never even write those two separately; we'd immediately combine them together, via S. Like this:

$$U \rightarrow S \rightarrow W$$

Leave the third rule for a minute; it doesn't link (yet) to the existing rules. The fourth rule does. That rule, by itself, would look like this:

$$W \rightarrow \begin{cases} \cancel{T} \\ \cancel{R} \end{cases}$$

Note the *split* arrows here; this is absolutely critical here, since the third rule links to R but not T.

Linking the fourth rule to the first and second, we get:

$$U \rightarrow S \rightarrow W \rightarrow \begin{cases} \cancel{T} \\ \cancel{R} \end{cases}$$

Finally, the third rule. By itself, that rule looks like this:

$$\cancel{R} \rightarrow Y$$

Linking that rule in to our growing rule chain:

$$U \rightarrow S \rightarrow W \rightarrow \begin{cases} \cancel{T} \\ \cancel{R} \rightarrow Y \end{cases}$$

I START SALIVATING when I see this game. Literally. (And by "literally," I mean "figuratively," which is now an accepted meaning of the word according to Merriam-Webster, which apparently doesn't care that we're getting dumber and dumber.) Anyway, this game *is* a very spicy meatball, and I would not blame you if saliva *actually, really, in fact* was produced upon reading it. It tends to evoke the exact opposite response in most people, but that will change. Stay with me.

At this point, the game is pretty well crushed. We have four rules, and they're all linked into one chain. This means we've made giant inferences. For example, if U is present then Y must also be present. Some of you are undoubtedly saying "Huh?" right about now. But look: If U is present, then S has to be present as well. And if S is there, then W is there as well. If W is there, then R must be absent. R's absence forces the presence of Y.

We've crushed it into grape jelly; to pulverize it down to grape juice we'll quickly jot down the contrapositive of the entire chain. Like this:

```
          T
            ↘
~~Y~~ → R → ~~W~~ → ~~S~~ → ~~U~~
```

This will take some getting used to; like always, you should practice, practice, *practice* this game until it makes sense. You'll get the hang of it. It's a big opportunity; you don't have to hit a home run on every single pitch but when they groove you a fastball, you should do your best to knock it out of the park.

Before we turn to the questions, an important note about the way the rule chain and contrapositive function: Please do *not* think that this is two worlds, or two scenarios. The first rule chain is 100% of the rules in the game. The contrapositive chain is also 100% of the rules in the game, looked at through a different lens. Think about this: If S is positive, what happens? This is pretty easy; look at the initial rules chain and see that W is present, T is absent, R is absent, and Y is present. But here's where the rubber meets the road: What if S is negative?

If S is negative, it does mean that U is absent, because we can follow the arrows from negative S to negative U in the bottom diagram. But does the absence of S mean that W is absent, R is present, etcetera? *No.* The absence of S tells us absolutely nothing about W, R, T, or Y because *the arrows only go one way.*

This is a critical juncture. For a lot of students, this won't make a lick of sense the first, second, or third time you hear it. But eventually, if you stick with it, it will make sense to everyone. Hang in there. We'll be doing this stuff again to get you more practice.

Back to the having dominated the game by linking all the rules together, the questions should be a piece of cake.

QUESTION 13

Which one of the following could be a complete and accurate list of the friends who appear together in a photograph?

(A) Raimundo, Selma, Ty, Wendy
(B) Raimundo, Ty, Yakira, Zack
(C) Raimundo, Wendy, Yakira, Zack
(D) Selma, Ty, Umiko, Yakira
(E) Selma, Ty, Umiko, Zack

It's a list question, which we can narrow down using the rules as weapons.

- If U, then S. This gets rid of nothing.
- If S, then W. This gets rid of both D and E.
- If W, then no T and no R. This gets rid of both A and C.
- If no R, then Y. We've only got B left, but we'd better check B to make sure that it doesn't violate this rule. And it does not. Note that the relationship between R and Y is like mom and dad taking care of the baby; any time one of them is gone the other must be there, but there's nothing wrong with them *both* being there.

Our answer is B, because it's the only one that satisfies all the rules.

QUESTION 14

If Ty and Zack appear together in a photograph, then which one of the following must be true?

(A) Selma also appears in the photograph.
(B) Yakira also appears in the photograph.
(C) Wendy also appears in the photograph.
(D) Raimundo does not appear in the photograph.
(E) Umiko does not appear in the photograph.

"If" questions first. (I'll say it every time as a means of drilling it into your head.) The presence of Z doesn't force anything, since Z was the wild card. But the presence of T does do things. Let's just jot down a quick list, like this:

If you really want to do this as an In-Out game you can, but since there aren't fixed spots I actually think that overcomplicates it. I'd just use a simple list, like this.

We're asked for a Must Be True. We must have already answered it.

A) No, this must be false.
B) This could be true, but doesn't have to be. Y and T have no relationship.
C) This must be false as well.
D) This could be true, but doesn't have to be. T and R have no relationship.
E) Yep. If T is there then W is gone, S is gone, and U is gone.

Our answer is E.

QUESTION 16

If Umiko and Zack appear together in a photograph, then exactly how many of the other friends must also appear in that photograph?

(A) four
(B) three
(C) two
(D) one
(E) zero

Again, Z doesn't do anything, since Z is the wild card. But the presence of U does *everything.* Like this:

We're asked how many *other* friends (not counting Z and U) must appear in the photograph. The answer is S, W, and Y, or three.

Our answer is B.

Note the LSAC's temporary benevolence here; the nastiest trick answer would have been "five," which would have trapped those who didn't read the word "other." Frequently, the LSAT will be this tough. Here, it's a bit more kind. But it's a good reminder to read every question as carefully as possible.

QUESTION 17

If exactly three friends appear together in a photograph, then each of the following could be true EXCEPT:

(A) Selma and Zack both appear in the photograph.
(B) Ty and Yakira both appear in the photograph.
(C) Wendy and Selma both appear in the photograph.
(D) Yakira and Zack both appear in the photograph.
(E) Zack and Raimundo both appear in the photograph.

The special condition here (exactly three friends) means that exactly four friends have to be out. So we could see this question in an In-Out format if we chose, like this:

It's possible to make one immediate inference here; U must be out. This is due to the fact that if U were in, S, W, and Y would have to be in as well, which would add up to more than three friends in the photograph. So U is out for this question:

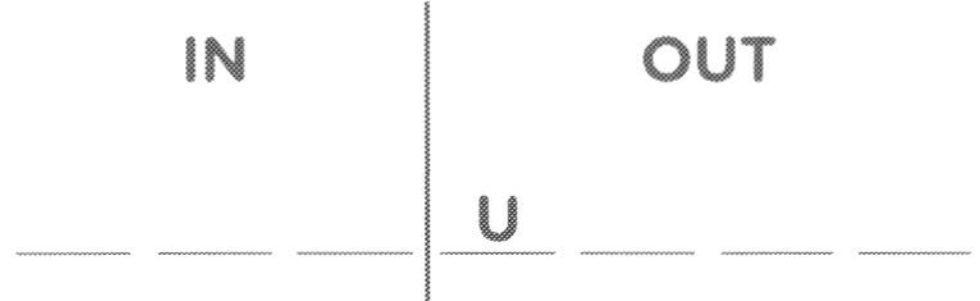

From here, there are several ways to get to three friends in the diagram. Let's check the answer choices, looking for one that won't work.

A) Oops, this would be a problem. Z doesn't do anything, but Z takes up a space. So does S, like this:

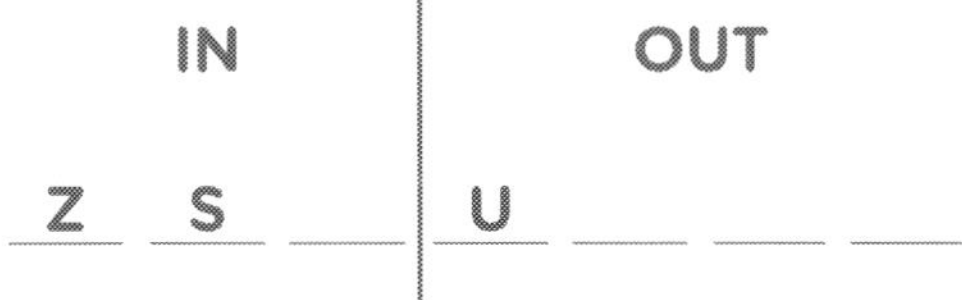

From here, we can see that W would have to be included, and so would Y. But that's four friends. No bueno. This will turn out to be the answer.

B) No problem; TYR would work.
C) No problem; SWY would work.
D) Not a problem; YZT would be fine.
E) No problem; ZRY for example.

Our answer is A, because it would result in more than three friends in the photo.

QUESTION 15

What is the maximum number of friends who could appear in a photograph that Yakira does not appear in?

(A) six
(B) five
(C) four
(D) three
(E) two

This question doesn't start with the word "if," so we skipped it on the first run through. But it's a hidden "if" question; the "that" here has the same "if" function that it had in all four of this game's rules. So we can make a new diagram:

The absence of Y triggers a positive R and a negative W, S, and U. But it has *no bearing* on T; those two variables aren't related. So if we're maximizing the number of folks in the photo, we'll bring T along. We'll also take Z, of course, since Z gets along with everybody.

So our answer is three, or D.

GROUP 2, GAME 5 FROM PREPTEST 45, DECEMBER 2004

GROUP 2, GAME 5
EXTRA PRACTICE

An album contains photographs picturing seven friends: Raimundo, Selma, Ty, Umiko, Wendy, Yakira, Zack. The friends appear either alone or in groups with one another, in accordance with the following:

Wendy appears in every photograph that Selma appears in.
Selma appears in every photograph that Umiko appears in.
Raimundo appears in every photograph that Yakira does not appear in.
Neither Ty nor Raimundo appears in any photograph that Wendy appears in.

13. Which one of the following could be a complete and accurate list of the friends who appear together in a photograph?

(A) Raimundo, Selma, Ty, Wendy
(B) Raimundo, Ty, Yakira, Zack
(C) Raimundo, Wendy, Yakira, Zack
(D) Selma, Ty, Umiko, Yakira
(E) Selma, Ty, Umiko, Zack

14. If Ty and Zack appear together in a photograph, then which one of the following must be true?

    (A) Selma also appears in the photograph.
    (B) Yakira also appears in the photograph.
    (C) Wendy also appears in the photograph.
    (D) Raimundo does not appear in the photograph.
    (E) Umiko does not appear in the photograph.

15. What is the maximum number of friends who could appear in a photograph that Yakira does not appear in?

    (A) six
    (B) five
    (C) four
    (D) three
    (E) two

16. If Umiko and Zack appear together in a photograph, then exactly how many of the other friends must also appear in that photograph?

    (A) four
    (B) three
    (C) two
    (D) one
    (E) zero

17. If exactly three friends appear together in a photograph, then each of the following could be true EXCEPT:

    (A) Selma and Zack both appear in the photograph.
    (B) Ty and Yakira both appear in the photograph.
    (C) Wendy and Selma both appear in the photograph.
    (D) Yakira and Zack both appear in the photograph.
    (E) Zack and Raimundo both appear in the photograph.

GROUP 2, GAME 5
EXTRA PRACTICE

An album contains photographs picturing seven friends: Raimundo, Selma, Ty, Umiko, Wendy, Yakira, Zack. The friends appear either alone or in groups with one another, in accordance with the following:

Wendy appears in every photograph that Selma appears in.
Selma appears in every photograph that Umiko appears in.
Raimundo appears in every photograph that Yakira does not appear in.
Neither Ty nor Raimundo appears in any photograph that Wendy appears in.

13. Which one of the following could be a complete and accurate list of the friends who appear together in a photograph?

(A) Raimundo, Selma, Ty, Wendy
(B) Raimundo, Ty, Yakira, Zack
(C) Raimundo, Wendy, Yakira, Zack
(D) Selma, Ty, Umiko, Yakira
(E) Selma, Ty, Umiko, Zack

14. If Ty and Zack appear together in a photograph, then which one of the following must be true?

    (A) Selma also appears in the photograph.
    (B) Yakira also appears in the photograph.
    (C) Wendy also appears in the photograph.
    (D) Raimundo does not appear in the photograph.
    (E) Umiko does not appear in the photograph.

15. What is the maximum number of friends who could appear in a photograph that Yakira does not appear in?

    (A) six
    (B) five
    (C) four
    (D) three
    (E) two

16. If Umiko and Zack appear together in a photograph, then exactly how many of the other friends must also appear in that photograph?

    (A) four
    (B) three
    (C) two
    (D) one
    (E) zero

17. If exactly three friends appear together in a photograph, then each of the following could be true EXCEPT:

    (A) Selma and Zack both appear in the photograph.
    (B) Ty and Yakira both appear in the photograph.
    (C) Wendy and Selma both appear in the photograph.
    (D) Yakira and Zack both appear in the photograph.
    (E) Zack and Raimundo both appear in the photograph.

GROUP 2, GAME 6

A locally known guitarist's demo CD contains exactly seven different songs—S, T, V, W, X, Y, and Z. Each song occupies exactly one of the CD's seven tracks. Some of the songs are rock classics; the others are new compositions. The following conditions must hold:

S occupies the fourth track of the CD.
Both W and Y precede S on the CD.
T precedes W on the CD.
A rock classic occupies the sixth track of the CD.
Each rock classic is immediately preceded on the CD by a new composition.
Z is a rock classic.

11. Which one of the following could be the order of the songs on the CD, from the first track through the seventh?

(A) T, W, V, S, Y, X, Z
(B) V, Y, T, S, W, Z, X
(C) X, Y, W, S, T, Z, S
(D) Y, T, W, S, X, Z, V
(E) Z, T, X, W, V, Y, S

12. Which one of the following is a pair of songs that must occupy consecutive tracks on the CD?

(A) S and V
(B) S and W
(C) T and Z
(D) T and Y
(E) V and Z

13. Which one of the following songs must be a new composition?

(A) S
(B) T
(C) W
(D) X
(E) Y

14. If W precedes Y on the CD, then which one of the following must be true?

(A) S is a rock classic.
(B) V is a rock classic.
(C) Y is a rock classic.
(D) T is a new composition.
(E) W is a new composition.

15. If there are exactly two songs on the CD that both precede V and are preceded by Y, then which one of the following could be true?

(A) V occupies the seventh track of the CD.
(B) X occupies the fifth track of the CD.
(C) Y occupies the third track of the CD.
(D) T is a rock classic.
(E) W is a rock classic.

EXPLANATION

Little things add up to a lot here. Follow the baby steps.

First, the general setup. We're putting seven songs in order; that's very familiar. We'll do that left to right; seven spots for seven things. And like the Thunderstorm game in Group 1 (Page 42) we've also got another piece of information about each spot. Let's start our diagram like this, with song names on the top and rock classic (R) and new composition (N) on the bottom:

S T V W X Y Z __ __ __ __ __ __ __

R / N __ __ __ __ __ __ __

As much as possible, we'll add pieces directly to the puzzle rather than making a list. So the first rule, obviously, looks like this:

__ __ __ S __ __ __

__ __ __ __ __ __ __

Now, because we *read all the rules before we write*, we'll add the second *and* third rule simultaneously. T goes before W; W and Y both go before S; S is fourth. So T...W, with Y, have to take up the first three spots. Like this:

(T ... W , Y) S __ __ __

__ __ __ __ __ __ __

Rock classic is sixth, no problem,

(T ... W , Y) S __ __ __

__ __ __ __ __ R __

Any time we have R, we have to have an N immediately in front of it. Let's notate that rule, conditionally, like this:

R → N R

~~N R~~ → ~~R~~

LIKE MANY (IF NOT ALL) of the games in Groups 1 and 2, this is one that you've simply gotta master. Real talk: If you're not *awesome* at this game, then you likely *suck* at the games overall. Please don't take offense; these are early days. You can, and will, get better. Do this game as many times as it takes until you own it.

A handful of inferences spring directly from this rule. We know the sixth spot is an R, so that obviously means the fifth spot is an N. But the first and last spots have to be N as well. The last spot can't be R because it's got an R preceding it; the first spot can't be R because it's preceded by nothing at all. Let's add those three to the diagram:

(T ... W , Y) S __ __ __

N __ __ __ N R N

The last rule says Z has to be a rock classic, and we don't need to bother writing that rule down at all, because there's only one place where Z can go at this point. We know it's not first, second, third, or fourth, because those spots are already occupied. If Z has to be a rock classic, then it also can't go fifth or seventh, because we've inferred that those spots are new compositions. So the only spot where Z can go is sixth, and we can write that straight into our diagram:

(T ... W , Y) S __ Z __

N __ __ __ N R N

Boom! That's an awesome inference right there. That's what it feels like when you're doing it right. We used *every* rule in the game to figure out that Z had to go sixth; that's definitely going to pay off. Finally, we're left with only two spots for X and V; the fifth and seventh spots. Let's go ahead and write those in.

(T ... W , Y) S X/V Z V/X

N __ __ __ N R N

The LSAT is about to give us five easy points. We deserve it.

QUESTION 11

Which one of the following could be the order of the songs on the CD, from the first track through the seventh?

(A) T, W, V, S, Y, X, Z
(B) V, Y, T, S, W, Z, X
(C) X, Y, W, S, T, Z, S
(D) Y, T, W, S, X, Z, V
(E) Z, T, X, W, V, Y, S

Process of elimination, using rules (and inferences!) to eliminate answers. Like this:

- S must go fourth. This gets rid of E.
- Z must go sixth (our big inference). This gets rid of A (and would also have eliminated E, if it wasn't already gone).
- T before W. This gets rid of C.
- W and Y before S. This gets rid of B.

Our answer is D.

It's worth noting here that our very *last* inference, that X and V have to go fifth and seventh, would have eliminated A, B, C, *and* E. When you achieve expert status, you might actually be able to answer a question like this that easily. But be careful with this strategy; only use it if you're *sure.*

QUESTION 15

If there are exactly two songs on the CD that both precede V and are preceded by Y, then which one of the following could be true?

(A) V occupies the seventh track of the CD.
(B) X occupies the fifth track of the CD.
(C) Y occupies the third track of the CD.
(D) T is a rock classic.
(E) W is a rock classic.

The only trick here is understanding the new rule. Read it carefully and make sure you understand it. If you end up having a problem answering the question (like if you eliminate all five answers, or think two or more of them could work) then you've probably misunderstood the rule. The rule looks like this:

Since V always has to go fifth or seventh, here, it must go fifth. (If it went seventh, then both Y and S would have to go fourth.) If V is fifth and Y is second, then T must go first and W must go third. Like this:

We're asked for something that could be true in this scenario. Let's see.

A) Nope, V is fifth.
B) Nope, V is fifth.
C) Nope, Y is second.
D) No, T has to be a new composition.
E) Okay, this is possible.

Our answer is E.

QUESTION 14

If W precedes Y on the CD, then which one of the following must be true?

(A) S is a rock classic.
(B) V is a rock classic.
(C) Y is a rock classic.
(D) T is a new composition.
(E) W is a new composition.

Should I say it, or do you already know which questions we tackle first? Okay fine, twist my arm—the If questions. If W is before Y, then the first three spots are T W Y. (Basically, all this new condition does is remove the brackets from our initial diagram.) Like this:

We're asked for something that must be true in our new diagram.

A) No, we have no clue whether S is a rock classic or a new composition.
B) No, this must be false.
C) No, we have no clue.
D) Yep.
E) No clue.

Our answer is D.

QUESTION 12

Which one of the following is a pair of songs that must occupy consecutive tracks on the CD?

(A) S and V
(B) S and W
(C) T and Z
(D) T and Y
(E) V and Z

Here's where our big inferences really pay off. Since V has to go fifth or seventh, and Z always goes sixth, V and Z are always consecutive.

Our answer is E.

QUESTION 13

Which one of the following songs must be a new composition?

(A) S
(B) T
(C) W
(D) X
(E) Y

And again, our big inferences pay off. Since V and X share the fifth and seventh spots, both of those guys have to be new compositions.

Only one of them is listed here, so our answer is D.

That's it! This is a game you can do in less than five minutes, with practice. From this perspective, the LSAT is largely a test of how hard you can work. Anybody can *say* "I'm a hard worker" on their personal statement. Please don't bother; your reader will think you're full of shit like everybody else. The LSAT, especially the games, is your chance to *show* how hard you can work. Get on it.

GROUP 2, GAME 6 FROM PREPTEST 51, DECEMBER 2006

GROUP 2, GAME 6
EXTRA PRACTICE

A locally known guitarist's demo CD contains exactly seven different songs—S, T, V, W, X, Y, and Z. Each song occupies exactly one of the CD's seven tracks. Some of the songs are rock classics; the others are new compositions. The following conditions must hold:

S occupies the fourth track of the CD.
Both W and Y precede S on the CD.
T precedes W on the CD.
A rock classic occupies the sixth track of the CD.
Each rock classic is immediately preceded on the CD by a new composition.
Z is a rock classic.

11. Which one of the following could be the order of the songs on the CD, from the first track through the seventh?

(A) T, W, V, S, Y, X, Z
(B) V, Y, T, S, W, Z, X
(C) X, Y, W, S, T, Z, S
(D) Y, T, W, S, X, Z, V
(E) Z, T, X, W, V, Y, S

12. Which one of the following is a pair of songs that must occupy consecutive tracks on the CD?

(A) S and V
(B) S and W
(C) T and Z
(D) T and Y
(E) V and Z

13. Which one of the following songs must be a new composition?

(A) S
(B) T
(C) W
(D) X
(E) Y

14. If W precedes Y on the CD, then which one of the following must be true?

(A) S is a rock classic.
(B) V is a rock classic.
(C) Y is a rock classic.
(D) T is a new composition.
(E) W is a new composition.

15. If there are exactly two songs on the CD that both precede V and are preceded by Y, then which one of the following could be true?

(A) V occupies the seventh track of the CD.
(B) X occupies the fifth track of the CD.
(C) Y occupies the third track of the CD.
(D) T is a rock classic.
(E) W is a rock classic.

GROUP 2, GAME 6
EXTRA PRACTICE

A locally known guitarist's demo CD contains exactly seven different songs—S, T, V, W, X, Y, and Z. Each song occupies exactly one of the CD's seven tracks. Some of the songs are rock classics; the others are new compositions. The following conditions must hold:

S occupies the fourth track of the CD.
Both W and Y precede S on the CD.
T precedes W on the CD.
A rock classic occupies the sixth track of the CD.
Each rock classic is immediately preceded on the CD by a new composition.
Z is a rock classic.

11. Which one of the following could be the order of the songs on the CD, from the first track through the seventh?

(A) T, W, V, S, Y, X, Z
(B) V, Y, T, S, W, Z, X
(C) X, Y, W, S, T, Z, S
(D) Y, T, W, S, X, Z, V
(E) Z, T, X, W, V, Y, S

12. Which one of the following is a pair of songs that must occupy consecutive tracks on the CD?

(A) S and V
(B) S and W
(C) T and Z
(D) T and Y
(E) V and Z

13. Which one of the following songs must be a new composition?

(A) S
(B) T
(C) W
(D) X
(E) Y

14. If W precedes Y on the CD, then which one of the following must be true?

(A) S is a rock classic.
(B) V is a rock classic.
(C) Y is a rock classic.
(D) T is a new composition.
(E) W is a new composition.

15. If there are exactly two songs on the CD that both precede V and are preceded by Y, then which one of the following could be true?

(A) V occupies the seventh track of the CD.
(B) X occupies the fifth track of the CD.
(C) Y occupies the third track of the CD.
(D) T is a rock classic.
(E) W is a rock classic.

GROUP **3**

GROUP 3, GAME 1

Exactly six guideposts, numbered 1 through 6, mark a mountain trail. Each guidepost pictures a different one of six animals—fox, grizzly, hare, lynx, moose, or porcupine. The following conditions must apply:

The grizzly is pictured on either guidepost 3 or guidepost 4.
The moose guidepost is numbered lower than the hare guidepost.
The lynx guidepost is numbered lower than the moose guidepost but higher than the fox guidepost.

1. Which one of the following could be an accurate list of the animals pictured on the guideposts, listed in order from guidepost 1 through guidepost 6?

(A) fox, lynx, grizzly, porcupine, moose, hare
(B) fox, lynx, moose, hare, grizzly, porcupine
(C) fox, moose, grizzly, lynx, hare, porcupine
(D) lynx, fox, moose, grizzly, hare, porcupine
(E) porcupine, fox, hare, grizzly, lynx, moose

2. Which one of the following animals CANNOT be the one pictured on guidepost 3?

(A) fox
(B) grizzly
(C) lynx
(D) moose
(E) porcupine

3. If the moose is pictured on guidepost 3, then which one of the following is the lowest numbered guidepost that could picture the porcupine?

(A) guidepost 1
(B) guidepost 2
(C) guidepost 4
(D) guidepost 5
(E) guidepost 6

4. If guidepost 5 does not picture the moose, then which one of the following must be true?

(A) The lynx is pictured on guidepost 2.
(B) The moose is pictured on guidepost 3.
(C) The grizzly is pictured on guidepost 4.
(D) The porcupine is pictured on guidepost 5.
(E) The hare is pictured on guidepost 6.

5. Which one of the following animals could be pictured on any one of the six guideposts?

(A) fox
(B) hare
(C) lynx
(D) moose
(E) porcupine

6. If the moose guidepost is numbered exactly one higher than the lynx guidepost, then which one of the following could be true?

(A) Guidepost 5 pictures the hare.
(B) Guidepost 4 pictures the moose.
(C) Guidepost 4 pictures the porcupine.
(D) Guidepost 3 pictures the lynx.
(E) Guidepost 3 pictures the porcupine.

EXPLANATION

A note at the beginning of Group 3: To this point, I've tried to be very diligent about explaining every single step along the way. But if you've mastered Groups 1 and 2, you shouldn't need quite as much help as this point. This isn't to say that I'm going to skip straight to the answers from here on out. But I will be picking up the pace a bit; expect a slightly brisker pace, and slightly bigger leaps, going forward. (Of course, as always, you'll also find lengthy digressions where useful to the reader or amusing to the author.)

For this first game in Group 3, the second and third rule link together here, in an obvious F . . . L . . . M . . . H chain. A deeper inference is the connection between that chain and the first rule, requiring G to go third or fourth. It's useful to play with the extremes here; an expert looks at this game and asks something like "can F go after G?" As it turns out, no. If G were third, and F were fourth, there wouldn't be room for L...M...H. Similarly, H can't go before G. (If G were fourth and H were third, there wouldn't be room in front of that for F... L... M.

So it's possible here to see an inference about G; a relation between G and the F...L... M...H chain. Our completed web of rules looks like this:

We can also pencil out our six spots, throwing G in the middle two spots, and placing F and H, respectively, in the first two and last two. Like this:

This isn't the only way to solve this game; you did not have to make all of these inferences. This is simply one way that an expert might have attacked this game on one particular day. (The same expert might not make exactly the same diagram tomorrow; the games are highly improvisational.) The critical part here is simply linking F...L...M...H. That part is required. If you didn't do that much, we'd recommend that you go back to Groups 1 and 2 before continuing further.

FUN GAME HERE. What, you're not having fun? You really should be, at least sometimes. These are *games.* No, they're not as amazing as Grand Theft Auto; I'll never neglect my Playstation on account of this stuff. But they're at least as fun as any crossword or Sudoku puzzle. My flight's delayed, my phone's dead, and the bar's closed? If you had a book of these games, I might beg you for it.

Seriously though, I do think this is a fun one. I like the symmetry of it, and I like making the connections. Oh, and it has a fox.

QUESTION 1

Which one of the following could be an accurate list of the animals pictured on the guideposts, listed in order from guidepost 1 through guidepost 6?

(A) fox, lynx, grizzly, porcupine, moose, hare
(B) fox, lynx, moose, hare, grizzly, porcupine
(C) fox, moose, grizzly, lynx, hare, porcupine
(D) lynx, fox, moose, grizzly, hare, porcupine
(E) porcupine, fox, hare, grizzly, lynx, moose

We'll always do the list questions by process of elimination, testing each rule to eliminate answer choices. Sometimes, when we have a linear chain of rules like F...L...M...H, we can test the entire chain at once. Like this:

- F...L...M...H This gets rid of C, D, and E.
- G must go third or fourth. This gets rid of B.

Our answer is A.

QUESTION 3

If the moose is pictured on guidepost 3, then which one of the following is the lowest numbered guidepost that could picture the porcupine?

(A) guidepost 1
(B) guidepost 2
(C) guidepost 4
(D) guidepost 5
(E) guidepost 6

If the moose is third, we get this:

The lowest numbered guidepost for P is fifth, so our answer is D.

It's critical that you do this question just the way we did it here; make your diagram and predict the answer, don't test answer choices. If you found yourself testing A, like "Can P go first? Hmm, let's see..." then you're wasting a ton of time that you might need elsewhere on the test.

QUESTION 4

If guidepost 5 does not picture the moose, then which one of the following must be true?

(A) The lynx is pictured on guidepost 2.
(B) The moose is pictured on guidepost 3.
(C) The grizzly is pictured on guidepost 4.
(D) The porcupine is pictured on guidepost 5.
(E) The hare is pictured on guidepost 6.

If the moose is not fifth, then it has to go either third or fourth, flip-flopping places with G. That puts F-L in the first two spots, leaving H and P to flip-flop in the last two. Like this:

We're asked for a Must Be True. Shouldn't be too tough.

A) Yes, this has to be true in our diagram. We *could* pick A here and move on, but it's only going to take 10 seconds to eliminate B-E and reach 100% certainty. Like so:
B) This could be true, but doesn't have to be.
C) Could be true; doesn't have to be.
D) Could be true, not must be true.
E) Could be true, not must be true.

Our answer is A.

QUESTION 6

If the moose guidepost is numbered exactly one higher than the lynx guidepost, then which one of the following could be true?

(A) Guidepost 5 pictures the hare.
(B) Guidepost 4 pictures the moose.
(C) Guidepost 4 pictures the porcupine.
(D) Guidepost 3 pictures the lynx.
(E) Guidepost 3 pictures the porcupine.

First, apply the new condition as a modifier to the initial chain of rules. Like this:

Since G has to go third or fourth, this modified web of rules leaves two outcomes:

We're looking for something that could be true in either of our two scenarios.

A) Yes, this looks like it would work in the second of our scenarios.
B) Nope. The fourth guidepost has to be L or G.
C) Nope, like we said, #4 is either L or G.
D) Guidepost 3 has to be either G or M.
E) No, like we said, #3 is either G or M.

Our answer is A, because it's the only one that works.

QUESTION 2

Which one of the following animals CANNOT be the one pictured on guidepost 3?

(A) fox
(B) grizzly
(C) lynx
(D) moose
(E) porcupine

There are two main ways to solve this question. The first, fastest, most expert way would be simply to infer the correct answer. Who can't go third? Well, neither F nor H can go third, because F has four things that have to go behind it (L, M, H, and G) and H has four things that must go ahead of it (F, L, M, and G). So F or H would be the answer here. Only F is listed, so the answer is A.

The second way to solve the problem would be testing the answer choices. Fortunately, the correct answer appears at the top of the list, so it hopefully wouldn't take too long to test. But if the correct answer was E, you might spend more time than we'd like sorting this one out.

In any case, our answer is A.

QUESTION 5

Which one of the following animals could be pictured on any one of the six guideposts?

(A) fox
(B) hare
(C) lynx
(D) moose
(E) porcupine

Easiest question of all time? Possibly. This game included one wild card, P. It's not always the case that the wild card can go in any spot, but in this case it can. Furthermore, none of F, L, M, H, or G are eligible to go in any spot.

So our answer here is E.

Piece of cake. As I've said before, and as I'm sure to say again, this is the bread and butter of the LSAT logic games. If you're not crushing this one, then you're not ready to take the LSAT.

GROUP 3, GAME 1 FROM PREPTEST 46, JUNE 2005

GROUP 3, GAME 1
EXTRA PRACTICE

Exactly six guideposts, numbered 1 through 6, mark a mountain trail. Each guidepost pictures a different one of six animals—fox, grizzly, hare, lynx, moose, or porcupine. The following conditions must apply:

The grizzly is pictured on either guidepost 3 or guidepost 4.
The moose guidepost is numbered lower than the hare guidepost.
The lynx guidepost is numbered lower than the moose guidepost but higher than the fox guidepost.

1. Which one of the following could be an accurate list of the animals pictured on the guideposts, listed in order from guidepost 1 through guidepost 6?

(A) fox, lynx, grizzly, porcupine, moose, hare
(B) fox, lynx, moose, hare, grizzly, porcupine
(C) fox, moose, grizzly, lynx, hare, porcupine
(D) lynx, fox, moose, grizzly, hare, porcupine
(E) porcupine, fox, hare, grizzly, lynx, moose

2. Which one of the following animals CANNOT be the one pictured on guidepost 3?

(A) fox
(B) grizzly
(C) lynx
(D) moose
(E) porcupine

3. If the moose is pictured on guidepost 3, then which one of the following is the lowest numbered guidepost that could picture the porcupine?

(A) guidepost 1
(B) guidepost 2
(C) guidepost 4
(D) guidepost 5
(E) guidepost 6

4. If guidepost 5 does not picture the moose, then which one of the following must be true?

(A) The lynx is pictured on guidepost 2.
(B) The moose is pictured on guidepost 3.
(C) The grizzly is pictured on guidepost 4.
(D) The porcupine is pictured on guidepost 5.
(E) The hare is pictured on guidepost 6.

5. Which one of the following animals could be pictured on any one of the six guideposts?

(A) fox
(B) hare
(C) lynx
(D) moose
(E) porcupine

6. If the moose guidepost is numbered exactly one higher than the lynx guidepost, then which one of the following could be true?

(A) Guidepost 5 pictures the hare.
(B) Guidepost 4 pictures the moose.
(C) Guidepost 4 pictures the porcupine.
(D) Guidepost 3 pictures the lynx.
(E) Guidepost 3 pictures the porcupine.

GROUP 3, GAME 1
EXTRA PRACTICE

Exactly six guideposts, numbered 1 through 6, mark a mountain trail. Each guidepost pictures a different one of six animals—fox, grizzly, hare, lynx, moose, or porcupine. The following conditions must apply:

The grizzly is pictured on either guidepost 3 or guidepost 4.
The moose guidepost is numbered lower than the hare guidepost.
The lynx guidepost is numbered lower than the moose guidepost but higher than the fox guidepost.

1. Which one of the following could be an accurate list of the animals pictured on the guideposts, listed in order from guidepost 1 through guidepost 6?

(A) fox, lynx, grizzly, porcupine, moose, hare
(B) fox, lynx, moose, hare, grizzly, porcupine
(C) fox, moose, grizzly, lynx, hare, porcupine
(D) lynx, fox, moose, grizzly, hare, porcupine
(E) porcupine, fox, hare, grizzly, lynx, moose

2. Which one of the following animals CANNOT be the one pictured on guidepost 3?

(A) fox
(B) grizzly
(C) lynx
(D) moose
(E) porcupine

3. If the moose is pictured on guidepost 3, then which one of the following is the lowest numbered guidepost that could picture the porcupine?

(A) guidepost 1
(B) guidepost 2
(C) guidepost 4
(D) guidepost 5
(E) guidepost 6

4. If guidepost 5 does not picture the moose, then which one of the following must be true?

(A) The lynx is pictured on guidepost 2.
(B) The moose is pictured on guidepost 3.
(C) The grizzly is pictured on guidepost 4.
(D) The porcupine is pictured on guidepost 5.
(E) The hare is pictured on guidepost 6.

5. Which one of the following animals could be pictured on any one of the six guideposts?

(A) fox
(B) hare
(C) lynx
(D) moose
(E) porcupine

6. If the moose guidepost is numbered exactly one higher than the lynx guidepost, then which one of the following could be true?

(A) Guidepost 5 pictures the hare.
(B) Guidepost 4 pictures the moose.
(C) Guidepost 4 pictures the porcupine.
(D) Guidepost 3 pictures the lynx.
(E) Guidepost 3 pictures the porcupine.

GROUP 3, GAME 2

A panel of five scientists will be formed. The panelists will be selected from among three botanists—F, G, and H—three chemists—K, L, and M—and three zoologists—P, Q, and R. Selection is governed by the following conditions:

The panel must include at least one scientist of each of the three types.
If more than one botanist is selected, then at most one zoologist is selected.
F and K cannot both be selected.
K and M cannot both be selected.
If M is selected, both P and R must be selected.

1. Which one of the following is an acceptable selection of scientists for the panel?

(A) F, G, K, P, Q
(B) G, H, K, L, M
(C) G, H, K, L, R
(D) H, K, M, P, R
(E) H, L, M, P, Q

2. If M is the only chemist selected for the panel, which one of the following must be true?

(A) F and G are both selected.
(B) G and H are both selected.
(C) H and P are both selected.
(D) F, G, and H are all selected.
(E) P, Q, and R are all selected.

3. If four of the scientists selected are F, L, Q, and R, which one of the following must be the fifth scientist selected?

(A) G
(B) H
(C) K
(D) M
(E) P

4. If P is the only zoologist selected, which one of the following must be true?

(A) If K is selected, G cannot be selected.
(B) If L is selected, F cannot be selected.
(C) If exactly one chemist is selected, it must be K.
(D) If exactly two chemists are selected, F cannot be selected.
(E) If exactly two chemists are selected, G cannot be selected.

5. If both G and H are among the scientists selected, then the panel must include either

(A) F or else K
(B) F or else M
(C) K or else M
(D) M or else Q
(E) P or else Q

EXPLANATION

Because we're selecting exactly five scientists out of nine, and leaving exactly four out, this game is ripe for an In-Out attack. Like this:

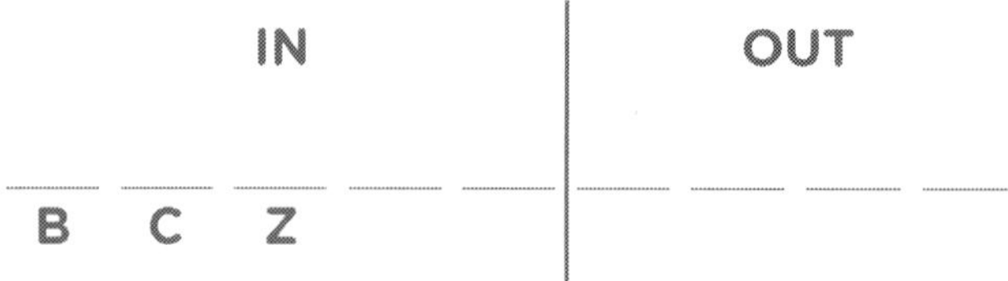

Notice that we've reserved a spot in the "In" group for one botanist, one chemist, and one zoologist; the other two spots in the "In" group can be any of these three types. Next, we'll diagram the rules. Take your time with these! Don't just scribble down the first thing that comes to mind. Take a minute to digest each rule, making sure you understand each one, simplify them as best you can, and look for connections.

First, if we have more than one botanist, we can only have one zoologist. Contrapositive: if we have more than one zoologist, we must only have one botanist. One way to diagram it (not the only way, but a way that makes sense to us) is this:

$$B^{>1} \rightarrow Z^{1}$$

$$Z^{>1} \rightarrow B^{1}$$

Next, we'll do the three rules involving F, K, M, P, and R. The lynchpin is M; that's the one that links the whole web together. Here's the web:

And here's the contrapositive of that web:

$K \rightarrow \not{F}$
$K \rightarrow \not{M}$
$\not{P} \rightarrow \not{M}$
$\not{R} \rightarrow \not{M}$

HERE'S A GAME that, historically, I tend to have overcomplicated. My usual approach was always to make two worlds, one with M and one without M, since M is the game's major asshole, and makes a lot of things happen. This isn't a terrible approach to the game, but since all the questions are "If" questions it's probably unnecessary. Ben Olson finally convinced me of the value of doing the "If" questions first, especially if you don't immediately see any shortcuts. If you want an extra challenge, try doing this game with two worlds based on M. It works, certainly, but I think it's simpler to do it the way we've done it here.

Again, I invite you to contact me directly if you need more help; it's easy for me to post a short video on my website explaining this rule chain, but I'll only bother with it if you ask. I'm nathan@foxlsat.com, and I love hearing from readers. Don't be shy!

We haven't made any crushing inferences; this game has a lot of flexibility unless you start making worlds. But most students won't immediately see the best way to make worlds here (see my sidebar) so it might be best to simply attack the questions. We've got a list question, which shouldn't be too tough, followed by four "If" questions, which are usually pretty manageable. Let's see what we've got.

QUESTION 1

Which one of the following is an acceptable selection of scientists for the panel?

(A) F, G, K, P, Q
(B) G, H, K, L, M
(C) G, H, K, L, R
(D) H, K, M, P, R
(E) H, L, M, P, Q

Process of elimination. Grab a rule, use that rule to eliminate as many answer choices as possible, move on to the next rule. No need to test the rules in order; grab whichever rule you think might be easy to test first.

- If K, no F and no M. This gets rid of A, B, and D. Sweet!
- If M, then P and R. This gets rid of E.

Looks like the answer is C, but if we weren't 100 percent sure, it wouldn't take long to get there. Let's just make sure that C has at least once scientist of each type (yes it does), and let's make sure that if C has more than one botanist (which it does) then it has no more than one zoologist (it has one).

So we're all good, and our answer is C.

QUESTION 2

If M is the only chemist selected for the panel, which one of the following must be true?

(A) F and G are both selected.
(B) G and H are both selected.
(C) H and P are both selected.
(D) F, G, and H are all selected.
(E) P, Q, and R are all selected.

M is the game's big asshole, so putting M in the In group should make a lot happen. The steps, quickly, are: 1) If M is the *only* chemist, then M is in and both K and L are out. 2) If M is in, then both P and R have to be in. 3) Since P and R are zoologists, that means we can't have more than one botanist. So we can reserve the remaining two spots in the out group (alongside K and L) for two out of the three of F, G, and H. It doesn't matter which botanist we pick; what matters is that the Out group is now full. There's no room for Q to be out, so Q has to be in. Like this:

$B^{2,3} \rightarrow Z^1$

$Z^{2,3} \rightarrow B^1$

F/G/H	M	P	R	Q	K	L	(F/G/H	)
B	C	Z	Z	Z			B	B

Now all we have to do is identify an answer that must be true in this scenario.

A) We can have F or G, but we don't have to have either and actually *can't* have both of these botanists. No way.
B) Same explanation here; we can have either, but not both.
C) We do have to have P, but we don't necessarily have to have H. Still looking.
D) No, we can only have one of these guys.
E) Yep. In order to avoid having too many botanists, we end up taking all three zoologists.

Our answer is E.

QUESTION 3

If four of the scientists selected are F, L, Q, and R, which one of the following must be the fifth scientist selected?

(A) G
(B) H
(C) K
(D) M
(E) P

Let's break this one down into three steps. First, place F, L, Q, and R into the In group, and put K into the Out group since F hates K:

IN					OUT			
F	L	Q	R		K			
B	C	Z	Z					

Next, since Q and R are both zoologists, that means we can only have one botanist. We already have F, so G and H must be out. Like this:

IN					OUT			
F	L	Q	R		K	G	H	
B	C	Z	Z					

This leaves us with only M and P; one has to be in, and the other has to be out. But if M were in, P would have to be in as well. That won't work, so M must be out. Our final diagram for this question is:

F	L	Q	R	P	K	G	H	M
B	C	Z	Z	Z		B	B	

As it turns out, that last step is the answer.

The fifth scientist selected must be P, so our answer is E.

QUESTION 4

If P is the only zoologist selected, which one of the following must be true?

(A) If K is selected, G cannot be selected.
(B) If L is selected, F cannot be selected.
(C) If exactly one chemist is selected, it must be K.
(D) If exactly two chemists are selected, F cannot be selected.
(E) If exactly two chemists are selected, G cannot be selected.

If P is the *only* zoologist selected, then Q and R (the other zoologists) must be out. And since the inclusion of R is a necessary condition for the inclusion of M, then M must be out as well. Like this:

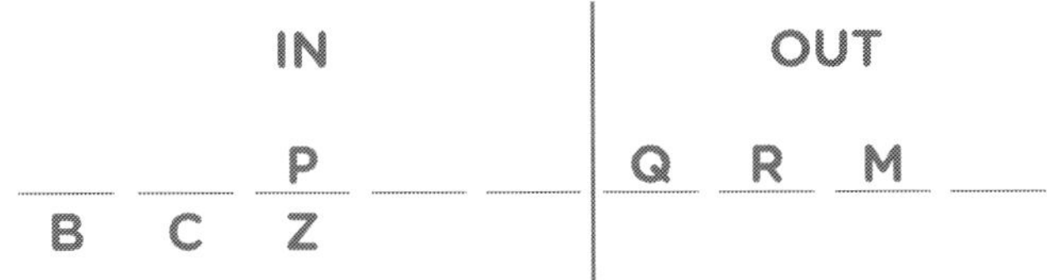

This leaves us with only one Out spot, and as frequently happens in In-Out games, we can Seat the Assholes first. (See Page 73 for the introduction to this concept.) F and K are assholes, since they hate each other. So one of them, doesn't matter who, must fill the only remaining spot in the Out group. This fills the Out group, and means everyone else must be In. Like this:

K → ~~F~~
~~P~~ → ~~M~~
~~R~~

G	L	P	H	F/K	Q	R	M	K/F
B	C	Z	B					

This is a very common, very important pattern to recognize. It should be trivial, from here, to identify a Must Be True.

A) No, G is definitely selected.
B) No, L is definitely selected and we can still have F.
C) No, this is must be false since L, a chemist, is already selected.
D) Well, yeah. The only way to get two chemists on board would be to add K to L, which would put F in the Out group. This must be it.
E) Nope, G is already selected regardless of how many chemists we pick.

Our answer is D.

QUESTION 5

If both G and H are among the scientists selected, then the panel must include either

(A) F or else K
(B) F or else M
(C) K or else M
(D) M or else Q
(E) P or else Q

If G and H, both botanists, are selected, then we have at most one zoologist. Since M requires *two* zoologists (both P and R) we know that M must be out. Like this:

IN					OUT			
G			H				M	
B	C	Z			Z	Z		

Two out of the three of P, Q, and R must fill those two Out spots for zoologists, and M is already out, so once again, we're left with only one spot in the Out group. And once again, the assholes F and K must fill that spot. Once we do this, the nice guy L is forced into the In group. At this point we won't care whether we have P, Q, or R as our lone zoologist, and we also won't care whether F or K fills the final In spot. Like this:

G	L	P/Q/R	H	F/K	P/Q/R		M	F/K
B	C	Z	B		Z	Z		

Time to answer the question. We're looking for a Must Be True:

A) Yep, we're definitely going to have one of these two. This must be the answer.
B) No, it's possible to leave out both F and M.
C) No, it's possible to leave out both K and M.
D) No, it's possible to leave out both M and Q.
E) No, it's possible to leave out both P and Q.

Our answer is A.

This game is quite a bit tougher than the typical Game 1 on more modern tests; this game, if it appeared on a current LSAT, would more likely be game 3 or 4. But it's still a fairly common type of game, and it has a lot to teach us (especially regarding Seating the Assholes First) about the modern test.

GROUP 3, GAME 2
EXTRA PRACTICE

A panel of five scientists will be formed. The panelists will be selected from among three botanists—F, G, and H—three chemists—K, L, and M—and three zoologists—P, Q, and R. Selection is governed by the following conditions:

The panel must include at least one scientist of each of the three types.
If more than one botanist is selected, then at most one zoologist is selected.
F and K cannot both be selected.
K and M cannot both be selected.
If M is selected, both P and R must be selected.

1. Which one of the following is an acceptable selection of scientists for the panel?

(A) F, G, K, P, Q
(B) G, H, K, L, M
(C) G, H, K, L, R
(D) H, K, M, P, R
(E) H, L, M, P, Q

2. If M is the only chemist selected for the panel, which one of the following must be true?

   (A) F and G are both selected.
   (B) G and H are both selected.
   (C) H and P are both selected.
   (D) F, G, and H are all selected.
   (E) P, Q, and R are all selected.

3. If four of the scientists selected are F, L, Q, and R, which one of the following must be the fifth scientist selected?

   (A) G
   (B) H
   (C) K
   (D) M
   (E) P

4. If P is the only zoologist selected, which one of the following must be true?

   (A) If K is selected, G cannot be selected.
   (B) If L is selected, F cannot be selected.
   (C) If exactly one chemist is selected, it must be K.
   (D) If exactly two chemists are selected, F cannot be selected.
   (E) If exactly two chemists are selected, G cannot be selected.

5. If both G and H are among the scientists selected, then the panel must include either

   (A) F or else K
   (B) F or else M
   (C) K or else M
   (D) M or else Q
   (E) P or else Q

GROUP 3, GAME 2
EXTRA PRACTICE

A panel of five scientists will be formed. The panelists will be selected from among three botanists—F, G, and H—three chemists—K, L, and M—and three zoologists—P, Q, and R. Selection is governed by the following conditions:

The panel must include at least one scientist of each of the three types.
If more than one botanist is selected, then at most one zoologist is selected.
F and K cannot both be selected.
K and M cannot both be selected.
If M is selected, both P and R must be selected.

1. Which one of the following is an acceptable selection of scientists for the panel?

(A) F, G, K, P, Q
(B) G, H, K, L, M
(C) G, H, K, L, R
(D) H, K, M, P, R
(E) H, L, M, P, Q

2. If M is the only chemist selected for the panel, which one of the following must be true?

   (A) F and G are both selected.
   (B) G and H are both selected.
   (C) H and P are both selected.
   (D) F, G, and H are all selected.
   (E) P, Q, and R are all selected.

3. If four of the scientists selected are F, L, Q, and R, which one of the following must be the fifth scientist selected?

   (A) G
   (B) H
   (C) K
   (D) M
   (E) P

4. If P is the only zoologist selected, which one of the following must be true?

   (A) If K is selected, G cannot be selected.
   (B) If L is selected, F cannot be selected.
   (C) If exactly one chemist is selected, it must be K.
   (D) If exactly two chemists are selected, F cannot be selected.
   (E) If exactly two chemists are selected, G cannot be selected.

5. If both G and H are among the scientists selected, then the panel must include either

   (A) F or else K
   (B) F or else M
   (C) K or else M
   (D) M or else Q
   (E) P or else Q

GROUP 3, GAME 3

A cruise line is scheduling seven week-long voyages for the ship *Freedom*. Each voyage will occur in exactly one of the first seven weeks of the season: weeks 1 through 7. Each voyage will be to exactly one of four destinations: Guadeloupe, Jamaica, Martinique, or Trinidad. Each destination will be scheduled for at least one of the weeks. The following conditions apply to *Freedom*'s schedule:

Jamaica will not be its destination in week 4.
Trinidad will be its destination in week 7.
Freedom will make exactly two voyages to Martinique, and at least one voyage to Guadeloupe will occur in some week between those two voyages.
Guadeloupe will be its destination in the week preceding any voyage it makes to Jamaica.
No destination will be scheduled for consecutive weeks.

11. Which one of the following is an acceptable schedule of destinations for *Freedom*, in order from week 1 through week 7?

(A) Guadeloupe, Jamaica, Martinique, Trinidad, Guadeloupe, Martinique, Trinidad
(B) Guadeloupe, Martinique, Trinidad, Martinique, Guadeloupe, Jamaica, Trinidad
(C) Jamaica, Martinique, Guadeloupe, Martinique, Guadeloupe, Jamaica, Trinidad
(D) Martinique, Trinidad, Guadeloupe, Jamaica, Martinique, Guadeloupe, Trinidad
(E) Martinique, Trinidad, Guadeloupe, Trinidad, Guadeloupe, Jamaica, Martinique

12. Which one of the following CANNOT be true about *Freedom*'s schedule of voyages?

(A) *Freedom* makes a voyage to Trinidad in week 6.
(B) *Freedom* makes a voyage to Martinique in week 5.
(C) *Freedom* makes a voyage to Jamaica in week 6.
(D) *Freedom* makes a voyage to Jamaica in week 3.
(E) *Freedom* makes a voyage to Guadeloupe in week 3.

13. If *Freedom* makes a voyage to Trinidad in week 5, which one of the following could be true?

(A) *Freedom* makes a voyage to Trinidad in week 1.
(B) *Freedom* makes a voyage to Martinique in week 2.
(C) *Freedom* makes a voyage to Guadeloupe in week 3.
(D) *Freedom* makes a voyage to Martinique in week 4.
(E) *Freedom* makes a voyage to Jamaica in week 6.

14. If *Freedom* makes a voyage to Guadeloupe in week 1 and a voyage to Jamaica in week 5, which one of the following must be true?

(A) *Freedom* makes a voyage to Jamaica in week 2.
(B) *Freedom* makes a voyage to Trinidad in week 2.
(C) *Freedom* makes a voyage to Martinique in week 3.
(D) *Freedom* makes a voyage to Guadeloupe in week 6.
(E) *Freedom* makes a voyage to Martinique in week 6.

15. If *Freedom* makes a voyage to Guadeloupe in week 1 and to Trinidad in week 2, which one of the following must be true?

(A) *Freedom* makes a voyage to Martinique in week 3.
(B) *Freedom* makes a voyage to Martinique in week 4.
(C) *Freedom* makes a voyage to Martinique in week 5.
(D) *Freedom* makes a voyage to Guadeloupe in week 3.
(E) *Freedom* makes a voyage to Guadeloupe in week 5.

16. If *Freedom* makes a voyage to Martinique in week 3, which one of the following could be an accurate list of *Freedom*'s destinations in week 4 and week 5, respectively?

(A) Guadeloupe, Trinidad
(B) Jamaica, Guadeloupe
(C) Martinique, Trinidad
(D) Trinidad, Jamaica
(E) Trinidad, Martinique

17. Which one of the following must be true about *Freedom*'s schedule of voyages?

(A) *Freedom* makes a voyage to Guadeloupe either in week 1 or else in week 2.
(B) *Freedom* makes a voyage to Martinique either in week 2 or else in week 3.
(C) *Freedom* makes at most two voyages to Guadeloupe.
(D) *Freedom* makes at most two voyages to Jamaica.
(E) *Freedom* makes at most two voyages to Trinidad.

EXPLANATION

This is a game without any huge inferences. In fact, we're only going to make two tiny ones before we tackle the questions. First, the basic setup, which should seem very familiar by now:

We've incorporated the first two rules directly into the diagram, since that's the simplest way to deal with them. For the next three rules, we have this:

M^1 ... G ... M^2

J → G J

~~GJ~~ → ~~J~~

~~XX~~

From these rules, we can really only infer two things. First, obviously, since T is seventh, T can't go sixth. Next, we can infer that J can't go first, since G has to immediately precede any trip to J. Let's add those two to the diagram:

As much as we love making big inferences, and as much as we love making worlds, this simply isn't a game where we can take that approach. We're stuck, and we'd have to brutally overcomplicate things in order to go much further. (Six worlds based on the various possibilities for the two Ms? No thanks.)

We talked earlier about hitting the wall; that's exactly what's happened here. Making everything more complicated than it needs to be won't do us much good. So it's time to attack the questions.

QUESTION 11

Which one of the following is an acceptable schedule of destinations for *Freedom*, in order from week 1 through week 7?

(A) Guadeloupe, Jamaica, Martinique, Trinidad, Guadeloupe, Martinique, Trinidad
(B) Guadeloupe, Martinique, Trinidad, Martinique, Guadeloupe, Jamaica, Trinidad
(C) Jamaica, Martinique, Guadeloupe, Martinique, Guadeloupe, Jamaica, Trinidad
(D) Martinique, Trinidad, Guadeloupe, Jamaica, Martinique, Guadeloupe, Trinidad
(E) Martinique, Trinidad, Guadeloupe, Trinidad, Guadeloupe, Jamaica, Martinique

A list question. Though we haven't made many inferences, we're confident we've got a firm grasp on the rules they've given us, so this shouldn't be too tough.

- J isn't fourth. This gets rid of D.
- T must be seventh. This gets rid of E.
- Exactly two Ms, with no G somewhere between them. This gets rid of B.
- If J, then GJ. This gets rid of C.
- We're down to nothing but A, but we might as well test the last rule: Can't go to the same destination consecutively. Great, A does not violate this rule.

Our answer is A.

QUESTION 13

If *Freedom* makes a voyage to Trinidad in week 5, which one of the following could be true?

(A) *Freedom* makes a voyage to Trinidad in week 1.
(B) *Freedom* makes a voyage to Martinique in week 2.
(C) *Freedom* makes a voyage to Guadeloupe in week 3.
(D) *Freedom* makes a voyage to Martinique in week 4.
(E) *Freedom* makes a voyage to Jamaica in week 6.

Start with the special condition; simply drop T into space five:

This restricts J pretty significantly. At this point, J can only go second or third. These Js, in turn, each trigger an immediately preceding G. Without a better idea, let's go ahead and pencil these two scenarios:

One more step: Think about M...G...M. If GJ go first and second, we're going to need to put an additional MG...M into the third, fourth, and sixth spots. If GJ goes second and third, we'll need to put M first, and also fourth or sixth. Like this:

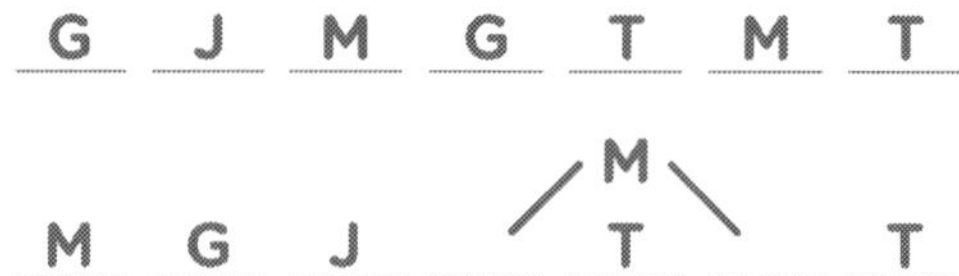

That feels like far enough. Let's see; we're asked to find something that could be true in one or both of our scenarios.

A) No, this doesn't happen in either scenario for this question.
B) Nope, this also can't happen.
C) Nope, can't happen.
D) Yes, this looks like it could happen in the second of our two scenarios.
E) No, because G would have to be in slot 5 which can't happen.

Tough question. Our answer is D, because it's the only one that will work.

QUESTION 14

If *Freedom* makes a voyage to Guadeloupe in week 1 and a voyage to Jamaica in week 5, which one of the following must be true?

(A) *Freedom* makes a voyage to Jamaica in week 2.
(B) *Freedom* makes a voyage to Trinidad in week 2.
(C) *Freedom* makes a voyage to Martinique in week 3.
(D) *Freedom* makes a voyage to Guadeloupe in week 6.
(E) *Freedom* makes a voyage to Martinique in week 6.

If J goes in spot five, then G has to immediately precede it in spot four. If G is in spot one, that gives us this:

G ___ ___ G J ___ T

The next step would be to think about M...G...M; the only way to satisfy this rule, at this point, will be to put M in the sixth spot, and also in either the second or third. Like this:

G (M, ___) G J M T

Should be answerable from here. We're looking for something that must be true. (Can you predict it, from here?)

A) This could be true, because G is already in the first spot, but it doesn't *have* to be true.
B) This could happen, but it doesn't have to.
C) Could happen, doesn't have to.
D) No, this must be false.
E) Yep. We've already incorporated this in our diagram, so this is what we were looking for. If you had the same instincts, then you're clearly starting to get it.

Our answer is E.

QUESTION 15

If *Freedom* makes a voyage to Guadeloupe in week 1 and to Trinidad in week 2, which one of the following must be true?

(A) *Freedom* makes a voyage to Martinique in week 3.
(B) *Freedom* makes a voyage to Martinique in week 4.
(C) *Freedom* makes a voyage to Martinique in week 5.
(D) *Freedom* makes a voyage to Guadeloupe in week 3.
(E) *Freedom* makes a voyage to Guadeloupe in week 5.

G in the first spot, and T in the second. Okay, let's jot that down:

G	T					T

We're left with only four spots, and we need to satisfy *two* rules within those four spots. We're still looking for M...G...M, so that's gonna be there for sure. We also need a J, which must be immediately preceded by a G. So there's only one way to do it; we have to drop M G J M in our four open spots. Like this:

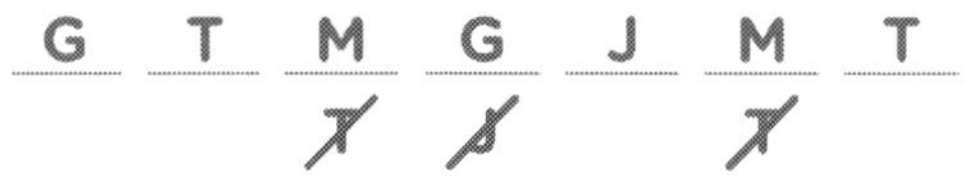

G	T	M	G	J	M	T
		~~T~~	~~J~~		~~T~~	

Finding a Must Be True from this point should be trivial, since we know everything.

A) Yes, this must be true. This is the answer, as long as B-E all suck.
B) This definitely sucks. The fourth spot has to be G.
C) Also sucks, the fifth spot is J.
D) No, the third spot is M.
E) No, the fifth spot is J.

Our answer is A.

QUESTION 16

If *Freedom* makes a voyage to Martinique in week 3, which one of the following could be an accurate list of *Freedom*'s destinations in week 4 and week 5, respectively?

(A) Guadeloupe, Trinidad
(B) Jamaica, Guadeloupe
(C) Martinique, Trinidad
(D) Trinidad, Jamaica
(E) Trinidad, Martinique

If M goes third, then it can't go fourth. So our starting diagram here looks like this:

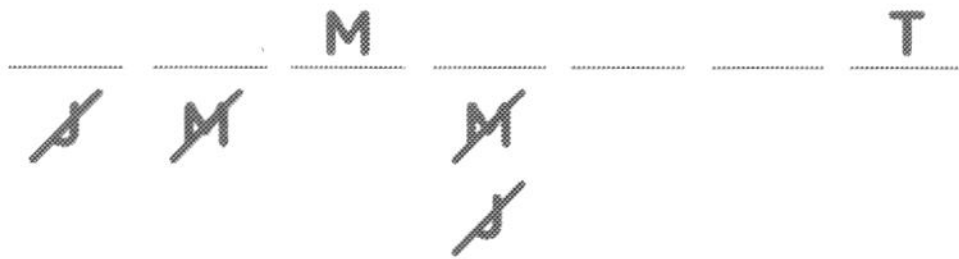

From there, the other M (and the G that goes between the Ms) must be either before or after the third spot. So we see two ways to do it, like this:

M G M ___ ___ ___ T

___ ___ M (G ... M , ___) T

We're asked about the fourth and fifth spots. Let's see:

A) Yes, this seems perfectly possible in our second scenario. Let's see if we can get rid of B-E.
B) No, J can't be fourth.
C) No, if M is third then the other M can't be fourth.
D) No, this would violate the J → GJ rule.
E) No, this wouldn't work in either scenario.

Our answer is A.

QUESTION 12

Which one of the following CANNOT be true about *Freedom*'s schedule of voyages?

(A) *Freedom* makes a voyage to Trinidad in week 6.
(B) *Freedom* makes a voyage to Martinique in week 5.
(C) *Freedom* makes a voyage to Jamaica in week 6.
(D) *Freedom* makes a voyage to Jamaica in week 3.
(E) *Freedom* makes a voyage to Guadeloupe in week 3.

Circling back, we find a Must Be False. Let's see what the answers have in store for us.

A) Wow, well, yeah. If T is seventh then T can't be sixth since you can't have consecutive trips to the same destination. We can skim the rest of the answer choices, but this is going to turn out to be the one.
B) This could have happened in our second scenario for question 16.
C) We might not have seen this happen before, but there's no reason to suspect it won't work. Especially when we *know* that A won't work. There's no point in testing it.
D) We saw this happen in question 13.
E) We haven't seen this happen, but why wouldn't it work?

Our answer is A, because it's clearly impossible.

QUESTION 17

Which one of the following must be true about *Freedom*'s schedule of voyages?

(A) *Freedom* makes a voyage to Guadeloupe either in week 1 or else in week 2.
(B) *Freedom* makes a voyage to Martinique either in week 2 or else in week 3.
(C) *Freedom* makes at most two voyages to Guadeloupe.
(D) *Freedom* makes at most two voyages to Jamaica.
(E) *Freedom* makes at most two voyages to Trinidad.

Finally, a Must Be True. Let's see.

A) This has happened in a lot of our previous work, but does it have to happen every single time? Why would it?
B) Definitely not; one of our scenarios for 13 disproves this.
C) No, why wouldn't three Gs work?
D) Oh, well, yeah. This better be true or else we'll be in trouble. If we had more than two Js, we'd also have to have more than two Gs to accompany them. Three Js, three Gs, two Ms; at least one T; that's nine players and we only have seven spots.
E) No, we could have three Ts.

Our answer is D, because it's impossible to have three or more Js.

GROUP 3, GAME 3
EXTRA PRACTICE

A cruise line is scheduling seven week-long voyages for the ship *Freedom*. Each voyage will occur in exactly one of the first seven weeks of the season: weeks 1 through 7. Each voyage will be to exactly one of four destinations: Guadeloupe, Jamaica, Martinique, or Trinidad. Each destination will be scheduled for at least one of the weeks. The following conditions apply to *Freedom*'s schedule:

Jamaica will not be its destination in week 4.
Trinidad will be its destination in week 7.
Freedom will make exactly two voyages to Martinique, and at least one voyage to Guadeloupe will occur in some week between those two voyages.
Guadeloupe will be its destination in the week preceding any voyage it makes to Jamaica.
No destination will be scheduled for consecutive weeks.

11. Which one of the following is an acceptable schedule of destinations for *Freedom*, in order from week 1 through week 7?

(A) Guadeloupe, Jamaica, Martinique, Trinidad, Guadeloupe, Martinique, Trinidad
(B) Guadeloupe, Martinique, Trinidad, Martinique, Guadeloupe, Jamaica, Trinidad
(C) Jamaica, Martinique, Guadeloupe, Martinique, Guadeloupe, Jamaica, Trinidad
(D) Martinique, Trinidad, Guadeloupe, Jamaica, Martinique, Guadeloupe, Trinidad
(E) Martinique, Trinidad, Guadeloupe, Trinidad, Guadeloupe, Jamaica, Martinique

12. Which one of the following CANNOT be true about *Freedom*'s schedule of voyages?

    (A) *Freedom* makes a voyage to Trinidad in week 6.
    (B) *Freedom* makes a voyage to Martinique in week 5.
    (C) *Freedom* makes a voyage to Jamaica in week 6.
    (D) *Freedom* makes a voyage to Jamaica in week 3.
    (E) *Freedom* makes a voyage to Guadeloupe in week 3.

13. If *Freedom* makes a voyage to Trinidad in week 5, which one of the following could be true?

    (A) *Freedom* makes a voyage to Trinidad in week 1.
    (B) *Freedom* makes a voyage to Martinique in week 2.
    (C) *Freedom* makes a voyage to Guadeloupe in week 3.
    (D) *Freedom* makes a voyage to Martinique in week 4.
    (E) *Freedom* makes a voyage to Jamaica in week 6.

14. If *Freedom* makes a voyage to Guadeloupe in week 1 and a voyage to Jamaica in week 5, which one of the following must be true?

    (A) *Freedom* makes a voyage to Jamaica in week 2.
    (B) *Freedom* makes a voyage to Trinidad in week 2.
    (C) *Freedom* makes a voyage to Martinique in week 3.
    (D) *Freedom* makes a voyage to Guadeloupe in week 6.
    (E) *Freedom* makes a voyage to Martinique in week 6.

15. If *Freedom* makes a voyage to Guadeloupe in week 1 and to Trinidad in week 2, which one of the following must be true?

    (A) *Freedom* makes a voyage to Martinique in week 3.
    (B) *Freedom* makes a voyage to Martinique in week 4.
    (C) *Freedom* makes a voyage to Martinique in week 5.
    (D) *Freedom* makes a voyage to Guadeloupe in week 3.
    (E) *Freedom* makes a voyage to Guadeloupe in week 5.

16. If *Freedom* makes a voyage to Martinique in week 3, which one of the following could be an accurate list of *Freedom*'s destinations in week 4 and week 5, respectively?

    (A) Guadeloupe, Trinidad
    (B) Jamaica, Guadeloupe
    (C) Martinique, Trinidad
    (D) Trinidad, Jamaica
    (E) Trinidad, Martinique

17. Which one of the following must be true about *Freedom*'s schedule of voyages?

    (A) *Freedom* makes a voyage to Guadeloupe either in week 1 or else in week 2.
    (B) *Freedom* makes a voyage to Martinique either in week 2 or else in week 3.
    (C) *Freedom* makes at most two voyages to Guadeloupe.
    (D) *Freedom* makes at most two voyages to Jamaica.
    (E) *Freedom* makes at most two voyages to Trinidad.

GROUP 3, GAME 3
EXTRA PRACTICE

A cruise line is scheduling seven week-long voyages for the ship *Freedom*. Each voyage will occur in exactly one of the first seven weeks of the season: weeks 1 through 7. Each voyage will be to exactly one of four destinations: Guadeloupe, Jamaica, Martinique, or Trinidad. Each destination will be scheduled for at least one of the weeks. The following conditions apply to *Freedom*'s schedule:

Jamaica will not be its destination in week 4.
Trinidad will be its destination in week 7.
Freedom will make exactly two voyages to Martinique, and at least one voyage to Guadeloupe will occur in some week between those two voyages.
Guadeloupe will be its destination in the week preceding any voyage it makes to Jamaica.
No destination will be scheduled for consecutive weeks.

11. Which one of the following is an acceptable schedule of destinations for *Freedom*, in order from week 1 through week 7?

(A) Guadeloupe, Jamaica, Martinique, Trinidad, Guadeloupe, Martinique, Trinidad
(B) Guadeloupe, Martinique, Trinidad, Martinique, Guadeloupe, Jamaica, Trinidad
(C) Jamaica, Martinique, Guadeloupe, Martinique, Guadeloupe, Jamaica, Trinidad
(D) Martinique, Trinidad, Guadeloupe, Jamaica, Martinique, Guadeloupe, Trinidad
(E) Martinique, Trinidad, Guadeloupe, Trinidad, Guadeloupe, Jamaica, Martinique

12. Which one of the following CANNOT be true about *Freedom*'s schedule of voyages?

(A) *Freedom* makes a voyage to Trinidad in week 6.
(B) *Freedom* makes a voyage to Martinique in week 5.
(C) *Freedom* makes a voyage to Jamaica in week 6.
(D) *Freedom* makes a voyage to Jamaica in week 3.
(E) *Freedom* makes a voyage to Guadeloupe in week 3.

13. If *Freedom* makes a voyage to Trinidad in week 5, which one of the following could be true?

(A) *Freedom* makes a voyage to Trinidad in week 1.
(B) *Freedom* makes a voyage to Martinique in week 2.
(C) *Freedom* makes a voyage to Guadeloupe in week 3.
(D) *Freedom* makes a voyage to Martinique in week 4.
(E) *Freedom* makes a voyage to Jamaica in week 6.

14. If *Freedom* makes a voyage to Guadeloupe in week 1 and a voyage to Jamaica in week 5, which one of the following must be true?

(A) *Freedom* makes a voyage to Jamaica in week 2.
(B) *Freedom* makes a voyage to Trinidad in week 2.
(C) *Freedom* makes a voyage to Martinique in week 3.
(D) *Freedom* makes a voyage to Guadeloupe in week 6.
(E) *Freedom* makes a voyage to Martinique in week 6.

15. If *Freedom* makes a voyage to Guadeloupe in week 1 and to Trinidad in week 2, which one of the following must be true?

(A) *Freedom* makes a voyage to Martinique in week 3.
(B) *Freedom* makes a voyage to Martinique in week 4.
(C) *Freedom* makes a voyage to Martinique in week 5.
(D) *Freedom* makes a voyage to Guadeloupe in week 3.
(E) *Freedom* makes a voyage to Guadeloupe in week 5.

16. If *Freedom* makes a voyage to Martinique in week 3, which one of the following could be an accurate list of *Freedom*'s destinations in week 4 and week 5, respectively?

(A) Guadeloupe, Trinidad
(B) Jamaica, Guadeloupe
(C) Martinique, Trinidad
(D) Trinidad, Jamaica
(E) Trinidad, Martinique

17. Which one of the following must be true about *Freedom*'s schedule of voyages?

(A) *Freedom* makes a voyage to Guadeloupe either in week 1 or else in week 2.
(B) *Freedom* makes a voyage to Martinique either in week 2 or else in week 3.
(C) *Freedom* makes at most two voyages to Guadeloupe.
(D) *Freedom* makes at most two voyages to Jamaica.
(E) *Freedom* makes at most two voyages to Trinidad.

GROUP 3, GAME 4

There are exactly three recycling centers in Rivertown: Center 1, Center 2, and Center 3. Exactly five kinds of material are recycled at these recycling centers: glass, newsprint, plastic, tin, and wood. Each recycling center recycles at least two but no more than three of these kinds of material. The following conditions must hold:

Any recycling center that recycles wood also recycles newsprint.
Every kind of material that Center 2 recycles is also recycled at Center 1.
Only one of the recycling centers recycles plastic, and that recycling center does not recycle glass.

18. Which one of the following could be an accurate account of all the kinds of material recycled at each recycling center in Rivertown?

(A) Center 1: newsprint, plastic, wood; Center 2: newsprint, wood; Center 3: glass, tin, wood
(B) Center 1: glass, newsprint, tin; Center 2: glass, newsprint, tin; Center 3: newsprint, plastic, wood
(C) Center 1: glass, newsprint, wood; Center 2: glass, newsprint, tin; Center 3: plastic, tin
(D) Center 1: glass, plastic, tin; Center 2: glass, tin; Center 3: newsprint, wood
(E) Center 1: newsprint, plastic, wood; Center 2: newsprint, plastic, wood; Center 3: glass, newsprint, tin

19. Which one of the following is a complete and accurate list of the recycling centers in Rivertown any one of which could recycle plastic?

(A) Center 1 only
(B) Center 3 only
(C) Center 1, Center 2
(D) Center 1, Center 3
(E) Center 1, Center 2, Center 3

20. If Center 2 recycles three kinds of material, then which one of the following kinds of material must Center 3 recycle?

(A) glass
(B) newsprint
(C) plastic
(D) tin
(E) wood

21. If each recycling center in Rivertown recycles exactly three kinds of material, then which one of the following could be true?

(A) Only Center 2 recycles glass.
(B) Only Center 3 recycles newsprint.
(C) Only Center 1 recycles plastic.
(D) Only Center 3 recycles tin.
(E) Only Center 1 recycles wood.

22. If Center 3 recycles glass, then which one of the following kinds of material must Center 2 recycle?

(A) glass
(B) newsprint
(C) plastic
(D) tin
(E) wood

23. If Center 1 is the only recycling center that recycles wood, then which one of the following could be a complete and accurate list of the kinds of material that one of the recycling centers recycles?

(A) plastic, tin
(B) newsprint, wood
(C) newsprint, tin
(D) glass, wood
(E) glass, tin

EXPLANATION

This game is quite a bit tougher, at least on its surface. Maybe the questions will turn out to be easy; we never know until we get there. But from a setup standpoint, this one seems a bit trickier. Here's how I see this one:

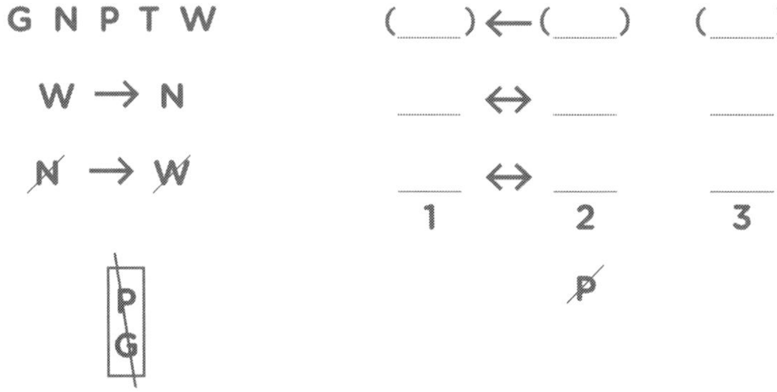

The lines without parentheses are spots that must be filled. So each group has two spots without parentheses and one spot with. Since anything that's in group 2 must also be in group 1, we have double arrows going between the mandatory spots in groups 1 and 2. For the *optional* spot, the arrow there only goes one way. If group 2 has three types of materials, then whatever that third thing is has to go in group 1 as well. But group 1 can have a random third thing in it that *doesn't* match group 2, as long as group 2 has only two types of materials.

Note also that we've made one inference; since anything in group 2 has to also be in group 1, and since plastic can only go once, this means that plastic can't be in group 2. (It can, however, be in group 1 as long as it's the third, optional, material.)

Beyond that, it seems like there's quite a bit of flexibility here. So rather than overcomplicate things, let's dive into the questions.

QUESTION 18

Which one of the following could be an accurate account of all the kinds of material recycled at each recycling center in Rivertown?

(A) Center 1: newsprint, plastic, wood; Center 2: newsprint, wood; Center 3: glass, tin, wood
(B) Center 1: glass, newsprint, tin; Center 2: glass, newsprint, tin; Center 3: newsprint, plastic, wood
(C) Center 1: glass, newsprint, wood; Center 2: glass, newsprint, tin; Center 3: plastic, tin
(D) Center 1: glass, plastic, tin; Center 2: glass, tin; Center 3: newsprint, wood
(E) Center 1: newsprint, plastic, wood; Center 2: newsprint, plastic, wood; Center 3: glass, newsprint, tin

List question—let's do the process of elimination.

- W → N This gets rid of A.
- Anything in group 2 has to be in group 1. This gets rid of C.
- P can only go once. This gets rid of E.
- P and G can't go together. This gets rid of D.

Our answer is B, because it can't be anything else.

QUESTION 20

If Center 2 recycles three kinds of material, then which one of the following kinds of material must Center 3 recycle?

(A) glass
(B) newsprint
(C) plastic
(D) tin
(E) wood

(Skipping 19 to tackle the "if" questions first.) No need to do a diagram here; the answer is "plastic." As we noted earlier, plastic can never go in group 2, and can only go in group 1 if it's the optional, third material in that group. But if group 2 has three things, then P can't go in group 1 either. Our inference really helped us out here.

So P has to go in group 3, and that's our answer: C.

QUESTION 21

If each recycling center in Rivertown recycles exactly three kinds of material, then which one of the following could be true?

(A) Only Center 2 recycles glass.
(B) Only Center 3 recycles newsprint.
(C) Only Center 1 recycles plastic.
(D) Only Center 3 recycles tin.
(E) Only Center 1 recycles wood.

Here, we'll make a diagram. The steps are basically these:

- P must go in group 3, and nowhere else, for the reasons we discussed previously.
- G can't go in group 3, because P is there.
- N must go in both groups 1 and 2, because without N you can't have W, and without N, W, and P you wouldn't be able to have three types of material.

The diagram looks like this:

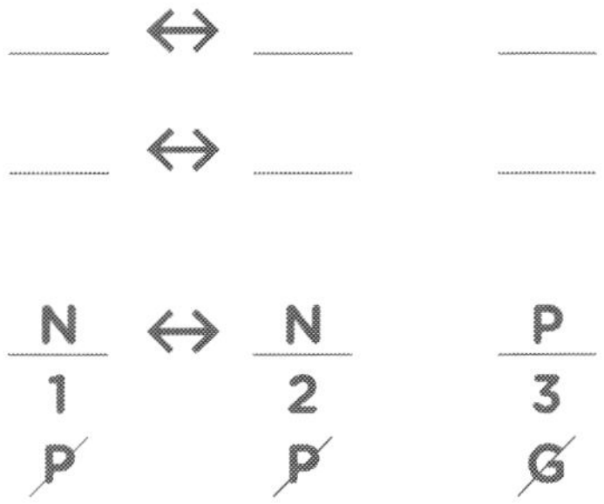

___	⇔	___	___
___	⇔	___	___
N	⇔	N	P
1		2	3
~~P~~		~~P~~	~~G~~

Hopefully that's enough to answer the question. We're looking for something that could be true. Let's see:

A) No, because everything in groups 1 and 2 has to match.
B) No, because N is already in both groups 1 and 2.
C) No, because P is already in group 3.
D) This seems possible. If we can get rid of E, this will be our answer.
E) No, because everything in groups 1 and 2 has to match.

Our answer is D, because it's the only one that will work.

Note that we didn't even bother testing it; if we're *certain* that the answer can't be A, B, C, or E, then the answer must be D. Any time you can shave on this test will help you answer the tougher questions. It's worth it.

QUESTION 22

If Center 3 recycles glass, then which one of the following kinds of material must Center 2 recycle?

(A) glass
(B) newsprint
(C) plastic
(D) tin
(E) wood

Again, a new diagram is in order. The steps are basically:

- If center 3 has G, it can't have P.
- The only other place P can possibly go is in the optional spot for group 1.
- Therefore, group 2 can only have two materials (no optional material).
- Group 1, since it has P, can't have G.
- This leaves only W, N, and T for the two empty spots in group 1. Since W requires N, there's no way to pick two out of the three of W, N, and T without including N. (If we leave N out, we'd also have to leave W out, leaving only T—a shortage.) So group 1 must have N.
- If group 1 has N, then group 2 must have N as well.

Here's the diagram:

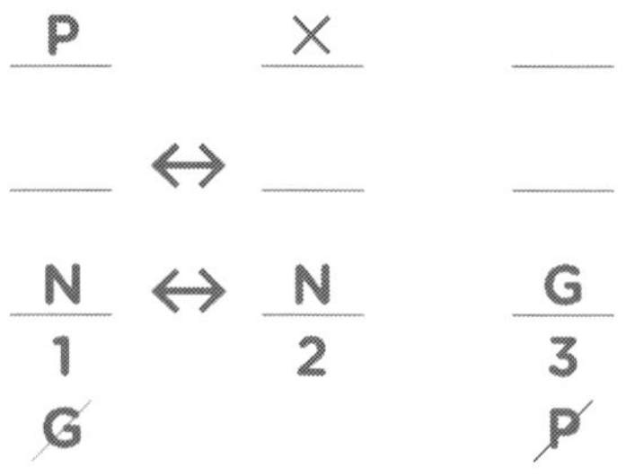

P		×		___
___	↔	___		___
N	↔	N		G
1		2		3
~~G~~				~~P~~

We're asked for something that must be in center 2, and the last step above got us there. Center 2 must have newsprint.

Our answer is B.

QUESTION 23

If Center 1 is the only recycling center that recycles wood, then which one of the following could be a complete and accurate list of the kinds of material that one of the recycling centers recycles?

(A) plastic, tin
(B) newsprint, wood
(C) newsprint, tin
(D) glass, wood
(E) glass, tin

Again, a new diagram. The steps are these:

- If group 1 is the *only* group with W, then that must be the optional material in group 1.
- Therefore group 2 has no optional material.
- If group 1 has W, it must also have N.
- If group 1 has N, then group 2 must as well.
- Group 2 can't have W or P.
- Because P can't go anywhere else, it must go in group 3.
- With P in group 3, G can't go there.
- Here's the step that almost everyone, including an LSAT professional, will miss. The rules say "exactly five kinds of materials *are* recycled." It hasn't come up so far, but this means that we do need to use each kind of material at least once. If that's true, then both group 1 and 2 are going to have to have G.
- For the same reason, Group 3 now has to have T.

Here's the finished diagram:

1		2	3
W		X	( )
G	↔	G	T
N	↔	N	P
~~P~~		~~P~~	~~W~~
		~~W~~	~~G~~

We're looking for a list that *could be* the complete list of materials recycled in one of the groups. We can probably eliminate a lot of wrong answers here, hopefully four of them.

A) This looks like it might be possible in group 3. Let's not test it though; let's just see if we can get rid of B-E.
B) No, this can't be the complete list in any of the groups. Group 1 must have three things, not two. Group 2 and 3 can't have W, if group 1 is the only group allowed to have W.
C) No, this is impossible. This is the answer choice that's very hard to eliminate if you forget that you have to use all five materials at least once.
D) No, this won't work.
E) Nope.

Our answer is A, because B-E won't work.

QUESTION 19

Which one of the following is a complete and accurate list of the recycling centers in Rivertown any one of which could recycle plastic?

(A) Center 1 only
(B) Center 3 only
(C) Center 1, Center 2
(D) Center 1, Center 3
(E) Center 1, Center 2, Center 3

We predicted this one in our initial setup. The only place P can go is groups 1 and 3. If that's an answer choice, it's our answer.

Yep. Our answer is D.

GROUP 3, GAME 4
EXTRA PRACTICE

There are exactly three recycling centers in Rivertown: Center 1, Center 2, and Center 3. Exactly five kinds of material are recycled at these recycling centers: glass, newsprint, plastic, tin, and wood. Each recycling center recycles at least two but no more than three of these kinds of material. The following conditions must hold:

Any recycling center that recycles wood also recycles newsprint.
Every kind of material that Center 2 recycles is also recycled at Center 1.
Only one of the recycling centers recycles plastic, and that recycling center does not recycle glass.

18. Which one of the following could be an accurate account of all the kinds of material recycled at each recycling center in Rivertown?

(A) Center 1: newsprint, plastic, wood; Center 2: newsprint, wood; Center 3: glass, tin, wood
(B) Center 1: glass, newsprint, tin; Center 2: glass, newsprint, tin; Center 3: newsprint, plastic, wood
(C) Center 1: glass, newsprint, wood; Center 2: glass, newsprint, tin; Center 3: plastic, tin
(D) Center 1: glass, plastic, tin; Center 2: glass, tin; Center 3: newsprint, wood
(E) Center 1: newsprint, plastic, wood; Center 2: newsprint, plastic, wood; Center 3: glass, newsprint, tin

19. Which one of the following is a complete and accurate list of the recycling centers in Rivertown any one of which could recycle plastic?

(A) Center 1 only
(B) Center 3 only
(C) Center 1, Center 2
(D) Center 1, Center 3
(E) Center 1, Center 2, Center 3

20. If Center 2 recycles three kinds of material, then which one of the following kinds of material must Center 3 recycle?

(A) glass
(B) newsprint
(C) plastic
(D) tin
(E) wood

21. If each recycling center in Rivertown recycles exactly three kinds of material, then which one of the following could be true?

(A) Only Center 2 recycles glass.
(B) Only Center 3 recycles newsprint.
(C) Only Center 1 recycles plastic.
(D) Only Center 3 recycles tin.
(E) Only Center 1 recycles wood.

22. If Center 3 recycles glass, then which one of the following kinds of material must Center 2 recycle?

(A) glass
(B) newsprint
(C) plastic
(D) tin
(E) wood

23. If Center 1 is the only recycling center that recycles wood, then which one of the following could be a complete and accurate list of the kinds of material that one of the recycling centers recycles?

(A) plastic, tin
(B) newsprint, wood
(C) newsprint, tin
(D) glass, wood
(E) glass, tin

GROUP 3, GAME 4
EXTRA PRACTICE

There are exactly three recycling centers in Rivertown: Center 1, Center 2, and Center 3. Exactly five kinds of material are recycled at these recycling centers: glass, newsprint, plastic, tin, and wood. Each recycling center recycles at least two but no more than three of these kinds of material. The following conditions must hold:

Any recycling center that recycles wood also recycles newsprint.
Every kind of material that Center 2 recycles is also recycled at Center 1.
Only one of the recycling centers recycles plastic, and that recycling center does not recycle glass.

18. Which one of the following could be an accurate account of all the kinds of material recycled at each recycling center in Rivertown?

(A) Center 1: newsprint, plastic, wood; Center 2: newsprint, wood; Center 3: glass, tin, wood
(B) Center 1: glass, newsprint, tin; Center 2: glass, newsprint, tin; Center 3: newsprint, plastic, wood
(C) Center 1: glass, newsprint, wood; Center 2: glass, newsprint, tin; Center 3: plastic, tin
(D) Center 1: glass, plastic, tin; Center 2: glass, tin; Center 3: newsprint, wood
(E) Center 1: newsprint, plastic, wood; Center 2: newsprint, plastic, wood; Center 3: glass, newsprint, tin

19. Which one of the following is a complete and accurate list of the recycling centers in Rivertown any one of which could recycle plastic?

(A) Center 1 only
(B) Center 3 only
(C) Center 1, Center 2
(D) Center 1, Center 3
(E) Center 1, Center 2, Center 3

20. If Center 2 recycles three kinds of material, then which one of the following kinds of material must Center 3 recycle?

(A) glass
(B) newsprint
(C) plastic
(D) tin
(E) wood

21. If each recycling center in Rivertown recycles exactly three kinds of material, then which one of the following could be true?

(A) Only Center 2 recycles glass.
(B) Only Center 3 recycles newsprint.
(C) Only Center 1 recycles plastic.
(D) Only Center 3 recycles tin.
(E) Only Center 1 recycles wood.

22. If Center 3 recycles glass, then which one of the following kinds of material must Center 2 recycle?

(A) glass
(B) newsprint
(C) plastic
(D) tin
(E) wood

23. If Center 1 is the only recycling center that recycles wood, then which one of the following could be a complete and accurate list of the kinds of material that one of the recycling centers recycles?

(A) plastic, tin
(B) newsprint, wood
(C) newsprint, tin
(D) glass, wood
(E) glass, tin

GROUP 3, GAME 5

A bakery makes exactly three kinds of cookie—oatmeal, peanut butter, and sugar. Exactly three batches of each kind of cookie are made each week (Monday through Friday) and each batch is made, from start to finish, on a single day. The following conditions apply:

No two batches of the same kind of cookie are made on the same day.
At least one batch of cookies is made on Monday.
The second batch of oatmeal cookies is made on the same day as the first batch of peanut butter cookies.
The second batch of sugar cookies is made on Thursday.

13. Which one of the following could be a complete and accurate list of the days on which the batches of each kind of cookie are made?

(A) oatmeal: Monday, Wednesday, Thursday peanut butter: Wednesday, Thursday, Friday sugar: Monday, Thursday, Friday
(B) oatmeal: Monday, Tuesday, Thursday peanut butter: Tuesday, Wednesday, Thursday sugar: Monday, Wednesday, Thursday
(C) oatmeal: Tuesday, Wednesday, Thursday peanut butter: Wednesday, Thursday, Friday sugar: Tuesday, Thursday, Friday
(D) oatmeal: Monday, Tuesday, Thursday peanut butter: Monday, Wednesday, Thursday sugar: Monday, Thursday, Friday
(E) oatmeal: Monday, Thursday, Friday peanut butter: Tuesday, Wednesday, Thursday sugar: Monday, Thursday, Friday

14. How many of the days, Monday through Friday, are such that at most two batches of cookies could be made on that day?

(A) one
(B) two
(C) three
(D) four
(E) five

15. If the first batch of peanut butter cookies is made on Tuesday, then each of the following could be true EXCEPT:

(A) Two different kinds of cookie have their first batch made on Monday.
(B) Two different kinds of cookie have their first batch made on Tuesday.
(C) Two different kinds of cookie have their second batch made on Wednesday.
(D) Two different kinds of cookie have their second batch made on Thursday.
(E) Two different kinds of cookie have their third batch made on Friday.

16. If no batch of cookies is made on Wednesday, then which one of the following must be true?

(A) Exactly three batches of cookies are made on Tuesday.
(B) Exactly three batches of cookies are made on Friday.
(C) At least two batches of cookies are made on Monday.
(D) At least two batches of cookies are made on Thursday.
(E) Fewer batches of cookies are made on Monday than on Tuesday.

17. If the number of batches made on Friday is exactly one, then which one of the following could be true?

(A) The first batch of sugar cookies is made on Monday.
(B) The first batch of oatmeal cookies is made on Tuesday.
(C) The third batch of oatmeal cookies is made on Friday.
(D) The first batch of peanut butter cookies is made on Wednesday.
(E) The second batch of peanut butter cookies is made on Tuesday.

18. If one kind of cookie's first batch is made on the same day as another kind of cookie's third batch, then which one of the following could be false?

(A) At least one batch of cookies is made on each of the five days.
(B) At least two batches of cookies are made on Wednesday.
(C) Exactly one batch of cookies is made on Monday.
(D) Exactly two batches of cookies are made on Tuesday.
(E) Exactly one batch of cookies is made on Friday.

EXPLANATION

Choosing a first step here is a no-brainer: We'll use the five days, Monday-Friday, as our foundation. LSAT history is littered with games like this, and this approach has always worked in the past.

			S^2	S^3
M	T	W	Th	F

Note the immediate inference: If the second batch of sugar cookies is on Thursday, then the third batch of sugar cookies can only be Friday.

Next, we need to dig into the rule that ties the second batch of oatmeal cookies to the first batch of peanut butter. This is the key to the game. Here's the rule, by itself:

That block is important, which becomes apparent when we view the block in context of the *other* oatmeal and peanut butter batches. Here's the big reveal:

O^1 ... [O^2 / P^1] ... O^3
... P^2 ... P^3

It might be obvious to some, but let's make sure we're all on the same page. The first batch of oatmeal (O^1) has to precede the P^1/O^2 block. The third batch of oatmeal (O^3) goes after the block, of course. And there will be plenty of room for that, because *both* the second and third batches of peanut butter (P^2 and P^3) have to follow the P^1/O^2 block.

So the P^1/O^2 block can't go Monday (where would O^1 go?) and it can't go Thursday or Friday, due to P^2 and P^3. As it turns out, there are only two places this block can go: Tuesday and Wednesday.

WHO ELSE IS HUNGRY? This game is now more than a decade old and I *still* get a craving for sweets about halfway through. How many cookies have been eaten by future lawyers on account of this single game?!? <Shakes fist at LSAC>

That realization is enough to crush the game, whether or not we actually pencil out the two worlds. But penciling the worlds makes a lot of sense here. There are only two places where P^1/O^2 can go, and when we place that block on either Tuesday or Wednesday, other pieces of the puzzle start to click. Here's what it looks like if the block goes on Tuesday:

O^1 O^2 (O^3 ___ ___)
P^1 (P^2 ... P^3 ___)

(S^1		)	S^2	S^3
M	T	W	Th	F

As you can see, in this scenario, O^1 is forced onto Monday. And here's what it looks like if the block is on Wednesday:

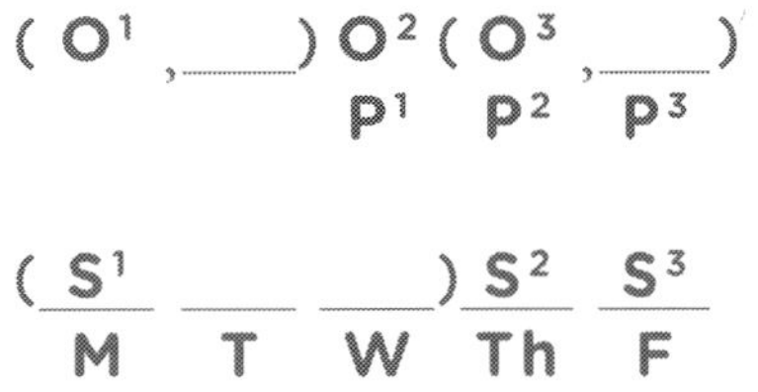

```
( O¹ ,____) O² ( O³ ,____)
            P¹   P²   P³

( S¹   ____  ____) S²   S³
  M     T     W    Th   F
```

In this scenario, P^2 must go Thursday, and P^3 must go Friday. In this world, we still haven't satisfied the rule that Monday has to have at least one batch, so we'll have to put either O^1 or S^1 on Monday in this world.

From here, the questions should be pretty manageable. Let's go!

QUESTION 13

Which one of the following could be a complete and accurate list of the days on which the batches of each kind of cookie are made?

(A) oatmeal: Monday, Wednesday, Thursday peanut butter: Wednesday, Thursday, Friday sugar: Monday, Thursday, Friday
(B) oatmeal: Monday, Tuesday, Thursday peanut butter: Tuesday, Wednesday, Thursday sugar: Monday, Wednesday, Thursday
(C) oatmeal: Tuesday, Wednesday, Thursday peanut butter: Wednesday, Thursday, Friday sugar: Tuesday, Thursday, Friday
(D) oatmeal: Monday, Tuesday, Thursday peanut butter: Monday, Wednesday, Thursday sugar: Monday, Thursday, Friday
(E) oatmeal: Monday, Thursday, Friday peanut butter: Tuesday, Wednesday, Thursday sugar: Monday, Thursday, Friday

Process of elimination. We'll take each rule one at a time and eliminate whatever we can with that rule before moving on to the next.

S^2 on Thursday. This gets rid of B.
Something has to go on Monday. This gets rid of C.
O^2 and P^1 are together. This gets rid of both D and E.

That's all the rules, leaving us with our answer: A.

QUESTION 15

If the first batch of peanut butter cookies is made on Tuesday, then each of the following could be true EXCEPT:

(A) Two different kinds of cookie have their first batch made on Monday.
(B) Two different kinds of cookie have their first batch made on Tuesday.
(C) Two different kinds of cookie have their second batch made on Wednesday.
(D) Two different kinds of cookie have their second batch made on Thursday.
(E) Two different kinds of cookie have their third batch made on Friday.

We anticipated this question with our first scenario. That scenario, again, is this:

$$O^1 \quad O^2 \, (\, O^3 \quad \_\_\_ \quad \_\_\_ \,)$$
$$P^1 \, (\, P^2 \ldots P^3 \quad \_\_\_ \,)$$

(S^1	___	___)	S^2	S^3
M	T	W	Th	F

If you hadn't made the scenario before you reached this question it wouldn't be the end of the world; you'd obviously need to draw it for this question, though. Anyway, they've told us that four answers could be true, which means that one of them (the right answer) must be false. Let's see.

A) This could be true, if S^1 is on Monday.
B) This could be true, if S^1 is on Tuesday.
C) This is impossible, since O^2 is already on Tuesday and S^2 is on Thursday.
D) This could be true, if P^2 is Thursday.
E) This could be true, if P^3 is Friday.

Our answer is C, since it's the one that won't work.

QUESTION 16

If no batch of cookies is made on Wednesday, then which one of the following must be true?

(A) Exactly three batches of cookies are made on Tuesday.
(B) Exactly three batches of cookies are made on Friday.
(C) At least two batches of cookies are made on Monday.
(D) At least two batches of cookies are made on Thursday.
(E) Fewer batches of cookies are made on Monday than on Tuesday.

If nothing's on Wednesday then we're obviously in the first scenario again. We're in a special version of that first scenario where we block out Wednesday, which makes this happen:

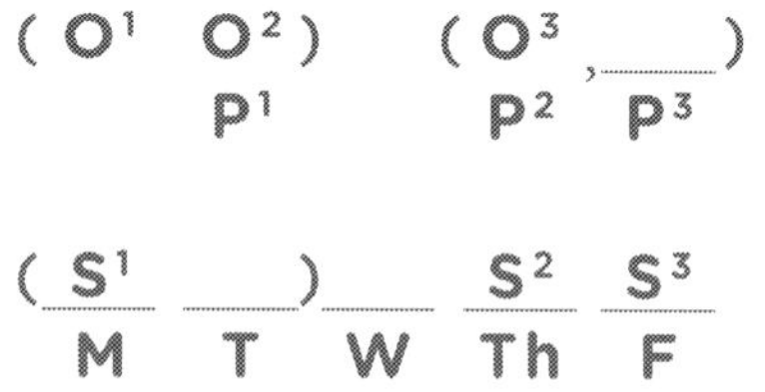

(O^1 O^2) (O^3 , ___)
P^1 P^2 P^3

(S^1 ___) ___ S^2 S^3
M T W Th F

We're asked to find something that must be true in this scenario.

A) Nope, this doesn't have to be true.
B) Nope, doesn't have to be true either.
C) Nope.
D) Yep. S^2 is always on Thursday, and in this scenario, P^2 got forced onto Thursday.
E) Nope, not necessarily.

Our answer is D.

QUESTION 17

If the number of batches made on Friday is exactly one, then which one of the following could be true?

(A) The first batch of sugar cookies is made on Monday.
(B) The first batch of oatmeal cookies is made on Tuesday.
(C) The third batch of oatmeal cookies is made on Friday.
(D) The first batch of peanut butter cookies is made on Wednesday.
(E) The second batch of peanut butter cookies is made on Tuesday.

Once again, the special condition puts us into world #1. (World #2 already has two batches on Friday.) If S^3 is the only batch we can place on Friday, we get this:

```
O¹   O² ( O³ , ___ )
     P¹   P²   P³

( S¹ , ___  ___ ) S²   S³
  M     T    W    Th   F
```

On to the answer choices, looking for something that could be true.

A) Yes, this does look like it can be true. But let's check that B-E all must be false, so we can be 100% sure.
B) No, O^1 is on Monday.
C) No, O^3 is either Wednesday or Thursday.
D) No, P^1 is Tuesday.
E) No, P^2 is on Wednesday.

Our answer is A.

QUESTION 18

If one kind of cookie's first batch is made on the same day as another kind of cookie's third batch, then which one of the following could be false?

(A) At least one batch of cookies is made on each of the five days.
(B) At least two batches of cookies are made on Wednesday.
(C) Exactly one batch of cookies is made on Monday.
(D) Exactly two batches of cookies are made on Tuesday.
(E) Exactly one batch of cookies is made on Friday.

The first step here is to realize that there is only one day that can possibly have the first batch, and the third batch, of any type of cookie. It's not Monday or Tuesday, because Monday and Tuesday can't have the third batch of anything. And it's not Thursday or Friday, because those days can't have the first batch of anything. So the day must be Wednesday. If you didn't get that part, you struggled mightily with this question.

We also must be in World 1 for this question, because in World 2, none of the third batches can be made on Wednesday. So let's start with World 1, and adapt it for this question. Here's World 1 again:

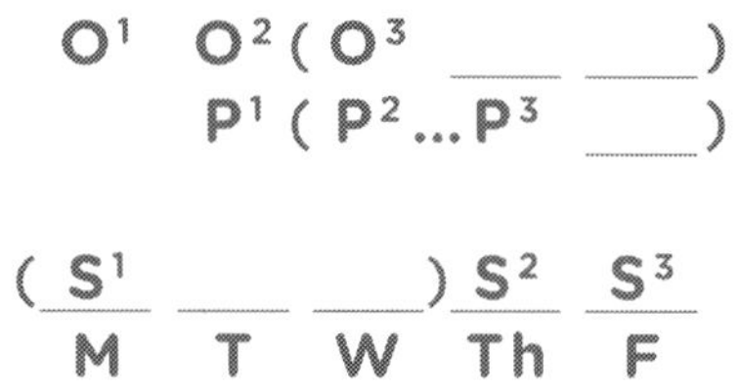

O^1 O^2 (O^3 ___ ___)
P^1 (P^2 ... P^3 ___)

(S^1 ___ ___) S^2 S^3
M T W Th F

Notice that the only batch #1 that can go on Wednesday, in this scenario, is S^1. Note also that the only batch #3 that can go on Wednesday here (or ever, for that matter) is O^3. So, to satisfy the restriction that this question poses, we need to put S^1 and O^3 on Wednesday, like this:

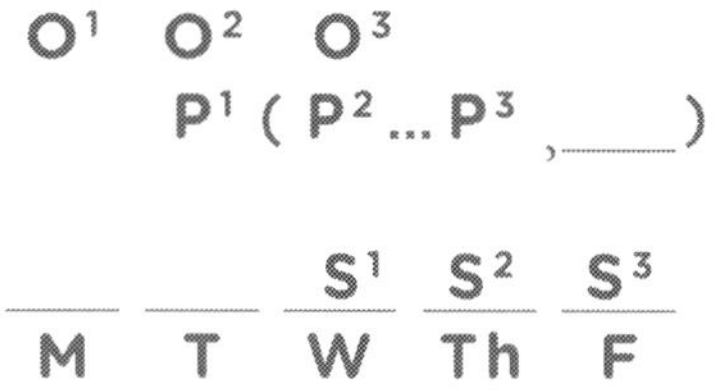

O^1 O^2 O^3
P^1 (P^2 ... P^3 , ___)

___ ___ S^1 S^2 S^3
M T W Th F

It can't be hard to answer from here. We're looking for something that could be false, which means that the four wrong answers all must be true.

A) We already have something on each of the five days, so this can't be false.
B) This also must be true.
C) Yes, the only thing that can go on Monday in this scenario is O^1.
D) Yes, the only things that can go on Tuesday here are O^2 and P^1.
E) This doesn't have to be true, because P^3 can join S^3 on Friday.

Our answer is E, because it's the only one that could be false.

QUESTION 14

How many of the days, Monday through Friday, are such that at most two batches of cookies could be made on that day?

(A) one
(B) two
(C) three
(D) four
(E) five

Our starting worlds answer this question quite nicely. Look at World #1 again:

O^1	O^2 (	O^3	___	___)
	P^1 (	P^2 …	P^3	___)
(S^1	___	___)	S^2	S^3
M	T	W	Th	F

In this World, it's possible to put three batches on each of Tuesday, Wednesday, Thursday, and Friday. Monday is the only day, in this scenario, that can't have three batches.

Now turn to World #2, and think about Monday:

(O^1	, ___)	O^2 (	O^3	, ___)
		P^1	P^2	P^3
(S^1	___	___)	S^2	S^3
M	T	W	Th	F

In this world, it's not possible to put three batches on Monday (because P^1 can't go Monday). Since it's impossible to put three batches on Monday in either world, and since we know we can put three batches on all the other days, it has to be one.

Our answer is A.

GROUP 3, GAME 5
EXTRA PRACTICE

A bakery makes exactly three kinds of cookie—oatmeal, peanut butter, and sugar. Exactly three batches of each kind of cookie are made each week (Monday through Friday) and each batch is made, from start to finish, on a single day. The following conditions apply:

No two batches of the same kind of cookie are made on the same day.
At least one batch of cookies is made on Monday.
The second batch of oatmeal cookies is made on the same day as the first batch of peanut butter cookies.
The second batch of sugar cookies is made on Thursday.

13. Which one of the following could be a complete and accurate list of the days on which the batches of each kind of cookie are made?

(A) oatmeal: Monday, Wednesday, Thursday peanut butter: Wednesday, Thursday, Friday sugar: Monday, Thursday, Friday
(B) oatmeal: Monday, Tuesday, Thursday peanut butter: Tuesday, Wednesday, Thursday sugar: Monday, Wednesday, Thursday
(C) oatmeal: Tuesday, Wednesday, Thursday peanut butter: Wednesday, Thursday, Friday sugar: Tuesday, Thursday, Friday
(D) oatmeal: Monday, Tuesday, Thursday peanut butter: Monday, Wednesday, Thursday sugar: Monday, Thursday, Friday
(E) oatmeal: Monday, Thursday, Friday peanut butter: Tuesday, Wednesday, Thursday sugar: Monday, Thursday, Friday

14. How many of the days, Monday through Friday, are such that at most two batches of cookies could be made on that day?

    (A) one
    (B) two
    (C) three
    (D) four
    (E) five

15. If the first batch of peanut butter cookies is made on Tuesday, then each of the following could be true EXCEPT:

    (A) Two different kinds of cookie have their first batch made on Monday.
    (B) Two different kinds of cookie have their first batch made on Tuesday.
    (C) Two different kinds of cookie have their second batch made on Wednesday.
    (D) Two different kinds of cookie have their second batch made on Thursday.
    (E) Two different kinds of cookie have their third batch made on Friday.

16. If no batch of cookies is made on Wednesday, then which one of the following must be true?

    (A) Exactly three batches of cookies are made on Tuesday.
    (B) Exactly three batches of cookies are made on Friday.
    (C) At least two batches of cookies are made on Monday.
    (D) At least two batches of cookies are made on Thursday.
    (E) Fewer batches of cookies are made on Monday than on Tuesday.

17. If the number of batches made on Friday is exactly one, then which one of the following could be true?

    (A) The first batch of sugar cookies is made on Monday.
    (B) The first batch of oatmeal cookies is made on Tuesday.
    (C) The third batch of oatmeal cookies is made on Friday.
    (D) The first batch of peanut butter cookies is made on Wednesday.
    (E) The second batch of peanut butter cookies is made on Tuesday.

18. If one kind of cookie's first batch is made on the same day as another kind of cookie's third batch, then which one of the following could be false?

    (A) At least one batch of cookies is made on each of the five days.
    (B) At least two batches of cookies are made on Wednesday.
    (C) Exactly one batch of cookies is made on Monday.
    (D) Exactly two batches of cookies are made on Tuesday.
    (E) Exactly one batch of cookies is made on Friday.

GROUP 3, GAME 5
EXTRA PRACTICE

A bakery makes exactly three kinds of cookie—oatmeal, peanut butter, and sugar. Exactly three batches of each kind of cookie are made each week (Monday through Friday) and each batch is made, from start to finish, on a single day. The following conditions apply:

No two batches of the same kind of cookie are made on the same day.
At least one batch of cookies is made on Monday.
The second batch of oatmeal cookies is made on the same day as the first batch of peanut butter cookies.
The second batch of sugar cookies is made on Thursday.

13. Which one of the following could be a complete and accurate list of the days on which the batches of each kind of cookie are made?

(A) oatmeal: Monday, Wednesday, Thursday
peanut butter: Wednesday, Thursday, Friday
sugar: Monday, Thursday, Friday
(B) oatmeal: Monday, Tuesday, Thursday peanut butter: Tuesday, Wednesday, Thursday sugar: Monday, Wednesday, Thursday
(C) oatmeal: Tuesday, Wednesday, Thursday
peanut butter: Wednesday, Thursday, Friday
sugar: Tuesday, Thursday, Friday
(D) oatmeal: Monday, Tuesday, Thursday peanut butter: Monday, Wednesday, Thursday sugar: Monday, Thursday, Friday
(E) oatmeal: Monday, Thursday, Friday peanut butter: Tuesday, Wednesday, Thursday sugar: Monday, Thursday, Friday

14. How many of the days, Monday through Friday, are such that at most two batches of cookies could be made on that day?

(A) one
(B) two
(C) three
(D) four
(E) five

15. If the first batch of peanut butter cookies is made on Tuesday, then each of the following could be true EXCEPT:

(A) Two different kinds of cookie have their first batch made on Monday.
(B) Two different kinds of cookie have their first batch made on Tuesday.
(C) Two different kinds of cookie have their second batch made on Wednesday.
(D) Two different kinds of cookie have their second batch made on Thursday.
(E) Two different kinds of cookie have their third batch made on Friday.

16. If no batch of cookies is made on Wednesday, then which one of the following must be true?

(A) Exactly three batches of cookies are made on Tuesday.
(B) Exactly three batches of cookies are made on Friday.
(C) At least two batches of cookies are made on Monday.
(D) At least two batches of cookies are made on Thursday.
(E) Fewer batches of cookies are made on Monday than on Tuesday.

17. If the number of batches made on Friday is exactly one, then which one of the following could be true?

(A) The first batch of sugar cookies is made on Monday.
(B) The first batch of oatmeal cookies is made on Tuesday.
(C) The third batch of oatmeal cookies is made on Friday.
(D) The first batch of peanut butter cookies is made on Wednesday.
(E) The second batch of peanut butter cookies is made on Tuesday.

18. If one kind of cookie's first batch is made on the same day as another kind of cookie's third batch, then which one of the following could be false?

(A) At least one batch of cookies is made on each of the five days.
(B) At least two batches of cookies are made on Wednesday.
(C) Exactly one batch of cookies is made on Monday.
(D) Exactly two batches of cookies are made on Tuesday.
(E) Exactly one batch of cookies is made on Friday.

GROUP 3, GAME 6

Exactly six of an artist's paintings, entitled *Quarterion*, *Redemption*, *Sipapu*, *Tesseract*, *Vale*, and *Zelkova*, are sold at auction. Three of the paintings are sold to a museum, and three are sold to a private collector. Two of the paintings are from the artist's first (earliest) period, two are from her second period, and two are from her third (most recent) period. The private collector and the museum each buy one painting from each period. The following conditions hold:

Sipapu, which is sold to the private collector, is from an earlier period than *Zelkova*, which is sold to the museum.
Quarterion is not from an earlier period than *Tesseract*.
Vale is from the artist's second period.

13. Which one of the following could be an accurate list of the paintings bought by the museum and the private collector, listed in order of the paintings' periods, from first to third?

(A) museum: *Quarterion*, *Vale*, *Zelkova* private collector: *Redemption*, *Sipapu*, *Tesseract*
(B) museum: *Redemption*, *Zelkova*, *Quarterion* private collector: *Sipapu*, *Vale*, *Tesseract*
(C) museum: *Sipapu*, *Zelkova*, *Quarterion* private collector: *Tesseract*, *Vale*, *Redemption*
(D) museum: *Tesseract*, *Quarterion*, *Zelkova* private collector: *Sipapu*, *Redemption*, *Vale*
(E) museum: *Zelkova*, *Tesseract*, *Redemption* private collector: *Sipapu*, *Vale*, *Quarterion*

14. If *Sipapu* is from the artist's second period, which one of the following could be two of the three paintings bought by the private collector?

(A) *Quarterion* and *Zelkova*
(B) *Redemption* and *Tesseract*
(C) *Redemption* and *Vale*
(D) *Redemption* and *Zelkova*
(E) *Tesseract* and *Zelkova*

15. Which one of the following is a complete and accurate list of the paintings, any one of which could be the painting from the artist's first period that is sold to the private collector?

(A) *Quarterion*, *Redemption*
(B) *Redemption*, *Sipapu*
(C) *Quarterion*, *Sipapu*, *Tesseract*
(D) *Quarterion*, *Redemption*, *Sipapu*, *Tesseract*
(E) *Redemption*, *Sipapu*, *Tesseract*, *Zelkova*

16. If *Sipapu* is from the artist's second period, then which one of the following paintings could be from the period immediately preceding *Quarterion*'s period and be sold to the same buyer as *Quarterion*?

(A) *Redemption*
(B) *Sipapu*
(C) *Tesseract*
(D) *Vale*
(E) *Zelkova*

17. If *Zelkova* is sold to the same buyer as *Tesseract* and is from the period immediately preceding *Tesseract*'s period, then which one of the following must be true?

(A) *Quarterion* is sold to the museum.
(B) *Quarterion* is from the artist's third period.
(C) *Redemption* is sold to the private collector.
(D) *Redemption* is from the artist's third period.
(E) *Redemption* is sold to the same buyer as *Vale*.

EXPLANATION

This was the third game in its section when it appeared on the official LSAT, in June of 2004. Game 3s have a tendency to be tough, but this one is actually much easier than it looks.

We're asked to put things in order (first period, second period, third period) and *also* put things in groups (museum / private collector). Many would call a game that contains both sequencing and grouping a "hybrid" game, but this nomenclature has a way of making things sound harder than they really are.

Don't get scared; frequently, the LSAT harbors sheep in wolves' clothing. Take a deep breath and read the rules carefully. Twice if you have to. Three times if necessary; no shame in that. Write down everything that you know for sure, and draw some sort of a picture to help you get organized. We got this.

Generally if we're putting things in order, we'll make a left-to-right sequence. Here, we'll use two parallel lines of three spots: one for the museum and one for the private collector. Like so:

Next let's look at the rules. The first one is a mouthful. It's really three rules in one. 1) S has to go to the private collector. 2) Z has to go to the museum. 3) S before Z. Let's add all that to our growing diagram:

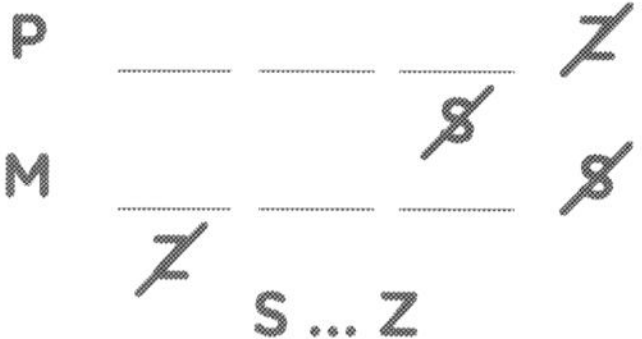

Be careful with the second rule. When the LSAT says "Q can't be before T," they're *hoping* that you'll make the incorrect inference that T has to be before Q. That's wrong here, because Q and T can actually go simultaneously. This is one of the LSAT's most common traps, and only novices fall for it. Let's take them at their word and write down exactly what they've said:

Finally, the last rule. Let's deal with "V must be second" by making it clear that V can't be first or third.

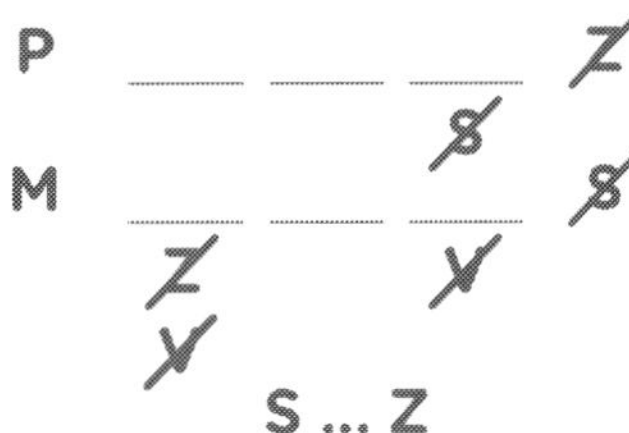

There aren't a ton of connections we can make here; not a single player was mentioned in more than one rule. Let's dive into the questions and see how we do.

QUESTION 13

Which one of the following could be an accurate list of the paintings bought by the museum and the private collector, listed in order of the paintings' periods, from first to third?

(A) museum: *Quarterion, Vale, Zelkova* private collector: *Redemption, Sipapu, Tesseract*
(B) museum: *Redemption, Zelkova, Quarterion* private collector: *Sipapu, Vale, Tesseract*
(C) museum: *Sipapu, Zelkova, Quarterion* private collector: *Tesseract, Vale, Redemption*
(D) museum: *Tesseract, Quarterion, Zelkova* private collector: *Sipapu, Redemption, Vale*
(E) museum: *Zelkova, Tesseract, Redemption* private collector: *Sipapu, Vale, Quarterion*

As always for list questions, it's a simple process of elimination. Grab a rule, check that rule against all remaining answer choices, see what's left. Let's go.

- S must be sold to the private collector. This gets rid of C.
- Z must be sold to the museum. This doesn't do anything. That's fine.
- S before Z. This gets rid of E.
- Q can't be before T. This gets rid of A.
- V must be in the second period. This gets rid of D.

Having tested all the rules, and having eliminated A, C, D, and E, our answer must be B.

QUESTION 14

If *Sipapu* is from the artist's second period, which one of the following could be two of the three paintings bought by the private collector?

(A) *Quarterion* and *Zelkova*
(B) *Redemption* and *Tesseract*
(C) *Redemption* and *Vale*
(D) *Redemption* and *Zelkova*
(E) *Tesseract* and *Zelkova*

The new condition S2 triggers a chain reaction. If S takes up the private collector spot for the second period, then V has to fill the museum spot for that period. Also, since S has to be before Z, and Z has to belong to the museum, we can write that in as well. Finally, since Q can't be before T, T now can't be in the third period at all (T can only go in the third period if Q accompanies it). Here's our final sketch for #14:

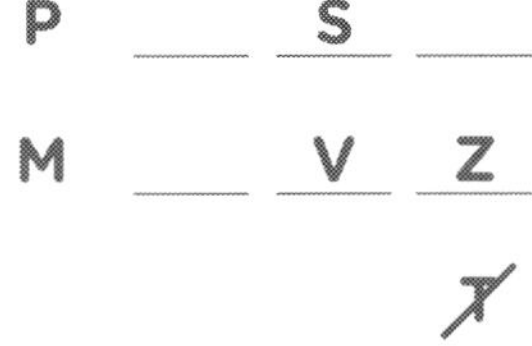

We're asked which could be two paintings owned by the private collector. The only thing we know is that S is owned by the private collector in this scenario, but S isn't mentioned in any of the answers. So the question is asking for the two *other* paintings that could be owned by the private collector. Well, we know that V and Z can't be on the list, since those both go to the museum. That gets rid of A, C, D, and E.

So our answer is B.

QUESTION 16

If *Sipapu* is from the artist's second period, then which one of the following paintings could be from the period immediately preceding *Quarterion*'s period and be sold to the same buyer as *Quarterion*?

(A) *Redemption*
(B) *Sipapu*
(C) *Tesseract*
(D) *Vale*
(E) *Zelkova*

Skipping #15 since it's not an "if" question, we make a new diagram for #16. Except we actually *don't* make a new diagram here, since the special condition for #16 is exactly the same special condition as #14, allowing us to immediately re-use that diagram. Here it is, again:

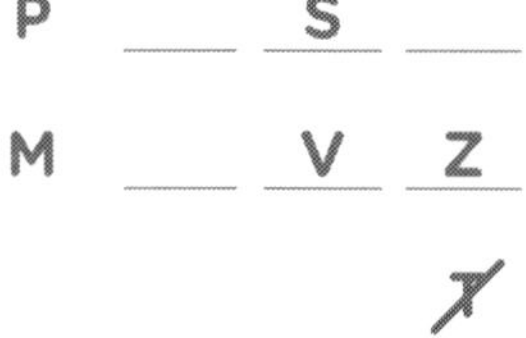

There are only three spots left for Q, and the only spot where Q would have anything before it is the third period private collector spot. If that's where Q goes, then S immediately precedes it.

So the answer here is B.

QUESTION 17

If *Zelkova* is sold to the same buyer as *Tesseract* and is from the period immediately preceding *Tesseract*'s period, then which one of the following must be true?

(A) *Quarterion* is sold to the museum.
(B) *Quarterion* is from the artist's third period.
(C) *Redemption* is sold to the private collector.
(D) *Redemption* is from the artist's third period.
(E) *Redemption* is sold to the same buyer as *Vale*.

S is always before Z, so here it's S before ZT. That means ZT must be the second and third paintings sold to the museum, and S must be the first painting sold to the private collector. Like this:

P	S	___	___
M	___	Z	T

That forces V into the second spot for the private collector:

P	S	V	___
M	___	Z	T

Q can't go before T, so Q must take the third spot for the private collector:

P	S	V	Q
M	R	Z	T

We can also fill in the remaining spot R to the artist's first period, sold to the museum. We now know everything and can confidently answer this Must Be True question.

A) Definitely not. Q is actually forced into the private collector's, um, collection. No way.
B) Yep, we've already proven this has to be true for this scenario.
C) No, R has to go the museum.
D) No, R has to be in the *first* period.
E) No, again, R has to go the museum.

Our answer is B.

QUESTION 15

Which one of the following is a complete and accurate list of the paintings, any one of which could be the painting from the artist's first period that is sold to the private collector?

(A) *Quarterion, Redemption*
(B) *Redemption, Sipapu*
(C) *Quarterion, Sipapu, Tesseract*
(D) *Quarterion, Redemption, Sipapu, Tesseract*
(E) *Redemption, Sipapu, Tesseract, Zelkova*

Returning to #15, which we skipped in our first go-around in the hopes that the "if" questions might give us some scenarios which would help. Unfortunately, here, they do not. We only filled in one P1 slot with S in our diagram for #17.

Let's see then. We know that Z can't be sold to the private collector, so that gets rid of E. We know that V can't go in the *first* private collector slot, since V always has to go second. But that doesn't help us much here, since V isn't listed in any of the answer choices.

How about everybody else—Q, R, S, and T? Is there any reason why any of them can't go first? Look at our diagram for #14. Seems like Q, R, and T could easily have gone in the P1 spot there. We already know that S can go in P1. So if QRST is an answer, we're gonna have to be happy with that. Yep, it sure is.

Our answer is D.

GROUP 3, GAME 6
EXTRA PRACTICE

Exactly six of an artist's paintings, entitled *Quarterion*, *Redemption*, *Sipapu*, *Tesseract*, *Vale*, and *Zelkova*, are sold at auction. Three of the paintings are sold to a museum, and three are sold to a private collector. Two of the paintings are from the artist's first (earliest) period, two are from her second period, and two are from her third (most recent) period. The private collector and the museum each buy one painting from each period. The following conditions hold:

Sipapu, which is sold to the private collector, is from an earlier period than *Zelkova*, which is sold to the museum.

Quarterion is not from an earlier period than *Tesseract*.

Vale is from the artist's second period.

13. Which one of the following could be an accurate list of the paintings bought by the museum and the private collector, listed in order of the paintings' periods, from first to third?

(A) museum: *Quarterion*, *Vale*, *Zelkova* private collector: *Redemption*, *Sipapu*, *Tesseract*

(B) museum: *Redemption*, *Zelkova*, *Quarterion* private collector: *Sipapu*, *Vale*, *Tesseract*

(C) museum: *Sipapu*, *Zelkova*, *Quarterion* private collector: *Tesseract*, *Vale*, *Redemption*

(D) museum: *Tesseract*, *Quarterion*, *Zelkova* private collector: *Sipapu*, *Redemption*, *Vale*

(E) museum: *Zelkova*, *Tesseract*, *Redemption* private collector: *Sipapu*, *Vale*, *Quarterion*

14. If *Sipapu* is from the artist's second period, which one of the following could be two of the three paintings bought by the private collector?

    (A) *Quarterion* and *Zelkova*
    (B) *Redemption* and *Tesseract*
    (C) *Redemption* and *Vale*
    (D) *Redemption* and *Zelkova*
    (E) *Tesseract* and *Zelkova*

15. Which one of the following is a complete and accurate list of the paintings, any one of which could be the painting from the artist's first period that is sold to the private collector?

    (A) *Quarterion*, *Redemption*
    (B) *Redemption*, *Sipapu*
    (C) *Quarterion*, *Sipapu*, *Tesseract*
    (D) *Quarterion*, *Redemption*, *Sipapu*, *Tesseract*
    (E) *Redemption*, *Sipapu*, *Tesseract*, *Zelkova*

16. If *Sipapu* is from the artist's second period, then which one of the following paintings could be from the period immediately preceding *Quarterion*'s period and be sold to the same buyer as *Quarterion*?

    (A) *Redemption*
    (B) *Sipapu*
    (C) *Tesseract*
    (D) *Vale*
    (E) *Zelkova*

17. If *Zelkova* is sold to the same buyer as *Tesseract* and is from the period immediately preceding *Tesseract*'s period, then which one of the following must be true?

    (A) *Quarterion* is sold to the museum.
    (B) *Quarterion* is from the artist's third period.
    (C) *Redemption* is sold to the private collector.
    (D) *Redemption* is from the artist's third period.
    (E) *Redemption* is sold to the same buyer as *Vale*.

GROUP 3, GAME 6
EXTRA PRACTICE

Exactly six of an artist's paintings, entitled *Quarterion*, *Redemption*, *Sipapu*, *Tesseract*, *Vale*, and *Zelkova*, are sold at auction. Three of the paintings are sold to a museum, and three are sold to a private collector. Two of the paintings are from the artist's first (earliest) period, two are from her second period, and two are from her third (most recent) period. The private collector and the museum each buy one painting from each period. The following conditions hold:

Sipapu, which is sold to the private collector, is from an earlier period than *Zelkova*, which is sold to the museum.

Quarterion is not from an earlier period than *Tesseract*.

Vale is from the artist's second period.

13. Which one of the following could be an accurate list of the paintings bought by the museum and the private collector, listed in order of the paintings' periods, from first to third?

(A) museum: *Quarterion*, *Vale*, *Zelkova* private collector: *Redemption*, *Sipapu*, *Tesseract*
(B) museum: *Redemption*, *Zelkova*, *Quarterion* private collector: *Sipapu*, *Vale*, *Tesseract*
(C) museum: *Sipapu*, *Zelkova*, *Quarterion* private collector: *Tesseract*, *Vale*, *Redemption*
(D) museum: *Tesseract*, *Quarterion*, *Zelkova* private collector: *Sipapu*, *Redemption*, *Vale*
(E) museum: *Zelkova*, *Tesseract*, *Redemption* private collector: *Sipapu*, *Vale*, *Quarterion*

14. If *Sipapu* is from the artist's second period, which one of the following could be two of the three paintings bought by the private collector?

    (A) *Quarterion* and *Zelkova*
    (B) *Redemption* and *Tesseract*
    (C) *Redemption* and *Vale*
    (D) *Redemption* and *Zelkova*
    (E) *Tesseract* and *Zelkova*

15. Which one of the following is a complete and accurate list of the paintings, any one of which could be the painting from the artist's first period that is sold to the private collector?

    (A) *Quarterion*, *Redemption*
    (B) *Redemption*, *Sipapu*
    (C) *Quarterion*, *Sipapu*, *Tesseract*
    (D) *Quarterion*, *Redemption*, *Sipapu*, *Tesseract*
    (E) *Redemption*, *Sipapu*, *Tesseract*, *Zelkova*

16. If *Sipapu* is from the artist's second period, then which one of the following paintings could be from the period immediately preceding *Quarterion*'s period and be sold to the same buyer as *Quarterion*?

    (A) *Redemption*
    (B) *Sipapu*
    (C) *Tesseract*
    (D) *Vale*
    (E) *Zelkova*

17. If *Zelkova* is sold to the same buyer as *Tesseract* and is from the period immediately preceding *Tesseract*'s period, then which one of the following must be true?

    (A) *Quarterion* is sold to the museum.
    (B) *Quarterion* is from the artist's third period.
    (C) *Redemption* is sold to the private collector.
    (D) *Redemption* is from the artist's third period.
    (E) *Redemption* is sold to the same buyer as *Vale*.

GROUP **4**

GROUP 4, GAME 1

There are exactly six groups in this year's Civic Parade: firefighters, gymnasts, jugglers, musicians, puppeteers, and veterans. Each group marches as a unit; the groups are ordered from first, at the front of the parade, to sixth, at the back. The following conditions apply:

At least two groups march behind the puppeteers but ahead of the musicians.
Exactly one group marches behind the firefighters but ahead of the veterans.
The gymnasts are the first, third, or fifth group.

1. Which one of the following could be an accurate list of the groups in the Civic Parade in order from first to last?

(A) firefighters, puppeteers, veterans, musicians, gymnasts, jugglers
(B) gymnasts, puppeteers, jugglers, musicians, firefighters, veterans
(C) veterans, puppeteers, firefighters, gymnasts, jugglers, musicians
(D) jugglers, puppeteers, gymnasts, firefighters, musicians, veterans
(E) musicians, veterans, jugglers, firefighters, gymnasts, puppeteers

2. If the gymnasts march immediately ahead of the veterans, then which one of the following could be the fourth group?

(A) gymnasts
(B) jugglers
(C) musicians
(D) puppeteers
(E) veterans

3. If the veterans march immediately behind the puppeteers, then which one of the following could be the second group?

(A) firefighters
(B) gymnasts
(C) jugglers
(D) musicians
(E) veterans

4. If the jugglers are the fifth group, then which one of the following must be true?

(A) The puppeteers are the first group.
(B) The firefighters are the first group.
(C) The veterans are the second group.
(D) The gymnasts are the third group.
(E) The musicians are the sixth group.

5. Which one of the following groups CANNOT march immediately behind the gymnasts?

(A) firefighters
(B) jugglers
(C) musicians
(D) puppeteers
(E) veterans

EXPLANATION

Fairly straightforward game here; by now, you should be getting more accustomed to games of this type. If not, there's no shame in reviewing the Ordering games from Groups 1-3 before proceeding. It's best to not get ahead of yourself because once you feel overwhelmed it's easy to get discouraged. We've said it many times, but it bears repeating: baby steps. Take them. It's good for you.

If you're ready to move on, then let's go!

Note the difference in how we'd diagram rules one and two:

F G J M P V

P ____ ____ ...M

F ____ V

There's some spacing flexibility with P and M. We know there are at least two spots between them, but the dots indicate that there might be more. On the other hand, with F and V, we know that there is *exactly* one spot between them. Hence, no dots.

G can only go first, third, or fifth, and there are a couple different ways you might include this in your diagram. Here, we'll show you both at once:

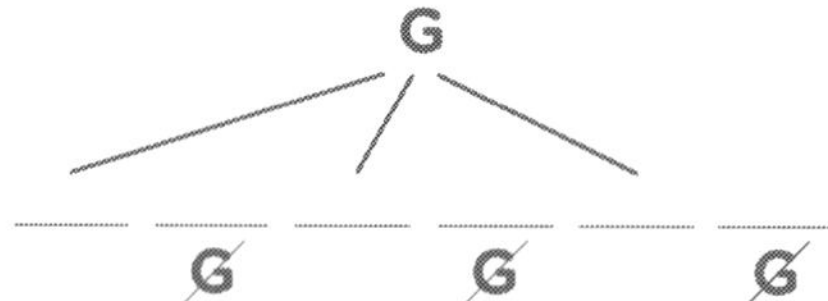

So our final diagram looks like this:

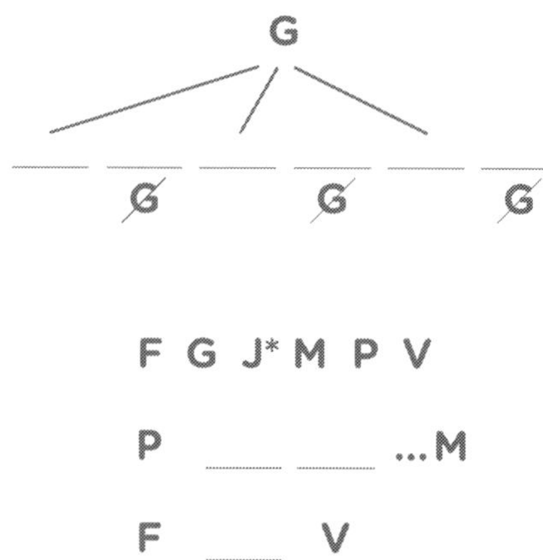

Note that we've given J an asterisk, since we've noticed that it's the only player that's not specifically implicated in any rule.

A BRIEF COMMENT on the rule about G. You don't *need* to include both the top part (G goes first, third, or fifth) and the bottom part (G can't go second, fourth, or sixth), the way we're presenting it here. It's a bit like wearing both belt and suspenders. But just because that move is dorky doesn't mean it won't keep your pants up. The logic games are largely about disaster avoidance, and accidentally putting G in the wrong spot is a bit like letting your pants fall down. Writing the rule both ways doesn't cost a lot, in terms of time. Five seconds? I'm not in the business of trying to save five seconds. I'm in the business of making sure that I avoid losing five minutes, or five questions, on some stupid mistake. As long as I don't lose my pants, I'm confident I'll do just fine on these games. Especially a very common, very predictable one like this.

QUESTION 1

Which one of the following could be an accurate list of the groups in the Civic Parade in order from first to last?

(A) firefighters, puppeteers, veterans, musicians, gymnasts, jugglers
(B) gymnasts, puppeteers, jugglers, musicians, firefighters, veterans
(C) veterans, puppeteers, firefighters, gymnasts, jugglers, musicians
(D) jugglers, puppeteers, gymnasts, firefighters, musicians, veterans
(E) musicians, veterans, jugglers, firefighters, gymnasts, puppeteers

A list question; we'll just follow a simple process of elimination:

P_ _...M: This gets rid of A, B, and E. That's a bit unusual, but it's true.
F_V: This gets rid of C. It seems like the answer must be D, but let's definitely check the last rule before we get too excited.
G is first, third, or fifth. This doesn't eliminate D.

Having checked this rule, we can now be 100% sure that the answer is D.

QUESTION 2

If the gymnasts march immediately ahead of the veterans, then which one of the following could be the fourth group?

(A) gymnasts
(B) jugglers
(C) musicians
(D) puppeteers
(E) veterans

Seems like there are two ways an FGV block might work out; the G has to be either third or fifth. Like this:

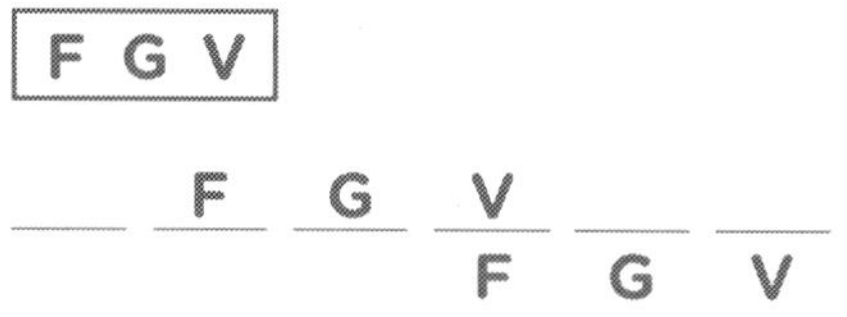

[F G V]

__ F G V __ __
F G V

If G is third, this will work out. But if G is fifth, then there's no room for P_ _ ... M. So we'll kill the second diagram, and fill out the first. Like this:

P F G V (M , J)
~~F G V~~

From here, finding the answer is trivial. We're asked about the fourth spot, and the fourth spot is definitely V.

So that's our answer, E.

QUESTION 3

If the veterans march immediately behind the puppeteers, then which one of the following could be the second group?

(A) firefighters
(B) gymnasts
(C) jugglers
(D) musicians
(E) veterans

If V is immediately behind P, we get this:

That leaves G and J to float around a bit. Of course G can only go first, third, or fifth. In this case it would have to be first or fifth; if it went third, then FPV_...M wouldn't fit. That might be enough to answer the question. We're asked to identify someone who could go second. Let's see.

A) Sure, why not? If G went first, then F would love to go second in this scenario. There's no point in even testing it; instead, let's see if we can eliminate B-E.
B) No, G can't ever go second.
C) No, because there would be no way for FPV_...M to fit if J went second.
D) No way, there are way too many players that have to precede M.
E) Nope; both F and P have to go before V, so V can't go second.

Having eliminated B-E, our answer is A. No need to test it.

QUESTION 4

If the jugglers are the fifth group, then which one of the following must be true?

(A) The puppeteers are the first group.
(B) The firefighters are the first group.
(C) The veterans are the second group.
(D) The gymnasts are the third group.
(E) The musicians are the sixth group.

If J is fifth, there are only two odd places left for G. Let's start there.

In the first of those two scenarios, where G is first, it seems there's only one way to satisfy *both* the P_ _...M rule and the F_V rule simultaneously. Like so:

In the second scenario, the one where G is third, there's also only one way to satisfy both the P_ _...M rule and the F_V rule. This:

P F G V J M

So our two scenarios for J coming fifth look like this:

G F P V J M

P F G V J M

We're asked to find a Must Be True, so we're looking for something that's true in *both* of these scenarios.

A) P goes first in one scenario, but not in the other.
B) No, F goes second in both scenarios.
C) No, V is fourth in both scenarios. (This is also a horrible answer because V can never ever go second, no matter what, based on the F_V rule.)
D) G goes third in one scenario, but not the other.
E) As it turns out, yes. M is last in both scenarios. Looks good.

So our answer is E.

QUESTION 5

Which one of the following groups CANNOT march immediately behind the gymnasts?

(A) firefighters
(B) jugglers
(C) musicians
(D) puppeteers
(E) veterans

Let's use our previous work here, at least to narrow the field. In previous questions, we've seen F directly follow G (from the correct answer, D, in #1. We've also seen V directly follow G, in #2. We learned from #3 that M will follow G whenever G ends up in the fifth spot. Question #4, unfortunately, doesn't help us eliminate any answers because we've already seen both V and F directly following G.

At this point, we know the answer has to be either J or P. It feels like P will probably work, since G can go first and P likes to go early. Let's try G first and P second:

G P _ _ _ _ _

We could arbitrarily put F third here, V fifth, and M last, without violating any rules:

G P F _ V M

Fill the only remaining player, J, into that last spot and we've proven that P can directly follow G.

So the correct answer must be the only one we've never seen and never tested—which is J.

Our answer is B.

GROUP 4, GAME 1
EXTRA PRACTICE

There are exactly six groups in this year's Civic Parade: firefighters, gymnasts, jugglers, musicians, puppeteers, and veterans. Each group marches as a unit; the groups are ordered from first, at the front of the parade, to sixth, at the back. The following conditions apply:

At least two groups march behind the puppeteers but ahead of the musicians.
Exactly one group marches behind the firefighters but ahead of the veterans.
The gymnasts are the first, third, or fifth group.

1. Which one of the following could be an accurate list of the groups in the Civic Parade in order from first to last?

(A) firefighters, puppeteers, veterans, musicians, gymnasts, jugglers
(B) gymnasts, puppeteers, jugglers, musicians, firefighters, veterans
(C) veterans, puppeteers, firefighters, gymnasts, jugglers, musicians
(D) jugglers, puppeteers, gymnasts, firefighters, musicians, veterans
(E) musicians, veterans, jugglers, firefighters, gymnasts, puppeteers

2. If the gymnasts march immediately ahead of the veterans, then which one of the following could be the fourth group?

(A) gymnasts
(B) jugglers
(C) musicians
(D) puppeteers
(E) veterans

3. If the veterans march immediately behind the puppeteers, then which one of the following could be the second group?

(A) firefighters
(B) gymnasts
(C) jugglers
(D) musicians
(E) veterans

4. If the jugglers are the fifth group, then which one of the following must be true?

(A) The puppeteers are the first group.
(B) The firefighters are the first group.
(C) The veterans are the second group.
(D) The gymnasts are the third group.
(E) The musicians are the sixth group.

5. Which one of the following groups CANNOT march immediately behind the gymnasts?

(A) firefighters
(B) jugglers
(C) musicians
(D) puppeteers
(E) veterans

GROUP 4, GAME 1
EXTRA PRACTICE

There are exactly six groups in this year's Civic Parade: firefighters, gymnasts, jugglers, musicians, puppeteers, and veterans. Each group marches as a unit; the groups are ordered from first, at the front of the parade, to sixth, at the back. The following conditions apply:

At least two groups march behind the puppeteers but ahead of the musicians.
Exactly one group marches behind the firefighters but ahead of the veterans.
The gymnasts are the first, third, or fifth group.

1. Which one of the following could be an accurate list of the groups in the Civic Parade in order from first to last?

(A) firefighters, puppeteers, veterans, musicians, gymnasts, jugglers
(B) gymnasts, puppeteers, jugglers, musicians, firefighters, veterans
(C) veterans, puppeteers, firefighters, gymnasts, jugglers, musicians
(D) jugglers, puppeteers, gymnasts, firefighters, musicians, veterans
(E) musicians, veterans, jugglers, firefighters, gymnasts, puppeteers

2. If the gymnasts march immediately ahead of the veterans, then which one of the following could be the fourth group?

(A) gymnasts
(B) jugglers
(C) musicians
(D) puppeteers
(E) veterans

3. If the veterans march immediately behind the puppeteers, then which one of the following could be the second group?

(A) firefighters
(B) gymnasts
(C) jugglers
(D) musicians
(E) veterans

4. If the jugglers are the fifth group, then which one of the following must be true?

(A) The puppeteers are the first group.
(B) The firefighters are the first group.
(C) The veterans are the second group.
(D) The gymnasts are the third group.
(E) The musicians are the sixth group.

5. Which one of the following groups CANNOT march immediately behind the gymnasts?

(A) firefighters
(B) jugglers
(C) musicians
(D) puppeteers
(E) veterans

GROUP 4, GAME 2

In a repair facility there are exactly six technicians: Stacy, Urma, Wim, Xena, Yolanda, and Zane. Each technician repairs machines of at least one of the following three types— radios, televisions, and VCRs—and no other types. The following conditions apply:

Xena and exactly three other technicians repair radios.
Yolanda repairs both televisions and VCRs.
Stacy does not repair any type of machine that Yolanda repairs.
Zane repairs more types of machines than Yolanda repairs.
Wim does not repair any type of machine that Stacy repairs.
Urma repairs exactly two types of machines.

13. For exactly how many of the six technicians is it possible to determine exactly which of the three types of machines each repairs?

(A) one
(B) two
(C) three
(D) four
(E) five

14. Which one of the following must be true?

(A) Of the types of machines repaired by Stacy there is exactly one type that Urma also repairs.
(B) Of the types of machines repaired by Yolanda there is exactly one type that Xena also repairs.
(C) Of the types of machines repaired by Wim there is exactly one type that Xena also repairs.
(D) There is more than one type of machine that both Wim and Yolanda repair.
(E) There is more than one type of machine that both Urma and Wim repair.

15. Which one of the following must be false?

(A) Exactly one of the six technicians repairs exactly one type of machine.
(B) Exactly two of the six technicians repair exactly one type of machine each.
(C) Exactly three of the six technicians repair exactly one type of machine each.
(D) Exactly one of the six technicians repairs exactly two types of machines.
(E) Exactly three of the six technicians repair exactly two types of machines each.

16. Which one of the following pairs of technicians could repair all and only the same types of machines as each other?

(A) Stacy and Urma
(B) Urma and Yolanda
(C) Urma and Xena
(D) Wim and Xena
(E) Xena and Yolanda

17. Which one of the following must be true?

(A) There is exactly one type of machine that both Urma and Wim repair.
(B) There is exactly one type of machine that both Urma and Xena repair.
(C) There is exactly one type of machine that both Urma and Yolanda repair.
(D) There is exactly one type of machine that both Wim and Yolanda repair.
(E) There is exactly one type of machine that both Xena and Yolanda repair.

EXPLANATION

This game is crushable, since the rules link together in fairly straightforward ways that lead to a lot of baby steps. This horse might already be beat to death, but we'll keep pounding away: *It's all about the baby steps.* As an LSAT teacher, I hear a lot of "Oh, once you guys set up the games they're soooooo easy!" Yeah, well, that's the point. These setups aren't memorized; there's no magic formula. Watch carefully as I walk through the baby steps, and soon you'll be able to do the setups for yourself.

On this one, you could probably use either the technicians or the devices as your base. We'll use the devices, since we prefer fewer groups when all else is equal. Like this:

The first rule tells us that R has exactly four spots, including X. We'll just throw X right into the R group, and we'll denote "R has four spots" in two different ways simultaneously: A superscript "4" and four spots. There can't be a fifth or sixth spot, and our diagram proves it. Like this:

___		
___		
___		
X	___	___
R^4	T	V

Yes, that's overkill. Good. We *like* overkill. What we just did takes five seconds and might save us a mistake that would cost five minutes. And even if we weren't going to make a mistake, more certainty is always good. Certainty breeds confidence. Confidence breeds a calm, focused approach. A calm, focused approach breeds correct answers like bunny rabbits on Cialis. We're not rushing, because once we start racking up the points, we're going to get them *all.*

The second and third rule combine, obviously, via Y. If this wasn't obvious to you, then you really need to slow down and look for the connections. If Y has to go in both the T and V groups, and if Y and S can't ever go together, and if S has to go somewhere, then S has to go in the R group only. In turn, this means Y can't go in the R group. So both Y and S are finished. Like this:

___		
___		
S		
X	Y	Y
R^4	T	V
~~Y~~	~~S~~	~~S~~

If Z repairs more types than Y, then Z must repair all three machines. We can just throw that right into the diagram, and be done with Z. If W can't go with S, then W can't go in the R group. Since that's the only place S can go, that's all we need to do with that rule. Our diagram now looks like this:

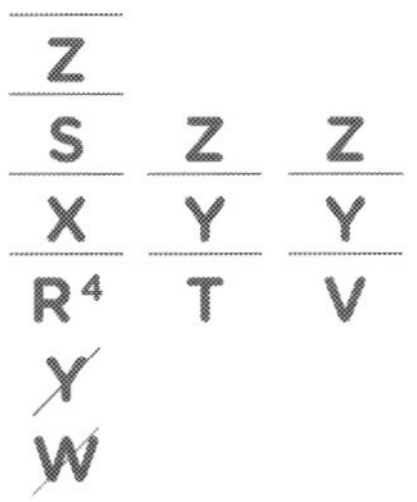

Z		
S	Z	Z
X	Y	Y
R^4	T	V
~~Y~~		
~~W~~		

We're left with only one possibility for the fourth spot in the R group. It can't be Y, and can't be W, so it has to be U. Let's throw that in:

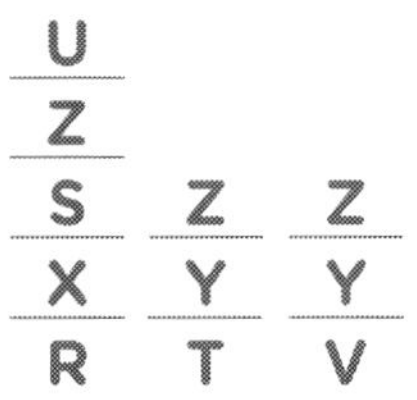

U		
Z		
S	Z	Z
X	Y	Y
R	T	V

The final rule tells us that we need to use exactly one more U, to go along with the one in the R group. To recap:

- S must go in the R group, and nowhere else.
- Y must go in the T and V groups, and nowhere else.
- Z must go in all three groups.
- We still need to use at least one W, in either the T or V group, and there's nothing wrong with W going in both groups.
- We need to use exactly one more U, in either the T or V group, and not both.
- We don't have to use any more X, but we are allowed to put X in either T, or V, or both.

We're left with very little flexibility, which means that the battle is over. At this point, all that's left is to stroll out onto the battlefield to loot the corpses. That's a metaphor. To be clear, the questions are the dead soldiers. Let's see what's in their pockets.

QUESTION 13

For exactly how many of the six technicians is it possible to determine exactly which of the three types of machines each repairs?

(A) one
(B) two
(C) three
(D) four
(E) five

There's no list question, and there also aren't any "if" questions. So we'll just do them all in order. For how many repair techs do we know *exactly* which machines they repair? Well, as discussed above, we know exactly where S, Y, and Z go. We still have some flexibility with W, U, and X.

So the answer is three, or C.

QUESTION 14

Which one of the following must be true?

(A) Of the types of machines repaired by Stacy there is exactly one type that Urma also repairs.
(B) Of the types of machines repaired by Yolanda there is exactly one type that Xena also repairs.
(C) Of the types of machines repaired by Wim there is exactly one type that Xena also repairs.
(D) There is more than one type of machine that both Wim and Yolanda repair.
(E) There is more than one type of machine that both Urma and Wim repair.

Which one of these five things do we know with certainty? Let's see.

A) Since we know that S and U both have to repair R, and we also know that S can't go anywhere else, this is going to be the answer. But let's skim B-E just to be sure.
B) Nope, Y and X haven't gone together yet, and there's no reason we have to use any more of either.
C) Nope, we do have to use one more W, but it wouldn't have to go with an X.
D) There does have to be one machine that's repaired by W and Y, and there *could* be two, but there doesn't have to be.
E) No, this actually can't be true.

Our answer is A.

QUESTION 15

Which one of the following must be false?

(A) Exactly one of the six technicians repairs exactly one type of machine.
(B) Exactly two of the six technicians repair exactly one type of machine each.
(C) Exactly three of the six technicians repair exactly one type of machine each.
(D) Exactly one of the six technicians repairs exactly two types of machines.
(E) Exactly three of the six technicians repair exactly two types of machines each.

Only one of these five things must be false, and the other four could be true.

A) S definitely has to repair exactly one type of machine, but everybody else either has to, or could, repair more than one. So this could be true.
B) This could be true, since S has to go exactly once and either X or W could also go exactly once.
C) This could also be true, since S has to go exactly once and both X and W could also go exactly once.
D) This must be false, since both Y and U are required to go exactly twice. This will be the answer.
E) This could be true, since Y and U have to go exactly twice and X and W are also eligible to do so.

Our answer is D.

QUESTION 16

Which one of the following pairs of technicians could repair all and only the same types of machines as each other?

(A) Stacy and Urma
(B) Urma and Yolanda
(C) Urma and Xena
(D) Wim and Xena
(E) Xena and Yolanda

This question is worded a bit oddly, but all it's asking is "Which two could have the exact same list?" Shouldn't be too tough to scan through the answers and eliminate the four that *can't* have the exact same list.

A) S has to go exactly once, and U has to go twice, so they're definitely not going to have the same list.
B) U has to go in the R group, and Y can't, so this is out.
C) This could be true, since U and X are already together in the R group and could also go together in either T or V.
D) X has to go in the R group, and W can't, so this is out.
E) X has to go in the R group, and Y can't, so this is out.

Our answer is C.

QUESTION 17

Which one of the following must be true?

(A) There is exactly one type of machine that both Urma and Wim repair.
(B) There is exactly one type of machine that both Urma and Xena repair.
(C) There is exactly one type of machine that both Urma and Yolanda repair.
(D) There is exactly one type of machine that both Wim and Yolanda repair.
(E) There is exactly one type of machine that both Xena and Yolanda repair.

There's just one more corpse to loot, and it's a Must Be True. Hard to see how this will be a problem because this game has very little flexibility.

A) There's no reason to suspect that this must be true, so we can calmly proceed to the next choice.
B) U and X do have to go together in the R group, but there's no reason they can't go together again in either the T or V group, which would make this false.
C) This has to be true, since U has to go in either the T or V group and Y is already in both groups. This will be the answer.
D) This doesn't have to be true, since W could go in *both* the T and V groups.
E) This doesn't have to be true, since X might not go in either the T or V groups.

Our answer is C.

It's the type of logic game that warms an LSAT teacher's heart. All you have to do is make a bunch of baby steps, then wander around harvesting points. This is how easy it can be.

GROUP 4, GAME 2 FROM PREPTEST 48, DECEMBER 2005

GROUP 4, GAME 2
EXTRA PRACTICE

In a repair facility there are exactly six technicians: Stacy, Urma, Wim, Xena, Yolanda, and Zane. Each technician repairs machines of at least one of the following three types— radios, televisions, and VCRs—and no other types. The following conditions apply:

Xena and exactly three other technicians repair radios.
Yolanda repairs both televisions and VCRs.
Stacy does not repair any type of machine that Yolanda repairs.
Zane repairs more types of machines than Yolanda repairs.
Wim does not repair any type of machine that Stacy repairs.
Urma repairs exactly two types of machines.

13. For exactly how many of the six technicians is it possible to determine exactly which of the three types of machines each repairs?

(A) one
(B) two
(C) three
(D) four
(E) five

14. Which one of the following must be true?

(A) Of the types of machines repaired by Stacy there is exactly one type that Urma also repairs.
(B) Of the types of machines repaired by Yolanda there is exactly one type that Xena also repairs.
(C) Of the types of machines repaired by Wim there is exactly one type that Xena also repairs.
(D) There is more than one type of machine that both Wim and Yolanda repair.
(E) There is more than one type of machine that both Urma and Wim repair.

15. Which one of the following must be false?

(A) Exactly one of the six technicians repairs exactly one type of machine.
(B) Exactly two of the six technicians repair exactly one type of machine each.
(C) Exactly three of the six technicians repair exactly one type of machine each.
(D) Exactly one of the six technicians repairs exactly two types of machines.
(E) Exactly three of the six technicians repair exactly two types of machines each.

16. Which one of the following pairs of technicians could repair all and only the same types of machines as each other?

(A) Stacy and Urma
(B) Urma and Yolanda
(C) Urma and Xena
(D) Wim and Xena
(E) Xena and Yolanda

17. Which one of the following must be true?

(A) There is exactly one type of machine that both Urma and Wim repair.
(B) There is exactly one type of machine that both Urma and Xena repair.
(C) There is exactly one type of machine that both Urma and Yolanda repair.
(D) There is exactly one type of machine that both Wim and Yolanda repair.
(E) There is exactly one type of machine that both Xena and Yolanda repair.

GROUP 4, GAME 2
EXTRA PRACTICE

In a repair facility there are exactly six technicians: Stacy, Urma, Wim, Xena, Yolanda, and Zane. Each technician repairs machines of at least one of the following three types— radios, televisions, and VCRs—and no other types. The following conditions apply:

Xena and exactly three other technicians repair radios.
Yolanda repairs both televisions and VCRs.
Stacy does not repair any type of machine that Yolanda repairs.
Zane repairs more types of machines than Yolanda repairs.
Wim does not repair any type of machine that Stacy repairs.
Urma repairs exactly two types of machines.

13. For exactly how many of the six technicians is it possible to determine exactly which of the three types of machines each repairs?

(A) one
(B) two
(C) three
(D) four
(E) five

14. Which one of the following must be true?

(A) Of the types of machines repaired by Stacy there is exactly one type that Urma also repairs.
(B) Of the types of machines repaired by Yolanda there is exactly one type that Xena also repairs.
(C) Of the types of machines repaired by Wim there is exactly one type that Xena also repairs.
(D) There is more than one type of machine that both Wim and Yolanda repair.
(E) There is more than one type of machine that both Urma and Wim repair.

15. Which one of the following must be false?

(A) Exactly one of the six technicians repairs exactly one type of machine.
(B) Exactly two of the six technicians repair exactly one type of machine each.
(C) Exactly three of the six technicians repair exactly one type of machine each.
(D) Exactly one of the six technicians repairs exactly two types of machines.
(E) Exactly three of the six technicians repair exactly two types of machines each.

16. Which one of the following pairs of technicians could repair all and only the same types of machines as each other?

(A) Stacy and Urma
(B) Urma and Yolanda
(C) Urma and Xena
(D) Wim and Xena
(E) Xena and Yolanda

17. Which one of the following must be true?

(A) There is exactly one type of machine that both Urma and Wim repair.
(B) There is exactly one type of machine that both Urma and Xena repair.
(C) There is exactly one type of machine that both Urma and Yolanda repair.
(D) There is exactly one type of machine that both Wim and Yolanda repair.
(E) There is exactly one type of machine that both Xena and Yolanda repair.

GROUP 4, GAME 3

A rowing team uses a boat with exactly six seats arranged in single file and numbered sequentially 1 through 6, from the front of the boat to the back. Six athletes—Lee, Miller, Ovitz, Singh, Valerio, and Zita—each row at exactly one of the seats. The following restrictions must apply:

Miller rows closer to the front than Singh.
Singh rows closer to the front than both Lee and Valerio.
Valerio and Zita each row closer to the front than Ovitz.

6. Which one of the following could be an accurate matching of athletes to seats?

(A) Miller: seat 1; Valerio: seat 5; Lee: seat 6
(B) Singh: seat 3; Valerio: seat 4; Zita: seat 5
(C) Miller: seat 1; Valerio: seat 3; Lee: seat 6
(D) Lee: seat 3; Valerio: seat 4; Ovitz: seat 5
(E) Zita: seat 2; Valerio: seat 3; Ovitz: seat 6

7. If Valerio rows at seat 5, then which one of the following must be true?

(A) Miller rows at seat 1.
(B) Singh rows at seat 2.
(C) Zita rows at seat 3.
(D) Lee rows at seat 4.
(E) Ovitz rows at seat 6.

8. If Lee rows at seat 3, then each of the following could be true EXCEPT:

(A) Zita rows immediately behind Valerio.
(B) Ovitz rows immediately behind Valerio.
(C) Ovitz rows immediately behind Zita.
(D) Valerio rows immediately behind Lee.
(E) Singh rows immediately behind Zita.

9. Which one of the following CANNOT be true?

(A) Ovitz rows closer to the front than Singh.
(B) Zita rows closer to the front than Miller.
(C) Lee rows closer to the front than Valerio.
(D) Singh rows closer to the front than Zita.
(E) Valerio rows closer to the front than Lee.

10. Exactly how many different seats could be the seat occupied by Zita?

(A) two
(B) three
(C) four
(D) five
(E) six

11. If Valerio rows closer to the front than Zita, then which one of the following must be true?

(A) Miller rows immediately in front of Singh.
(B) Lee rows immediately in front of Valerio.
(C) Zita rows immediately in front of Ovitz.
(D) Singh rows immediately in front of Lee.
(E) Singh rows immediately in front of Valerio.

12. Suppose the restriction that Miller rows closer to the front than Singh is replaced by the restriction that Singh rows closer to the front than Miller. If the other two restrictions remain in effect, then each of the following could be an accurate matching of athletes to seats EXCEPT:

(A) Singh: seat 1; Zita: seat 2; Miller: seat 6
(B) Singh: seat 1; Valerio: seat 3; Ovitz: seat 5
(C) Singh: seat 3; Lee: seat 4; Valerio: seat 5
(D) Valerio: seat 3; Miller: seat 4; Lee: seat 5
(E) Valerio: seat 4; Miller: seat 5; Ovitz: seat 6

EXPLANATION

As setups go, they don't get much easier than this. We have three rules, they're all easy to understand, and they all link together easily. Start thinking about what type of touchdown dance you're gonna do.

Don't bother writing rules one and two separately. We know they're going to link, so let's just link them together immediately:

L
M ... S
V

Note that L and V are separated. I can't stress this enough. If you write something like "L&V" you're going to be screwed because the next step links the third rule to just V, *not* L. Like this:

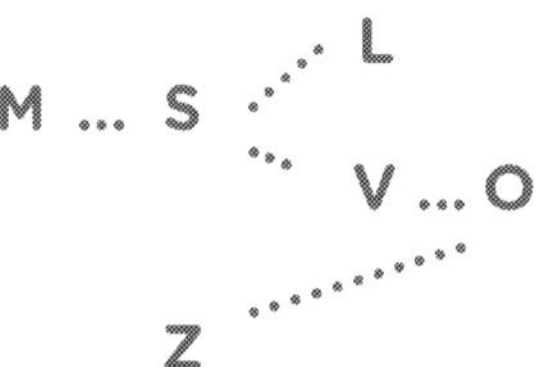

Again, it's really important that you keep V and Z separated. Incorrectly lumping variables together might be the most common mistake we see.

Notice the placement of the Z and V. We've got the Z floating way out there; we want to know, at a glance, that the Z has no relationship to anybody but O.

Making this web of rules was pretty easy, and it won't get any harder from here.

We just looked ahead at the questions, and #6 is a partial list. Let's skip this, since it's a not a full list question, and partial lists are usually harder and therefore might benefit from some further diagrams. We'll do the "if" questions first.

QUESTION 7

If Valerio rows at seat 5, then which one of the following must be true?

(A) Miller rows at seat 1.
(B) Singh rows at seat 2.
(C) Zita rows at seat 3.
(D) Lee rows at seat 4.
(E) Ovitz rows at seat 6.

If V goes fifth, then O must go sixth. Like this:

__ __ __ __ V O

M ... S ... L

Z

Notice that this leaves Z hanging out in space; once O is last then Z can go in any remaining spot. M...S...L is still in play.

So M...S...L, with Z, will take the first four spots. We can consolidate like this:

(M ... S ... L , Z) V O

The question asks for something that must be true. We'll hunt for it, while dodging answers that could be false.

A) No, M can be in seat one or seat two.
B) No, S can be in two or three.
C) No, Z can be in one, two, three, or four.
D) No, L can be in three or four.
E) Yes. O must follow V.

Our answer is E.

Yes, we knew O had to be sixth right away. And yes, we went a step further in our diagram than strictly necessary to answer this question. But it's hard to skip straight to E without wading through the traps of A, B, C, and D. Maybe we would have made it through safely without such a thorough diagram, but then again, maybe not. Remember: Overkill is good.

QUESTION 8

If Lee rows at seat 3, then each of the following could be true EXCEPT:

(A) Zita rows immediately behind Valerio.
(B) Ovitz rows immediately behind Valerio.
(C) Ovitz rows immediately behind Zita.
(D) Valerio rows immediately behind Lee.
(E) Singh rows immediately behind Zita.

Same idea here, but we can skip a step. If L goes third, then M and S have to take the first and second spots. That turns out to be enough to answer the question, but I wouldn't know that, and wouldn't much care. I'd keep rolling, and go ahead and finish the diagram. Two of the three remaining players, V and Z, both have to go before O. So O must go sixth, and V and Z can flip-flop in the fourth and fifth spots.

M S L (V , Z) O

Our answer is E.

QUESTION 11

If Valerio rows closer to the front than Zita, then which one of the following must be true?

(A) Miller rows immediately in front of Singh.
(B) Lee rows immediately in front of Valerio.
(C) Zita rows immediately in front of Ovitz.
(D) Singh rows immediately in front of Lee.
(E) Singh rows immediately in front of Valerio.

Make a new web, starting with the new rule:

V ... Z

Adding all the old, existing rules:

L
M ... S ... V ... Z ... O

And condense to this:

M S (V ... Z ... O , L)

Looking for a Must be True,

A) Yes, this must be true. I'm 99 percent certain that this is the answer, but it will only take me 10 more seconds to reach 100 percent.
B) Nope, L doesn't have to go anywhere near V.
C) No, L can go between them.
D) No, L can be very far from S.
E) No, L can go between them.

Our answer is A.

QUESTION 6

Which one of the following could be an accurate matching of athletes to seats?

(A) Miller: seat 1; Valerio: seat 5; Lee: seat 6
(B) Singh: seat 3; Valerio: seat 4; Zita: seat 5
(C) Miller: seat 1; Valerio: seat 3; Lee: seat 6
(D) Lee: seat 3; Valerio: seat 4; Ovitz: seat 5
(E) Zita: seat 2; Valerio: seat 3; Ovitz: seat 6

Okay, let's tackle this partial list question. We know that only one of the answer choices could be true, which means that four of them must be false. Process of elimination might be our best bet.

A) No, if V is fifth then O would have to be sixth.
B) No, if S is third, V is fourth and Z is fifth, then both L and O would be forced into the sixth spot. This is out.
C) We don't immediately see why this is wrong, so we'll see if we can eliminate D and E.
D) No, if LVO is third-fifth, then MS would have to be first and second, leaving Z for the sixth spot, which is after O. (Which can't happen.)
E) No. If Z is second and V is third, then both M and S would have to be first.

Our answer is C, because it can't be A, B, D, or E.

QUESTION 9

Which one of the following CANNOT be true?

(A) Ovitz rows closer to the front than Singh.
(B) Zita rows closer to the front than Miller.
(C) Lee rows closer to the front than Valerio.
(D) Singh rows closer to the front than Zita.
(E) Valerio rows closer to the front than Lee.

Hopefully our web of rules will answer this one for us.

A) Bingo. S goes before V, and V goes before O, so O can't go before S. This is the answer.

There's no reason to individually discuss B, C, D, or E. Unless you accidentally lumped two variables together, there's no reason to suspect that any of them won't work.

Our answer is A.

QUESTION 10

Exactly how many different seats could be the seat occupied by Zita?

(A) two
(B) three
(C) four
(D) five
(E) six

Our initial web of rules suggests that Z can go everywhere except last. In the diagrams we've already made, we've confirmed that Z can go in every spot except the final one.

So our answer is five, or D.

QUESTION 12

Suppose the restriction that Miller rows closer to the front than Singh is replaced by the restriction that Singh rows closer to the front than Miller. If the other two restrictions remain in effect, then each of the following could be an accurate matching of athletes to seats EXCEPT:

(A) Singh: seat 1; Zita: seat 2; Miller: seat 6
(B) Singh: seat 1; Valerio: seat 3; Ovitz: seat 5
(C) Singh: seat 3; Lee: seat 4; Valerio: seat 5
(D) Valerio: seat 3; Miller: seat 4; Lee: seat 5
(E) Valerio: seat 4; Miller: seat 5; Ovitz: seat 6

No problem, right? Just take our initial web of rules and switch M and S. Like this:

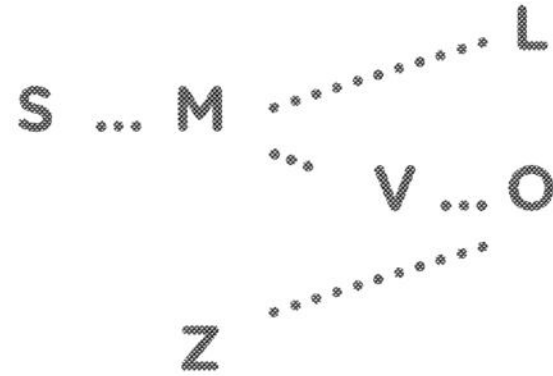

JUST KIDDING. That's exactly what the makers of the test are hoping you'll do. It didn't say "replace S with M in every rule that mentions either one of them." It's only suspending one rule, M...S, and replacing it with S... M. Be careful, because the above diagram is dead wrong, which becomes clear if we start from scratch with this new rule. Here we go:

S ... M

Now tack on the original rules:

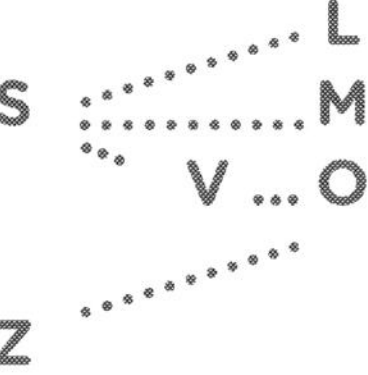

See how it's different? We're asked to find a "could be true... EXCEPT," which means that the correct answer is something that must be false.

A) There's no reason this wouldn't work.
B) No problem.
C) This is a problem. In our new diagram, S has to go before L, M, V, and O. That means it can't go third.
D) No problem.
E) No problem here either.

Our answer is C, because it's the one that won't work.

GROUP 4, GAME 3
EXTRA PRACTICE

A rowing team uses a boat with exactly six seats arranged in single file and numbered sequentially 1 through 6, from the front of the boat to the back. Six athletes—Lee, Miller, Ovitz, Singh, Valerio, and Zita—each row at exactly one of the seats. The following restrictions must apply:

Miller rows closer to the front than Singh.
Singh rows closer to the front than both Lee and Valerio.
Valerio and Zita each row closer to the front than Ovitz.

6. Which one of the following could be an accurate matching of athletes to seats?

(A) Miller: seat 1; Valerio: seat 5; Lee: seat 6
(B) Singh: seat 3; Valerio: seat 4; Zita: seat 5
(C) Miller: seat 1; Valerio: seat 3; Lee: seat 6
(D) Lee: seat 3; Valerio: seat 4; Ovitz: seat 5
(E) Zita: seat 2; Valerio: seat 3; Ovitz: seat 6

7. If Valerio rows at seat 5, then which one of the following must be true?

(A) Miller rows at seat 1.
(B) Singh rows at seat 2.
(C) Zita rows at seat 3.
(D) Lee rows at seat 4.
(E) Ovitz rows at seat 6.

8. If Lee rows at seat 3, then each of the following could be true EXCEPT:

(A) Zita rows immediately behind Valerio.
(B) Ovitz rows immediately behind Valerio.
(C) Ovitz rows immediately behind Zita.
(D) Valerio rows immediately behind Lee.
(E) Singh rows immediately behind Zita.

9. Which one of the following CANNOT be true?

(A) Ovitz rows closer to the front than Singh.
(B) Zita rows closer to the front than Miller.
(C) Lee rows closer to the front than Valerio.
(D) Singh rows closer to the front than Zita.
(E) Valerio rows closer to the front than Lee.

10. Exactly how many different seats could be the seat occupied by Zita?

(A) two
(B) three
(C) four
(D) five
(E) six

11. If Valerio rows closer to the front than Zita, then which one of the following must be true?

(A) Miller rows immediately in front of Singh.
(B) Lee rows immediately in front of Valerio.
(C) Zita rows immediately in front of Ovitz.
(D) Singh rows immediately in front of Lee.
(E) Singh rows immediately in front of Valerio.

12. Suppose the restriction that Miller rows closer to the front than Singh is replaced by the restriction that Singh rows closer to the front than Miller. If the other two restrictions remain in effect, then each of the following could be an accurate matching of athletes to seats EXCEPT:

(A) Singh: seat 1; Zita: seat 2; Miller: seat 6
(B) Singh: seat 1; Valerio: seat 3; Ovitz: seat 5
(C) Singh: seat 3; Lee: seat 4; Valerio: seat 5
(D) Valerio: seat 3; Miller: seat 4; Lee: seat 5
(E) Valerio: seat 4; Miller: seat 5; Ovitz: seat 6

GROUP 4, GAME 3
EXTRA PRACTICE

A rowing team uses a boat with exactly six seats arranged in single file and numbered sequentially 1 through 6, from the front of the boat to the back. Six athletes—Lee, Miller, Ovitz, Singh, Valerio, and Zita—each row at exactly one of the seats. The following restrictions must apply:

Miller rows closer to the front than Singh.
Singh rows closer to the front than both Lee and Valerio.
Valerio and Zita each row closer to the front than Ovitz.

6. Which one of the following could be an accurate matching of athletes to seats?

(A) Miller: seat 1; Valerio: seat 5; Lee: seat 6
(B) Singh: seat 3; Valerio: seat 4; Zita: seat 5
(C) Miller: seat 1; Valerio: seat 3; Lee: seat 6
(D) Lee: seat 3; Valerio: seat 4; Ovitz: seat 5
(E) Zita: seat 2; Valerio: seat 3; Ovitz: seat 6

7. If Valerio rows at seat 5, then which one of the following must be true?

(A) Miller rows at seat 1.
(B) Singh rows at seat 2.
(C) Zita rows at seat 3.
(D) Lee rows at seat 4.
(E) Ovitz rows at seat 6.

8. If Lee rows at seat 3, then each of the following could be true EXCEPT:

(A) Zita rows immediately behind Valerio.
(B) Ovitz rows immediately behind Valerio.
(C) Ovitz rows immediately behind Zita.
(D) Valerio rows immediately behind Lee.
(E) Singh rows immediately behind Zita.

9. Which one of the following CANNOT be true?

(A) Ovitz rows closer to the front than Singh.
(B) Zita rows closer to the front than Miller.
(C) Lee rows closer to the front than Valerio.
(D) Singh rows closer to the front than Zita.
(E) Valerio rows closer to the front than Lee.

10. Exactly how many different seats could be the seat occupied by Zita?

(A) two
(B) three
(C) four
(D) five
(E) six

11. If Valerio rows closer to the front than Zita, then which one of the following must be true?

(A) Miller rows immediately in front of Singh.
(B) Lee rows immediately in front of Valerio.
(C) Zita rows immediately in front of Ovitz.
(D) Singh rows immediately in front of Lee.
(E) Singh rows immediately in front of Valerio.

12. Suppose the restriction that Miller rows closer to the front than Singh is replaced by the restriction that Singh rows closer to the front than Miller. If the other two restrictions remain in effect, then each of the following could be an accurate matching of athletes to seats EXCEPT:

(A) Singh: seat 1; Zita: seat 2; Miller: seat 6
(B) Singh: seat 1; Valerio: seat 3; Ovitz: seat 5
(C) Singh: seat 3; Lee: seat 4; Valerio: seat 5
(D) Valerio: seat 3; Miller: seat 4; Lee: seat 5
(E) Valerio: seat 4; Miller: seat 5; Ovitz: seat 6

GROUP 4, GAME 4

Each side of four cassette tapes—Tapes 1 through 4—contains exactly one of the following four genres: folk, hip-hop, jazz, and rock. The following conditions must apply:

Each genre is found on exactly two of the eight sides.
Tape 1 has jazz on at least one side, but neither hip-hop nor rock.
Tape 2 has no jazz.
Folk is not on any tape numbered exactly one higher than a tape that has any rock on it.

7. Which one of the following could be an accurate matching of tapes with the musical genres found on them?

(A) Tape 1: folk and jazz; Tape 2: folk and jazz; Tape 3: hip-hop and rock; Tape 4: hip-hop and rock
(B) Tape 1: folk and jazz; Tape 2: folk and rock; Tape 3: hip-hop and jazz; Tape 4: hip-hop and rock
(C) Tape 1: folk and jazz; Tape 2: folk and rock; Tape 3: two sides of jazz; Tape 4: two sides of hip-hop
(D) Tape 1: hip-hop and jazz; Tape 2: folk and hiphop; Tape 3: folk and jazz; Tape 4: two sides of rock
(E) Tape 1: two sides of jazz; Tape 2: folk and rock; Tape 3: hip-hop and rock; Tape 4: folk and hip-hop

8. Which one of the following must be true?

(A) If Tape 1 has two sides of jazz, Tape 4 has at least one side of rock.
(B) If Tape 2 has two sides of folk, Tape 3 has at least one side of hip-hop.
(C) If Tape 2 has two sides of rock, Tape 4 has at least one side of folk.
(D) If Tape 3 has two sides of folk, Tape 2 has at least one side of jazz.
(E) If Tape 4 has two sides of hip-hop, Tape 3 has at least one side of folk.

9. Which one of the following could be true?

(A) Tape 1 has jazz on both sides while Tape 4 has folk and hip-hop.
(B) Tape 2 has hip-hop on one side while Tape 3 has hip-hop and jazz.
(C) Tape 3 has folk on both sides while Tape 4 has jazz and rock.
(D) Tape 3 has jazz on one side while Tape 4 has folk on both sides.
(E) Tapes 2 and 3 each have jazz on one side.

10. Which one of the following could be true?

(A) Tape 1 has two sides of folk.
(B) Tape 2 has both hip-hop and jazz.
(C) Tape 4 has both folk and rock.
(D) Tapes 1 and 4 each have a side of hip-hop.
(E) Tapes 3 and 4 each have a side of folk.

11. Which one of the following CANNOT be true?

(A) Tape 2 has rock on both sides while Tape 3 has hip-hop on both sides.
(B) Tape 3 has rock on both sides while Tape 2 has hip-hop on both sides.
(C) Tape 3 has rock on both sides while Tape 4 has hip-hop on both sides.
(D) Tape 4 has rock on both sides while Tape 2 has hip-hop on both sides.
(E) Tape 4 has rock on both sides while Tape 3 has hip-hop on both sides.

EXPLANATION

We'll start by noticing that this game, even though it has "tapes" with two sides each, does not have "front" or "back" sides, or "side 1, side 2." So if jazz has to go on Tape 1, it doesn't matter *which* side that is. It's really just two types of music on each tape. Might not matter much, but we might be rewarded for not making assumptions here.

The rules are fairly straightforward, and it's not a stretch to reach a setup that looks like this:

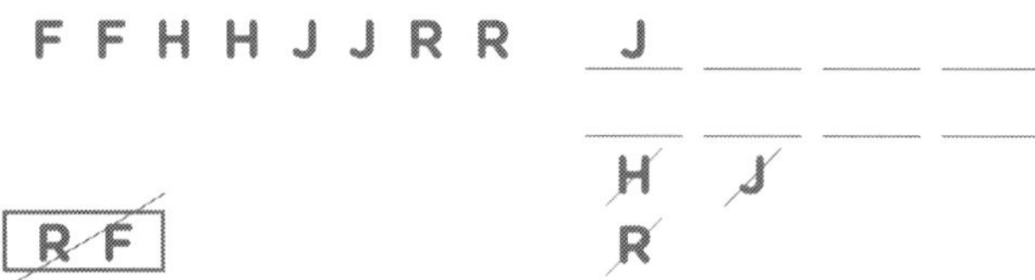

We could probably go straight to the questions from here, but it might be worth looking at the other side of Tape 1. We know it can't be H or R there, so what can it be? Well, it could be either J or F. It's worth writing that in:

That actually simplifies the setup a bit; we don't need "not H" and "not R" underneath Tape 1 if we've already filled both sides of Tape 1 with J and J/F. This is a good example of how the "not" rules can sometimes be converted into more useful "must" rules.

That's it; there aren't any grand inferences to make in this game. There's no choice but to tackle the questions.

QUESTION 7

Which one of the following could be an accurate matching of tapes with the musical genres found on them?

(A) Tape 1: folk and jazz; Tape 2: folk and jazz; Tape 3: hip-hop and rock; Tape 4: hip-hop and rock
(B) Tape 1: folk and jazz; Tape 2: folk and rock; Tape 3: hip-hop and jazz; Tape 4: hip-hop and rock
(C) Tape 1: folk and jazz; Tape 2: folk and rock; Tape 3: two sides of jazz; Tape 4: two sides of hip-hop
(D) Tape 1: hip-hop and jazz; Tape 2: folk and hiphop; Tape 3: folk and jazz; Tape 4: two sides of rock
(E) Tape 1: two sides of jazz; Tape 2: folk and rock; Tape 3: hip-hop and rock; Tape 4: folk and hip-hop

The game kicks off with a list question, which we'll always approach with a process of elimination driven by the rules.

- Tape 1 has J on at least one side, but no H and no R. This gets rid of D.
- Tape 2 has no J. This gets rid of A.
- Never RF. This gets rid of E.
- Two of each type. This gets rid of C. Note that we tested this rule last on purpose, because it seemed like it would take the longest to test.

Our answer is B.

There aren't any "if" questions in this game, so we'll tackle the remaining questions in order.

QUESTION 8

Which one of the following must be true?

(A) If Tape 1 has two sides of jazz, Tape 4 has at least one side of rock.
(B) If Tape 2 has two sides of folk, Tape 3 has at least one side of hip-hop.
(C) If Tape 2 has two sides of rock, Tape 4 has at least one side of folk.
(D) If Tape 3 has two sides of folk, Tape 2 has at least one side of jazz.
(E) If Tape 4 has two sides of hip-hop, Tape 3 has at least one side of folk.

A bit of a tricky one here; each answer choice contains its own "if." We'll probably have to make some diagrams to sort out which one of these has to be true and which four of them could be false. Let's see.

A) This doesn't have to be true; we can make it false. Like this:

J	F	R	H
J	F	R	H

B) This doesn't have to be true; look at the diagram we made immediately above. It's got F on both sides of Tape 2, and it doesn't have any H on Tape 3.

C) Yes, this has to be true. If we put R on both sides of Tape 2, we can't put F on Tape 3. We can either put one F on Tape 1 and one on Tape 3, or both Fs on Tape 4, like this:

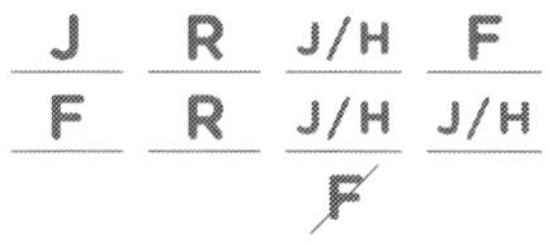

J	R	J/H	F
F	R	J/H	J/H
		~~F~~	

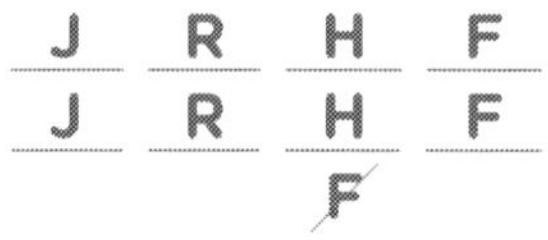

J	R	H	F
J	R	H	F
		~~F~~	

So, yup! If Tape 2 has two sides of rock, Tape 4 has at least one side of folk. We can probably pick this answer and move on, but let's go ahead and prove to ourselves that D and E can both be false.

D) Wait, what? This answer doesn't even make any sense, since J can never go on Tape 2. This is instantly out.

E) Nope. Look at the diagram that we did for A one last time. That one has H on both sides of tape 4, and it doesn't have any F on Tape 3. This is out.

Our answer is C, because it's the only one that has to be true.

QUESTION 9

Which one of the following could be true?

(A) Tape 1 has jazz on both sides while Tape 4 has folk and hip-hop.
(B) Tape 2 has hip-hop on one side while Tape 3 has hip-hop and jazz.
(C) Tape 3 has folk on both sides while Tape 4 has jazz and rock.
(D) Tape 3 has jazz on one side while Tape 4 has folk on both sides.
(E) Tapes 2 and 3 each have jazz on one side.

If there's one that could be true, then there are four that must be false. Let's go.

A) Nope. If we put J on both sides of Tape 1 and F and H on Tape 4, we can't put any R on Tape 3. That means both Rs have to go on Tape 2, but it leaves us with nowhere to put the remaining F. Like this:

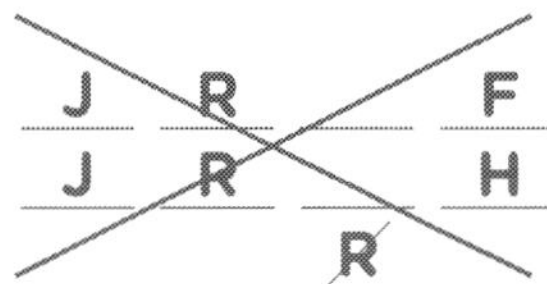

We've crossed this diagram out because it won't work, and we don't want to forget that when we're doing later questions.

B) Sure, why not? Like this:

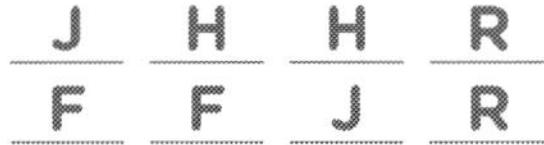

This will work. Here, there's no reason to test C-E. We're 100% sure this will work, which means it's the answer. No point wasting any more time; let's move on.

Our answer is B.

QUESTION 10

Which one of the following could be true?

(A) Tape 1 has two sides of folk.
(B) Tape 2 has both hip-hop and jazz.
(C) Tape 4 has both folk and rock.
(D) Tapes 1 and 4 each have a side of hip-hop.
(E) Tapes 3 and 4 each have a side of folk.

Another Could Be True.

A) No, this can't be true because Tape 1 has to have at least one J.
B) No, this can't be true because Tape 2 can never have J.
C) It's hard to see why this would be a problem. Rather than test it, let's see if we can eliminate D and E.
D) No, because Tape 1 can never have H.
E) Nope. Look:

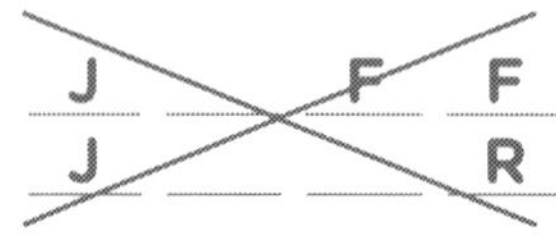

Where would the two Rs go? One of them could go on Tape 4, but the other one would violate the RF rule. We've crossed this diagram out, since it won't work.

Our answer is C.

QUESTION 11

Which one of the following CANNOT be true?

(A) Tape 2 has rock on both sides while Tape 3 has hip-hop on both sides.
(B) Tape 3 has rock on both sides while Tape 2 has hip-hop on both sides.
(C) Tape 3 has rock on both sides while Tape 4 has hip-hop on both sides.
(D) Tape 4 has rock on both sides while Tape 2 has hip-hop on both sides.
(E) Tape 4 has rock on both sides while Tape 3 has hip-hop on both sides.

We're looking for something that can't be true (i.e. Must be False), which means that there are four answers that could be true.

A) It's hard to see why this would be a problem, since it would automatically satisfy the "no RF" rule. Let's not even bother testing it, in hopes that one of the answers will jump out at us as a troublemaker.
B) This one's trouble. Look:

J	H	R	___
J/F	H	R	___

Where can the two Fs go? One of them can go on Tape 1, sure, but the other one is going to violate the "no RF" rule. This is our answer, and there's no reason to prove that C-E will work.

Our answer is B.

Two nice takeaways from this game:

First, don't falsely believe that you've always got to make some sort of grand diagram for every single game. Here, we made zero inferences but still made it through the game pretty quickly. Yes, we had to do some testing for most of the questions. That's what happens when you don't/can't make inferences. No worries! This happens sometimes.

Second, it's important to be nimble in your approach to answering the questions. This means you have to have multiple ways of identifying the correct answer. On this game, we used process of elimination for #7 and #10, but positively identified the correct answers for #8, #9, and #11. (We continued testing D and E for #8 simply because it came early in the game and we wanted to be 100% sure. By the time we reached #9 and #11, we were feeling confident enough to move on without looking at all five answers.) Point is, we have two ways of answering every question, and we don't always know in advance which one we're going to use. Whichever route gets us there faster, that's the one we'll choose.

GROUP 4, GAME 4
EXTRA PRACTICE

Each side of four cassette tapes—Tapes 1 through 4—contains exactly one of the following four genres: folk, hip-hop, jazz, and rock. The following conditions must apply:

Each genre is found on exactly two of the eight sides.
Tape 1 has jazz on at least one side, but neither hip-hop nor rock.
Tape 2 has no jazz.
Folk is not on any tape numbered exactly one higher than a tape that has any rock on it.

7. Which one of the following could be an accurate matching of tapes with the musical genres found on them?

(A) Tape 1: folk and jazz; Tape 2: folk and jazz; Tape 3: hip-hop and rock; Tape 4: hip-hop and rock
(B) Tape 1: folk and jazz; Tape 2: folk and rock; Tape 3: hip-hop and jazz; Tape 4: hip-hop and rock
(C) Tape 1: folk and jazz; Tape 2: folk and rock; Tape 3: two sides of jazz; Tape 4: two sides of hip-hop
(D) Tape 1: hip-hop and jazz; Tape 2: folk and hiphop; Tape 3: folk and jazz; Tape 4: two sides of rock
(E) Tape 1: two sides of jazz; Tape 2: folk and rock; Tape 3: hip-hop and rock; Tape 4: folk and hip-hop

8. Which one of the following must be true?

(A) If Tape 1 has two sides of jazz, Tape 4 has at least one side of rock.
(B) If Tape 2 has two sides of folk, Tape 3 has at least one side of hip-hop.
(C) If Tape 2 has two sides of rock, Tape 4 has at least one side of folk.
(D) If Tape 3 has two sides of folk, Tape 2 has at least one side of jazz.
(E) If Tape 4 has two sides of hip-hop, Tape 3 has at least one side of folk.

9. Which one of the following could be true?

(A) Tape 1 has jazz on both sides while Tape 4 has folk and hip-hop.
(B) Tape 2 has hip-hop on one side while Tape 3 has hip-hop and jazz.
(C) Tape 3 has folk on both sides while Tape 4 has jazz and rock.
(D) Tape 3 has jazz on one side while Tape 4 has folk on both sides.
(E) Tapes 2 and 3 each have jazz on one side.

10. Which one of the following could be true?

(A) Tape 1 has two sides of folk.
(B) Tape 2 has both hip-hop and jazz.
(C) Tape 4 has both folk and rock.
(D) Tapes 1 and 4 each have a side of hip-hop.
(E) Tapes 3 and 4 each have a side of folk.

11. Which one of the following CANNOT be true?

(A) Tape 2 has rock on both sides while Tape 3 has hip-hop on both sides.
(B) Tape 3 has rock on both sides while Tape 2 has hip-hop on both sides.
(C) Tape 3 has rock on both sides while Tape 4 has hip-hop on both sides.
(D) Tape 4 has rock on both sides while Tape 2 has hip-hop on both sides.
(E) Tape 4 has rock on both sides while Tape 3 has hip-hop on both sides.

GROUP 4, GAME 4
EXTRA PRACTICE

Each side of four cassette tapes—Tapes 1 through 4—contains exactly one of the following four genres: folk, hip-hop, jazz, and rock. The following conditions must apply:

Each genre is found on exactly two of the eight sides.
Tape 1 has jazz on at least one side, but neither hip-hop nor rock.
Tape 2 has no jazz.
Folk is not on any tape numbered exactly one higher than a tape that has any rock on it.

7. Which one of the following could be an accurate matching of tapes with the musical genres found on them?

(A) Tape 1: folk and jazz; Tape 2: folk and jazz; Tape 3: hip-hop and rock; Tape 4: hip-hop and rock
(B) Tape 1: folk and jazz; Tape 2: folk and rock; Tape 3: hip-hop and jazz; Tape 4: hip-hop and rock
(C) Tape 1: folk and jazz; Tape 2: folk and rock; Tape 3: two sides of jazz; Tape 4: two sides of hip-hop
(D) Tape 1: hip-hop and jazz; Tape 2: folk and hiphop; Tape 3: folk and jazz; Tape 4: two sides of rock
(E) Tape 1: two sides of jazz; Tape 2: folk and rock; Tape 3: hip-hop and rock; Tape 4: folk and hip-hop

8. Which one of the following must be true?

(A) If Tape 1 has two sides of jazz, Tape 4 has at least one side of rock.
(B) If Tape 2 has two sides of folk, Tape 3 has at least one side of hip-hop.
(C) If Tape 2 has two sides of rock, Tape 4 has at least one side of folk.
(D) If Tape 3 has two sides of folk, Tape 2 has at least one side of jazz.
(E) If Tape 4 has two sides of hip-hop, Tape 3 has at least one side of folk.

9. Which one of the following could be true?

(A) Tape 1 has jazz on both sides while Tape 4 has folk and hip-hop.
(B) Tape 2 has hip-hop on one side while Tape 3 has hip-hop and jazz.
(C) Tape 3 has folk on both sides while Tape 4 has jazz and rock.
(D) Tape 3 has jazz on one side while Tape 4 has folk on both sides.
(E) Tapes 2 and 3 each have jazz on one side.

10. Which one of the following could be true?

(A) Tape 1 has two sides of folk.
(B) Tape 2 has both hip-hop and jazz.
(C) Tape 4 has both folk and rock.
(D) Tapes 1 and 4 each have a side of hip-hop.
(E) Tapes 3 and 4 each have a side of folk.

11. Which one of the following CANNOT be true?

(A) Tape 2 has rock on both sides while Tape 3 has hip-hop on both sides.
(B) Tape 3 has rock on both sides while Tape 2 has hip-hop on both sides.
(C) Tape 3 has rock on both sides while Tape 4 has hip-hop on both sides.
(D) Tape 4 has rock on both sides while Tape 2 has hip-hop on both sides.
(E) Tape 4 has rock on both sides while Tape 3 has hip-hop on both sides.

GROUP 4, GAME 5

A summer program offers at least one of the following seven courses: geography, history, literature, mathematics, psychology, sociology, zoology. The following restrictions on the program must apply:

If mathematics is offered, then either literature or sociology (but not both) is offered.
If literature is offered, then geography is also offered but psychology is not.
If sociology is offered, then psychology is also offered but zoology is not.
If geography is offered, then both history and zoology are also offered.

13. Which one of the following could be a complete and accurate list of the courses offered by the summer program?

(A) history, psychology
(B) geography, history, literature
(C) history, mathematics, psychology
(D) literature, mathematics, psychology
(E) history, literature, mathematics, sociology

14. If the summer program offers literature, then which one of the following could be true?

(A) Sociology is offered.
(B) History is not offered.
(C) Mathematics is not offered
(D) A total of two courses are offered
(E) Zoology is not offered

15. If history is not offered by the summer program, then which one of the following is another course that CANNOT be offered?

(A) literature
(B) mathematics
(C) psychology
(D) sociology
(E) zoology

16. If the summer program offers mathematics, then which one of the following must be true?

(A) Literature is offered.
(B) Psychology is offered.
(C) Sociology is offered.
(D) At least three courses are offered.
(E) At most four courses are offered.

17. Which one of the following must be false of the summer program?

(A) Both geography and psychology are offered.
(B) Both geography and mathematics are offered.
(C) Both psychology and mathematics are offered.
(D) Both history and mathematics are offered.
(E) Both geography and sociology are offered.

EXPLANATION

Let's leave Rule 1 alone for a minute, since it's got an inconvenient "either-or, but not both." That's not the easiest way to start, so let's kick this off with Rule 2 instead to get a good solid footing.

I've already been hollering about this until my voice is hoarse, but I'm going to keep yelling until I lose my voice entirely, then move on to sign language, then build a fucking bonfire and start sending smoke signals: Do NOT lump things together that shouldn't be lumped. Seriously. Do not do it.

L → G
L → ~~P~~

Are you picking up what I'm laying down? This is awful goddamned important. The reason it's important is that the very next rule links to P, but not G. If you lump P and G together, then you don't get to combine Rule 2 with Rule 3. If you don't combine those two rules together, then you're going to miss an inference. Here's the connection:

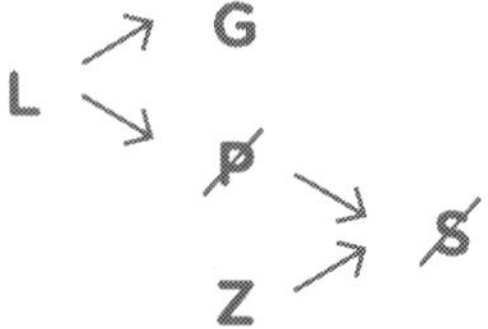

I skipped a step there; I did the contrapositive of Rule 3 in order to attach it to Rule 2. Don't get it? That's okay. Email me: nathan@foxlsat.com. I'm an LSAT nerd, and nothing pleases me more than helping folks like you understand stuff like this. Get in touch and I'll guide you toward some resources that will help you get it.

At this point, we've already made one inference: L and S hate each other. We can only reach this inference by linking Rule 2 with Rule 3. We can only link Rule 2 with Rule 3 if we avoid lumping variables together. Links = good. Lumps = bad. Okay? Onward.

The next rule changes the landscape a bit; we'll show you this one in two steps. First, just tack Rule 4 onto the G that already exists in our chain:

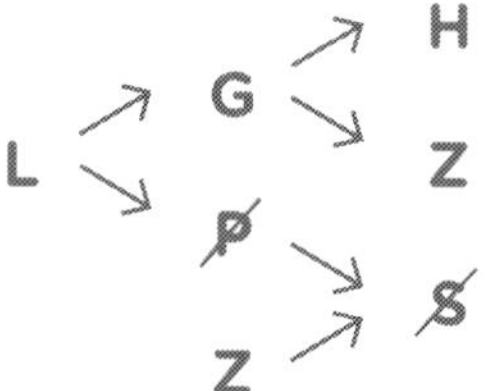

This is a bit messy, because it has Z in the diagram twice. Without changing any of the logic, we can rearrange the diagram to look like this:

H
G
L Z
P S

None of the individual relationships have changed here. All we've done is simplify. And at this point, oh boy, the game is almost over. Let's do the contrapositive of the whole chain, since these chains are awful important and it would be nice to see it both ways:

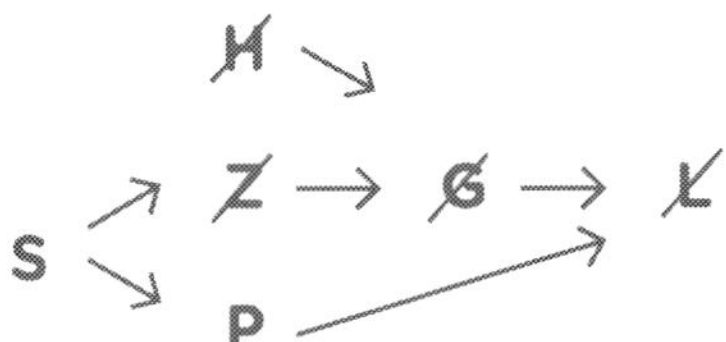

With that, this game is almost over. But we do need to return to rule #1, with its awkward "either-or, not both" construction. (Side note: The "but not both" part of that rule has already been made moot by our rules chains. We can see that L and S, after combining rules 2, 3, and 4 together, already hate each other. So the first rule really now means "if M then either L or S.")

At this point, we don't even need to write anything down for that first rule. We can just remember that M, if it's active, will either trigger L and a whole mess of other things, or S and a whole other mess of things. Time to attack the questions.

QUESTION 13

Which one of the following could be a complete and accurate list of the courses offered by the summer program?

(A) history, psychology
(B) geography, history, literature
(C) history, mathematics, psychology
(D) literature, mathematics, psychology
(E) history, literature, mathematics, sociology

Process of elimination, no sweat. We'll just grab each individual element of the top rules chain and test it, eliminating whatever we can.

- L → G This gets rid of both D and E. Sweet.
- G → H This does nothing.
- G → Z This gets rid of B.
- Z → ~~S~~ This does nothing.
- L → ~~P~~ This would eliminate D, if it weren't already out. (Suck it, D.)
- ~~P~~ → ~~S~~ This does nothing.
- Last, we'll test the toughest rule: If M, then L or S (not both). This gets rid of C.

Our answer is A, because it's the only one left.

QUESTION 14

If the summer program offers literature, then which one of the following could be true?

(A) Sociology is offered.
(B) History is not offered.
(C) Mathematics is not offered
(D) A total of two courses are offered
(E) Zoology is not offered

This has got to be a piece of cake; all we have to do is look at the diagram that starts with L and follow the arrows, eliminating four Must Be Falses.

A) No, L and S hate each other in two separate ways. (Via not Z, not G, and separately via P)
B) No, L triggers G, which triggers H.
C) Sure, M needs either L or S, but doesn't care which.
D) No, L triggers G, which in turn triggers both H and Z.
E) No, L triggers G, which triggers Z.

Our answer is C, because we've eliminated A, B, D, and E.

This game is tough on the surface, but our chain of rules has made it easy. We're licking our chops as we turn to the rest of these questions.

QUESTION 15

If history is not offered by the summer program, then which one of the following is another course that CANNOT be offered?

(A) literature
(B) mathematics
(C) psychology
(D) sociology
(E) zoology

If H isn't offered, then G can't be either. And if G can't be offered, then neither can L. Too easy.

Our answer is A.

QUESTION 16

If the summer program offers mathematics, then which one of the following must be true?

(A) Literature is offered.
(B) Psychology is offered.
(C) Sociology is offered.
(D) At least three courses are offered.
(E) At most four courses are offered.

If M is offered, then that's going to kick off either the L chain or the S chain. Let's just look at the answers and see which one will be true in both of those scenarios.

A) No, M doesn't care whether it goes with L or S.
B) No, if M goes with L then P actually *can't* go.
C) No, again, M is agnostic between L and S.
D) Well, yeah. If M brings L along, then G, Z, and H are all going to follow. And if M brings S along, then P has to come as well. Either way, there's a minimum of three.
E) No way. If M brings L, then there are going to be five players.

Our answer is D.

QUESTION 17

Which one of the following must be false of the summer program?

(A) Both geography and psychology are offered.
(B) Both geography and mathematics are offered.
(C) Both psychology and mathematics are offered.
(D) Both history and mathematics are offered.
(E) Both geography and sociology are offered.

No way to predict this one, we just have to dive into the answer choices.

A) Nope. This is a trap for people who lump G and not P together. In fact, G and P have nothing to do with one another.
B) Nope. G and M are forced to be together if M takes L.
C) Nope. P and M are forced to be together if M takes S.
D) Nope. H and M are forced to be together if M takes L.
E) Yes, this must be false because G requires Z, and Z hates S.

Our answer is E, because it's the only one that must be false.

Sorry for the incoming golf analogy, but this game is like a par five with a wimpy 100-yard carry over water. Standing on the tee, the water looks super-scary for beginners. But players with any skill at all don't even *see* the water; it simply isn't in play for anybody who can make solid contact. Once you learn how to link the rules together properly, this game is a piece of cake.

GROUP 4, GAME 5
EXTRA PRACTICE

A summer program offers at least one of the following seven courses: geography, history, literature, mathematics, psychology, sociology, zoology. The following restrictions on the program must apply:

If mathematics is offered, then either literature or sociology (but not both) is offered.
If literature is offered, then geography is also offered but psychology is not.
If sociology is offered, then psychology is also offered but zoology is not.
If geography is offered, then both history and zoology are also offered.

13. Which one of the following could be a complete and accurate list of the courses offered by the summer program?

(A) history, psychology
(B) geography, history, literature
(C) history, mathematics, psychology
(D) literature, mathematics, psychology
(E) history, literature, mathematics, sociology

14. If the summer program offers literature, then which one of the following could be true?

(A) Sociology is offered.
(B) History is not offered.
(C) Mathematics is not offered
(D) A total of two courses are offered
(E) Zoology is not offered

15. If history is not offered by the summer program, then which one of the following is another course that CANNOT be offered?

(A) literature
(B) mathematics
(C) psychology
(D) sociology
(E) zoology

16. If the summer program offers mathematics, then which one of the following must be true?

(A) Literature is offered.
(B) Psychology is offered.
(C) Sociology is offered.
(D) At least three courses are offered.
(E) At most four courses are offered.

17. Which one of the following must be false of the summer program?

(A) Both geography and psychology are offered.
(B) Both geography and mathematics are offered.
(C) Both psychology and mathematics are offered.
(D) Both history and mathematics are offered.
(E) Both geography and sociology are offered.

GROUP 4, GAME 5
EXTRA PRACTICE

A summer program offers at least one of the following seven courses: geography, history, literature, mathematics, psychology, sociology, zoology. The following restrictions on the program must apply:

If mathematics is offered, then either literature or sociology (but not both) is offered.
If literature is offered, then geography is also offered but psychology is not.
If sociology is offered, then psychology is also offered but zoology is not.
If geography is offered, then both history and zoology are also offered.

13. Which one of the following could be a complete and accurate list of the courses offered by the summer program?

(A) history, psychology
(B) geography, history, literature
(C) history, mathematics, psychology
(D) literature, mathematics, psychology
(E) history, literature, mathematics, sociology

14. If the summer program offers literature, then which one of the following could be true?

(A) Sociology is offered.
(B) History is not offered.
(C) Mathematics is not offered
(D) A total of two courses are offered
(E) Zoology is not offered

15. If history is not offered by the summer program, then which one of the following is another course that CANNOT be offered?

(A) literature
(B) mathematics
(C) psychology
(D) sociology
(E) zoology

16. If the summer program offers mathematics, then which one of the following must be true?

(A) Literature is offered.
(B) Psychology is offered.
(C) Sociology is offered.
(D) At least three courses are offered.
(E) At most four courses are offered.

17. Which one of the following must be false of the summer program?

(A) Both geography and psychology are offered.
(B) Both geography and mathematics are offered.
(C) Both psychology and mathematics are offered.
(D) Both history and mathematics are offered.
(E) Both geography and sociology are offered.

GROUP 4, GAME 6

Eight files will be ordered from first to eighth. Each file falls into exactly one of three categories: red files (H, M, O), green files (P, V, X), or yellow files (T, Z). The files must be ordered according to the following conditions:

H must be placed into some position before O, but H cannot immediately precede O.
X must be placed into some position before V.
X and V must be separated by the same number of files as separate H and O.
Z must immediately precede M.
The first file cannot be a red file.

1. Which of the following is an acceptable ordering of the files from first to eighth?

	1	2	3	4	5	6	7	8
(A)	H	X	O	V	Z	M	P	T
(B)	P	M	Z	H	X	O	V	T
(C)	P	Z	M	H	O	T	X	V
(D)	X	Z	M	V	H	T	P	O
(E)	Z	M	H	P	O	X	V	T

2. The largest possible number of files that can separate Z from H is
   (A) two
   (B) three
   (C) four
   (D) five
   (E) six

3. If each of the three red files is immediately followed by a green file, which one of the following must be a yellow file?
   (A) the first
   (B) the second
   (C) the third
   (D) the fourth
   (E) the fifth

4. The largest possible number of files that can separate X from V is

   (A) three
   (B) four
   (C) five
   (D) six
   (E) seven

5. If Z is placed in the fifth position, then which one of the following is a complete and accurate list of the positions, any one of which could be H's position?

   (A) first, third, fourth
   (B) first, second, third
   (C) second, third, fourth
   (D) second, third, fourth, sixth
   (E) third, fourth, sixth, seventh

EXPLANATION

This is an easy game masquerading as a hard one, so job one is simply don't freak out. At first glance, many students feel pretty intimidated by the following:

The game contains a lot of variables. Some games ask you to put five things in a row, or six things. Here we have eight things. More variables usually increases the complexity. There are two pieces of information for each spot (file name and file color) rather than just one. Again, this tends to complicate things.

The H_...O and X_...V rules have flexibility, rather than certainty. (Contrast that with the ZM rule, which is a lot easier to handle.) Flexible rules mean there are more ways to arrange things. More ways to arrange things usually means more complexity.

In light of these three complications, many students would be tempted to skip this game. Please resist this temptation. Sometimes games with complicated-sounding setups end up having relatively easy questions. This is an example of such a game.

Before I get into specifics, I have two big-picture pieces of advice here:

First, don't even bother trying to assess which games are hard and which games are easy. Instead, tackle the games in order and trust that the earlier ones are almost always the easier ones.

Second, don't overcomplicate the earlier games. I didn't make a ton of inferences on this game, and I didn't come up with any overcomplicated system of scenarios, or anything like that. That's okay! Simple, straightforward approaches to the earlier, easier games can be perfectly acceptable.

Okay, onto the specifics. After reading the "setup" (that's what I'm calling the paragraph part) and all of the rules, I arrived at the following diagram:

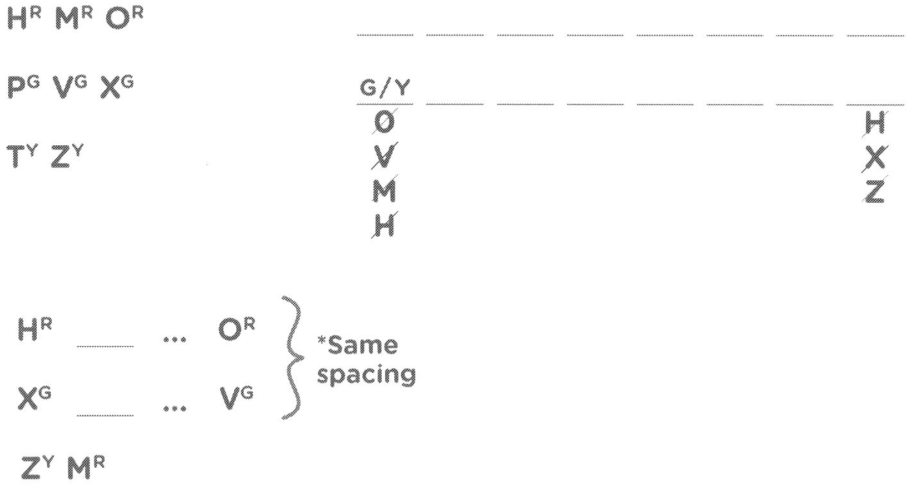

H^R M^R O^R

P^G V^G X^G

T^Y Z^Y

G/Y							
~~O~~							~~H~~
~~V~~							~~X~~
~~M~~							~~Z~~
~~H~~							

H^R ___ ... O^R
X^G ___ ... V^G
*Same spacing

Z^Y M^R

Try to stay disciplined and read all the rules before you start writing. You won't know what to write until you see the big picture, and there's no point in writing "X...V" and then scratching it out five seconds later (changing to "X_...V") when you realize that the rule has the same form as the H_...O rule. Measure twice, cut once.

Anyway, as you can see from the diagram I didn't make any huge revelations on this one. I briefly considered making six scenarios based on the ZM rule, but I quickly scrapped that because it's absolutely nuts to make six scenarios unless they are completely filled out, which I did not think they would be. I also briefly considered making scenarios based on the four players who can go first (TVPX) but again, I didn't think that these scenarios would lead to enough certainty to proceed. Sometimes you just have to dive into the questions, and this is one of those times.

QUESTION 1

Which of the following is an acceptable ordering of the files from first to eighth?

	1	2	3	4	5	6	7	8
(A)	H	X	O	V	Z	M	P	T
(B)	P	M	Z	H	X	O	V	T
(C)	P	Z	M	H	O	T	X	V
(D)	X	Z	M	V	H	T	P	O
(E)	Z	M	H	P	O	X	V	T

A list question, so we'll use the process of elimination. On a (seemingly) tricky question like this, it's important to answer this question with 100% certainty, to be sure that you understand the game properly.

A) Nope, the first file can't be red.
B) Violates the ZM rule.
C) Violates the H_...O rule.
D) Passes all the rules, and is therefore going to be the correct answer. Let's make sure E gets eliminated just to make sure.
E) Violates the X_...V rule.

Our answer is D.

QUESTION 3

If each of the three red files is immediately followed by a green file, which one of the following must be a yellow file?

(A) the first
(B) the second
(C) the third
(D) the fourth
(E) the fifth

Skipping #2 to tackle the "if" questions, we find that we can combine the new rule "every red is followed immediately by a green" with the starting rules.

H^R _G_ ... O^R _G_

Z^Y M^R _G_

} _Y_ __ __ __ __ __ __ __

I started with the stuff on the left, which quickly led to my inference on the right: that Y had to be first. Now, my Spidey Answer Sense is tingling... "Y must be first" could definitely be the answer.

Taking a quick glance at the question, sure enough, it's asking "Which one must be yellow?" Glancing at the answers, sure enough, one of the answers is "first." It feels pretty good when you can predict not only the answers, but even the questions themselves. With enough practice, you can get there too.

Our answer is A, with 100% certainty.

QUESTION 5

If Z is placed in the fifth position, then which one of the following is a complete and accurate list of the positions, any one of which could be H's position?

(A) first, third, fourth
(B) first, second, third
(C) second, third, fourth
(D) second, third, fourth, sixth
(E) third, fourth, sixth, seventh

Tackling the next "if" question gets us this new diagram:

The trick, as I see it, is to make the above diagram before looking at the answer choices. They gave me a new condition (Z5), which I've placed into the diagram. They've asked us where H can go, so before looking at the answer choices I've tried to make a prediction. I knew it couldn't be fifth or sixth (occupied by Z and M) and I knew it couldn't be seventh or eighth (not enough room for H_...O). I also know H can't go first, because it's red. But I don't see any reason why H couldn't go second, third, or fourth.

I didn't bother trying to prove this... having made the hypothesis, I looked at the answer choices. When I saw that "second, third, fourth" was an answer choice I was happy to pick it. The more you practice, the more you start to learn what exactly the test is trying to get out of you. This is perfect example of that.

Our answer is C.

QUESTION 2

The largest possible number of files that can separate Z from H is

(A) two
(B) three
(C) four
(D) five
(E) six

Here's my diagram:

___ H ___ ___ ___ ___ Z M

Z M ___ ___ ___ H ___ O

As much as I strive for certainty on the logic games, I actually didn't bother proving to myself that the answer was four here. If I'm trying to maximize the space between H and Z, I either need to put H as far left as I can and Z as far right as I can (that's what I'm doing on top... H can't go first because it's red, and Z can't go later than seventh because of M) or I can put Z as far left as I can (first) and H as late as I can (sixth, because of its relationship with O). And if you count it up, you'll find a wonderful coincidence: four spots between H and Z in both scenarios.

We know for sure that there was no way to put them further apart, and I don't see why either one of the four-spaces-apart scenarios wouldn't work. I'd say this is 99% certainty, and in this case, I think that's good enough.

So our answer is C.

QUESTION 4

The largest possible number of files that can separate X from V is

(A) three
(B) four
(C) five
(D) six
(E) seven

Here, we need to find the maximum separation for X and V. We already know that X can go first, so that's a good start. Obviously, to get maximum separation, V would then go last, but we know that can't be true because X and V have to maintain the same separation as H and O. If X is first and V is last, then H and O will have to fit between them, which won't work.

So let's try the next best thing:

X^G ___ ___ ___ ___ ___ V^G ___

The answer simply has to be "five" because there's no reason why this scenario won't work. The rule X_...V has already been satisfied, and so has the rule "red can't go first." There's plenty of room to satisfy H_...O and ZM, and H_...O has room to match the five-space separation of X and V.

My answer is C.

GROUP 4, GAME 6
EXTRA PRACTICE

Eight files will be ordered from first to eighth. Each file falls into exactly one of three categories: red files (H, M, O), green files (P, V, X), or yellow files (T, Z). The files must be ordered according to the following conditions:

H must be placed into some position before O, but H cannot immediately precede O.
X must be placed into some position before V.
X and V must be separated by the same number of files as separate H and O.
Z must immediately precede M.
The first file cannot be a red file.

1. Which of the following is an acceptable ordering of the files from first to eighth?

	1	2	3	4	5	6	7	8
(A)	H	X	O	V	Z	M	P	T
(B)	P	M	Z	H	X	O	V	T
(C)	P	Z	M	H	O	T	X	V
(D)	X	Z	M	V	H	T	P	O
(E)	Z	M	H	P	O	X	V	T

2. The largest possible number of files that can separate Z from H is
   (A) two
   (B) three
   (C) four
   (D) five
   (E) six

3. If each of the three red files is immediately followed by a green file, which one of the following must be a yellow file?

   (A) the first
   (B) the second
   (C) the third
   (D) the fourth
   (E) the fifth

4. The largest possible number of files that can separate X from V is

   (A) three
   (B) four
   (C) five
   (D) six
   (E) seven

5. If Z is placed in the fifth position, then which one of the following is a complete and accurate list of the positions, any one of which could be H's position?

   (A) first, third, fourth
   (B) first, second, third
   (C) second, third, fourth
   (D) second, third, fourth, sixth
   (E) third, fourth, sixth, seventh

GROUP 4, GAME 6
EXTRA PRACTICE

Eight files will be ordered from first to eighth. Each file falls into exactly one of three categories: red files (H, M, O), green files (P, V, X), or yellow files (T, Z). The files must be ordered according to the following conditions:

H must be placed into some position before O, but H cannot immediately precede O.
X must be placed into some position before V.
X and V must be separated by the same number of files as separate H and O.
Z must immediately precede M.
The first file cannot be a red file.

1. Which of the following is an acceptable ordering of the files from first to eighth?

	1	2	3	4	5	6	7	8
(A)	H	X	O	V	Z	M	P	T
(B)	P	M	Z	H	X	O	V	T
(C)	P	Z	M	H	O	T	X	V
(D)	X	Z	M	V	H	T	P	O
(E)	Z	M	H	P	O	X	V	T

2. The largest possible number of files that can separate Z from H is
   (A) two
   (B) three
   (C) four
   (D) five
   (E) six

3. If each of the three red files is immediately followed by a green file, which one of the following must be a yellow file?

   (A) the first
   (B) the second
   (C) the third
   (D) the fourth
   (E) the fifth

4. The largest possible number of files that can separate X from V is

   (A) three
   (B) four
   (C) five
   (D) six
   (E) seven

5. If Z is placed in the fifth position, then which one of the following is a complete and accurate list of the positions, any one of which could be H's position?

   (A) first, third, fourth
   (B) first, second, third
   (C) second, third, fourth
   (D) second, third, fourth, sixth
   (E) third, fourth, sixth, seventh

GROUP **5**

GROUP 5, GAME 1

Charlie makes a soup by adding exactly six kinds of foods— kale, lentils, mushrooms, onions, tomatoes, and zucchini—to a broth, one food at a time. No food is added more than once. The order in which Charlie adds the foods to the broth must be consistent with the following:

If the mushrooms are added third, then the lentils are added last.
If the zucchini is added first, then the lentils are added at some time before the onions.
Neither the tomatoes nor the kale is added fifth.
The mushrooms are added at some time before the tomatoes or the kale, but not before both.

1. Which one of the following could be the order in which the foods are added to the broth?

(A) kale, mushrooms, onions, lentils, tomatoes, zucchini
(B) kale, zucchini, mushrooms, tomatoes, lentils, onions
(C) lentils, mushrooms, zucchini, kale, onions, tomatoes
(D) zucchini, lentils, kale, mushrooms, onions, tomatoes
(E) zucchini, tomatoes, onions, mushrooms, lentils, kale

2. Which one of the following foods CANNOT be added first?

(A) kale
(B) lentils
(C) mushrooms
(D) onions
(E) tomatoes

3. If the lentils are added last, then which one of the following must be true?

(A) At least one of the foods is added at some time before the zucchini.
(B) At least two of the foods are added at some time before the kale.
(C) The mushrooms are added third.
(D) The zucchini is added third.
(E) The tomatoes are added fourth.

4. Which one of the following could be an accurate partial ordering of the foods added to the broth?

(A) lentils: second; mushrooms: third
(B) mushrooms: fourth; lentils: last
(C) onions: second; mushrooms: fifth
(D) zucchini: first; lentils: last
(E) zucchini: first; mushrooms: second

5. If the zucchini is added first, then which one of the following CANNOT be true?

(A) The kale is added second.
(B) The tomatoes are added second.
(C) The lentils are added third.
(D) The lentils are added fourth.
(E) The onions are added fourth.

EXPLANATION

Our last Group kicks off with a sequencing game from 2003; this one is a good example of how the games used to be quite a bit tougher than they are today. This game is a Game 1, which on modern tests are almost universally easy. This one *looks* easy on first glance, because it's just putting six things in order. But the "if-then" and "either-or, but not both" rules make this a much tougher game than many simple ordering games. That said, having worked our way through Groups 1-4, there shouldn't be too many surprises here. We're ready for this. Don't panic.

The first two rules are conditional, and there's a connection between the two. Lentils, of course, is the connection. Here are the two rules, with an inference that can be made by combining the two:

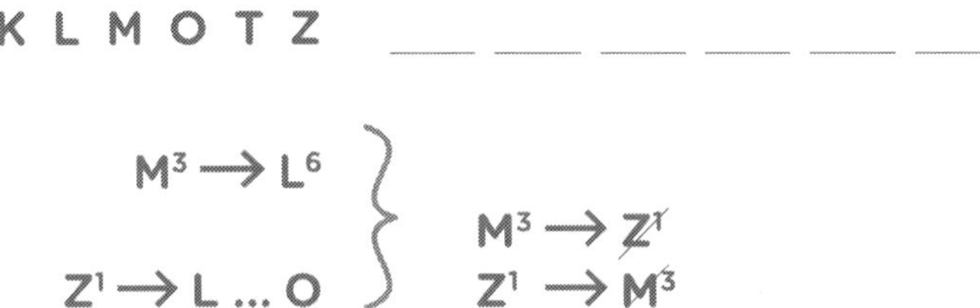

It's not the world's easiest inference, but it's a nice one. M can't be third while Z is first, because L can't be last while also being before O. Take all the time you need and make sure this sinks in. If you don't understand that connection, you probably won't understand the rest of the game. Have I mentioned that you can email me for help if you need it? Because you can: nathan@foxlsat.com.

The third rule is easy; we can add this as a simple "not" rule:

The fourth rule requires a bit of translation. You might be able to do it in your head, but if not, we'll give you a process that you can easily master for simplifying these "either-or, but not both" rules. Basically, if one side is true then the other side has to be false; write that down. Then, if the *other* side is true, then the first side has to be false. Write that down as well. You'll end up with two scenarios, and no more "but not both." Like this:

If M is before T, then M *can't* be before K (so K has to go before M). Like this:

K ... M ... T

Alternatively, if M is before K, then M *can't* be before T (so T has to go before M). Like this:

T ... M ... K

Taking those two diagrams together, we see that M is always in between T and K. So we can simplify further, to get this:

K/T ... M ... T/K

Some of you probably saw that immediately when you read this rule. But these "either-or" rules aren't always so transparent, so if you have to take it through this process of translation, there's no shame in that whatsoever. The resulting translation "M goes somewhere between T and K" is a lot easier to deal with than the clunky "either-or but not both" construction. It's better to sort this out once, before doing the questions, rather than dealing with an awkward rule for the entire game.

Baby steps: Since M always has to go between T and K, it can never go first or last. Let's add that to our growing repository of knowledge.

At this point, it's worth noticing the connection between rules 3 and 4, which both mention T and K. We can't make any specific inferences here, but it might be helpful to remember that, since T and K can't go fifth, one of them will frequently get forced into the last spot. This will happen any time M goes either fourth or fifth.

That's it! Let's tackle the questions.

QUESTION 1

Which one of the following could be the order in which the foods are added to the broth?

(A) kale, mushrooms, onions, lentils, tomatoes, zucchini
(B) kale, zucchini, mushrooms, tomatoes, lentils, onions
(C) lentils, mushrooms, zucchini, kale, onions, tomatoes
(D) zucchini, lentils, kale, mushrooms, onions, tomatoes
(E) zucchini, tomatoes, onions, mushrooms, lentils, kale

List question. We'll use our usual process of elimination.

- T and K can't go fifth. This gets rid of A.
- M goes somewhere between T and K. This gets rid of C.
- If M^3, then L^6. This gets rid of B.
- If Z^1, then L before O. This gets rid of E.

No sweat. Our answer is D because it's the only one left.

QUESTION 3

If the lentils are added last, then which one of the following must be true?

(A) At least one of the foods is added at some time before the zucchini.
(B) At least two of the foods are added at some time before the kale.
(C) The mushrooms are added third.
(D) The zucchini is added third.
(E) The tomatoes are added fourth.

Doing the "if" questions first (after the list question, of course) allows us to make some scenarios that might be helpful when we circle back to questions 2 and 4. For this one, if L is last, we start with this:

___ ___ ___ ___ ___ L

Since no matter where we put O, it will be before L, this means that Z can't be first. (If Z were first, L would have to be before O, which is impossible here.) Furthermore, since T and K can't go fifth (or last), M now can't go fourth or fifth (because it needs to be between T and K).

We don't see an obvious next step, so let's see if that's enough to answer the question. We're looking for something that must be true.

A) Well, yeah. We know Z can't be first. Another way of saying that is "something has to be before Z." This is the answer. Let's just scan B-E to be 100% sure.
B) No, K could be second here.
C) No, could go second.
D) No, there are a bunch of places where Z could go.
E) No, there are a bunch of places for T as well.

Our answer is A.

QUESTION 5

If the zucchini is added first, then which one of the following CANNOT be true?

(A) The kale is added second.
(B) The tomatoes are added second.
(C) The lentils are added third.
(D) The lentils are added fourth.
(E) The onions are added fourth.

If Z is first, then L has to be before O. This triggers our very first inference: When Z is first, M can't be third. Like this:

We can go a couple steps further here. If L is before O, then O now can't go second and L can't go last. Also, since M has to be between T and K, M now can't go second.

Z
O M T L
M K

Time to attack the answer choices, looking for a Must be False.

A) No, this could be true.
B) No, this could also be true. (Nerd note: T and K are equivalent according to the rules, which means that if A or B were the answer, then *both* A and B would have to be the answer. There can't be two correct answers, so A and B could be eliminated for this reason alone.)
C) Why would this be impossible?
D) Why would this be impossible?
E) Oh shit; it's hard to see why this would have to be impossible either.

Looks like we're going to have to do some testing. Intuition says the answer is probably not C, because putting L in the third spot leaves a lot of room behind it for O. Putting L third also keeps M from going third, which we knew was impossible. So let's not test that one first. Instead, let's try L fourth, which leaves less room for O and also leaves the third spot open for a potential M problem. This will make it clear that L fourth won't work, Like this:

See it? If L goes fourth, where will M go? We already knew that it couldn't go second or third. If L goes fourth then M can't go fifth either, since O would have to go sixth.

Our answer is D.

QUESTION 2

Which one of the following foods CANNOT be added first?

(A) kale
(B) lentils
(C) mushrooms
(D) onions
(E) tomatoes

This is actually a super-easy question.

The answer is C. M can't go first because it has to go between T and K.

QUESTION 4

Which one of the following could be an accurate partial ordering of the foods added to the broth?

(A) lentils: second; mushrooms: third
(B) mushrooms: fourth; lentils: last
(C) onions: second; mushrooms: fifth
(D) zucchini: first; lentils: last
(E) zucchini: first; mushrooms: second

Partial list questions tend to be a bit difficult. We'll probably have to do some testing.

A) This one doesn't require a test. If M is third, then L is supposed to go last, not second. This is out.
B) Here we get rewarded for noticing the connection (T and K) between the third and fourth rules. We said at the top that if M were fourth, either T or K would have to go last. So this is out.
C) It's hard to see why this would pose a problem. Let's see if we can get rid of D and E.
D) Nope. If Z is first, then L has to go before O, which means L can't go last.
E) No, because M has to go between T and K.

Our answer is C, because it can't be A, B, D, or E.

Pay close attention to the strategy we used here. Rather than try to prove that C would work, we simply eliminated the other four. It can be hard to prove that a Could Be True could actually be true; sometimes it's a lot faster to eliminate the four that must be false.

Again, this was a Game #1 from a 2003 test, when the games used to be more difficult. If this were a 2015 test, this would probably be Game #3 or #4.

GROUP 5, GAME 1
EXTRA PRACTICE

Charlie makes a soup by adding exactly six kinds of foods— kale, lentils, mushrooms, onions, tomatoes, and zucchini—to a broth, one food at a time. No food is added more than once. The order in which Charlie adds the foods to the broth must be consistent with the following:

If the mushrooms are added third, then the lentils are added last.
If the zucchini is added first, then the lentils are added at some time before the onions.
Neither the tomatoes nor the kale is added fifth.
The mushrooms are added at some time before the tomatoes or the kale, but not before both.

1. Which one of the following could be the order in which the foods are added to the broth?

(A) kale, mushrooms, onions, lentils, tomatoes, zucchini
(B) kale, zucchini, mushrooms, tomatoes, lentils, onions
(C) lentils, mushrooms, zucchini, kale, onions, tomatoes
(D) zucchini, lentils, kale, mushrooms, onions, tomatoes
(E) zucchini, tomatoes, onions, mushrooms, lentils, kale

2. Which one of the following foods CANNOT be added first?

(A) kale
(B) lentils
(C) mushrooms
(D) onions
(E) tomatoes

3. If the lentils are added last, then which one of the following must be true?

(A) At least one of the foods is added at some time before the zucchini.
(B) At least two of the foods are added at some time before the kale.
(C) The mushrooms are added third.
(D) The zucchini is added third.
(E) The tomatoes are added fourth.

4. Which one of the following could be an accurate partial ordering of the foods added to the broth?

(A) lentils: second; mushrooms: third
(B) mushrooms: fourth; lentils: last
(C) onions: second; mushrooms: fifth
(D) zucchini: first; lentils: last
(E) zucchini: first; mushrooms: second

5. If the zucchini is added first, then which one of the following CANNOT be true?

(A) The kale is added second.
(B) The tomatoes are added second.
(C) The lentils are added third.
(D) The lentils are added fourth.
(E) The onions are added fourth.

GROUP 5, GAME 1
EXTRA PRACTICE

Charlie makes a soup by adding exactly six kinds of foods— kale, lentils, mushrooms, onions, tomatoes, and zucchini—to a broth, one food at a time. No food is added more than once. The order in which Charlie adds the foods to the broth must be consistent with the following:

If the mushrooms are added third, then the lentils are added last.
If the zucchini is added first, then the lentils are added at some time before the onions.
Neither the tomatoes nor the kale is added fifth.
The mushrooms are added at some time before the tomatoes or the kale, but not before both.

1. Which one of the following could be the order in which the foods are added to the broth?

(A) kale, mushrooms, onions, lentils, tomatoes, zucchini
(B) kale, zucchini, mushrooms, tomatoes, lentils, onions
(C) lentils, mushrooms, zucchini, kale, onions, tomatoes
(D) zucchini, lentils, kale, mushrooms, onions, tomatoes
(E) zucchini, tomatoes, onions, mushrooms, lentils, kale

2. Which one of the following foods CANNOT be added first?

   (A) kale
   (B) lentils
   (C) mushrooms
   (D) onions
   (E) tomatoes

3. If the lentils are added last, then which one of the following must be true?

   (A) At least one of the foods is added at some time before the zucchini.
   (B) At least two of the foods are added at some time before the kale.
   (C) The mushrooms are added third.
   (D) The zucchini is added third.
   (E) The tomatoes are added fourth.

4. Which one of the following could be an accurate partial ordering of the foods added to the broth?

   (A) lentils: second; mushrooms: third
   (B) mushrooms: fourth; lentils: last
   (C) onions: second; mushrooms: fifth
   (D) zucchini: first; lentils: last
   (E) zucchini: first; mushrooms: second

5. If the zucchini is added first, then which one of the following CANNOT be true?

   (A) The kale is added second.
   (B) The tomatoes are added second.
   (C) The lentils are added third.
   (D) The lentils are added fourth.
   (E) The onions are added fourth.

GROUP 5, GAME 2

Barbara is shopping at a pet store to select fish for her new aquarium from among the following species: J, K, L, M, N, O, and P. For each of the seven species, the store has several fish available. Barbara makes her selection in a manner consistent with the following conditions:

If she selects one or more K, then she does not select any O.
If she selects one or more M, then she does not select any N.
If she selects one or more M, then she selects at least one O.
If she selects one or more N, then she selects at least one O.
If she selects one or more O, then she selects at least one P.
If she selects one or more P, then she selects at least one O.
If she selects any O at all, then she selects at least two O.

19. Which one of the following could be a complete and accurate list of the fish Barbara selects for her aquarium?

(A) three J, one K, two M
(B) one J, one K, one M, three O
(C) one J, one M, two O, one P
(D) one J, one N, one O, two P
(E) one M, one N, two O, one P

20. If Barbara does not select any fish of species P, then it could be true that she selects fish of species

(A) J and of species K
(B) J and of species M
(C) K and of species M
(D) K and of species N
(E) L and of species O

21. If Barbara selects fish of as many species as possible, then she cannot select any fish of which one of the following species?

(A) K
(B) L
(C) M
(D) N
(E) P

22. Which one of the following statements must be false?

(A) Barbara selects exactly four fish, at least one of which is a J.
(B) Barbara selects exactly four fish, at least one of which is an L.
(C) Barbara selects exactly three fish, at least one of which is an M.
(D) Barbara selects exactly three fish, at least one of which is an O.
(E) Barbara selects exactly three fish, at least one of which is a P.

23. If Barbara selects at least one fish for her aquarium, then which one of the following lists the minimum and maximum possible numbers, respectively, of different species of fish that Barbara selects?

(A) 1, 4
(B) 1, 5
(C) 1, 6
(D) 2, 5
(E) 2, 6

EXPLANATION

As we've discussed throughout the book, this type of game is eminently learnable. If we can link the rules together into a web, we should crush it. Two things to remember about this kind of game:

1) We don't have to tackle the rules in order. It's our game, and we can attack it however we choose.
2) We'll probably need to do the contrapositive of one or more rules in order to make the connections.

Since Rule 1 doesn't immediately link to Rule 2, and since Rule 2 neatly links to Rule 3, let's leave Rule 1 aside for the moment. Rule 2 and Rule 3 both have M as a trigger ("sufficient condition" would be a geekier way of saying it) so let's start there:

Now let's tie in Rule 1. We'll have to do the contrapositive of that rule in order to link to the O, like this:

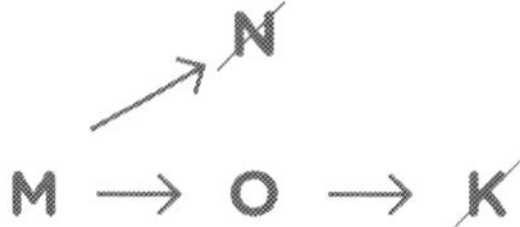

And just like that, we're killing this game. The importance of these first two steps can't be overstated, so please make sure you understand what we've done. (Nathan@foxlsat.com stands ready to help if you're at all confused.) Of course we didn't *have* to take the rules in exactly this order; there are many ways to tackle each game, and addressing the rules in order is certainly one option. But it's hard to see how writing those two rules separately, since they can't be linked, would have kicked anywhere near as much ass as the ass we're kicking so far. We have this game on the ropes.

The fourth rule seems like it might be a bit awkward, so let's let it sit. The fifth and sixth rules will play nice with our growing rule chain, so let's invite them to the party:

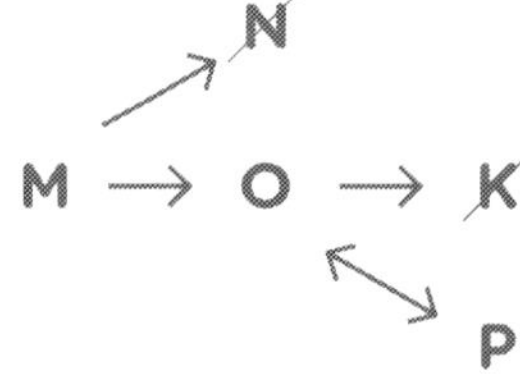

The OP arrow goes both ways, since both O→P and P→O are in play. Now let's see if we can get Rule 4 involved in the action. We'll do the contrapositive of Rule 4 and tack it on to the front:

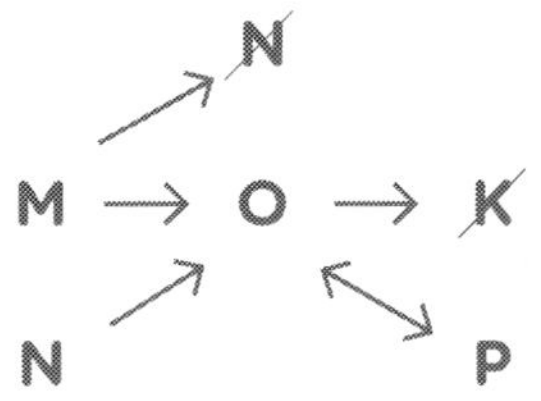

```
        ↗ N̸
M  →  O  →  K̸
    ↗     ↖↘
N             P
```

That's still a bit awkward (since we've got a negative N and a positive N in the same diagram) but if that's the best punch this game can throw at us, this one looks like an early knockout.

The final rule is a special condition for O. It's not all that useful to link it into the rules chain, since it doesn't trigger any other variables. Let's just add a "greater than or equal to two" sign to the O, so that we remember that any time we have O we have more than one. That makes this our final diagram:

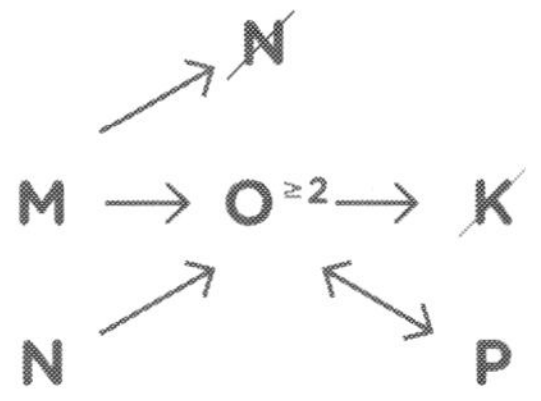

```
        ↗ N̸
M  →  O≥2 →  K̸
    ↗      ↖↘
N              P
```

It's probably worth looking at the contrapositive of this entire web. All we have to do is take the contrapositive of each element, one at a time, until we get this:

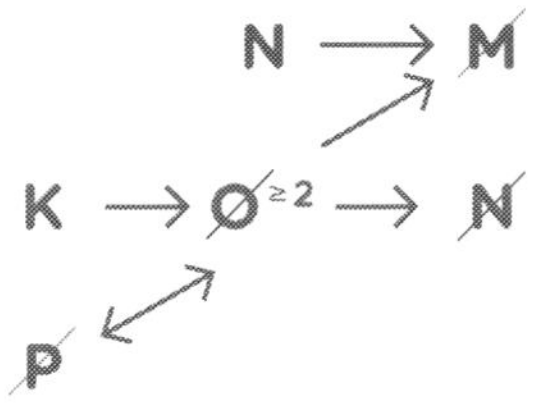

```
          N  →  M̸
             ↗
K  →  O̸≥2  →  N̸
    ↙↗
P̸
```

Overkill? Perhaps. But we're never afraid of winning too handily; if the ref stops the fight, that's fine by us. Watch how easy the questions become...

QUESTION 19

Which one of the following could be a complete and accurate list of the fish Barbara selects for her aquarium?

(A) three J, one K, two M
(B) one J, one K, one M, three O
(C) one J, one M, two O, one P
(D) one J, one N, one O, two P
(E) one M, one N, two O, one P

Process of elimination.

- If M then no N. This gets rid of E.
- If M, then O. This gets rid of A.
- If N, then O. This doesn't do anything for us.
- If O, then OO. This gets rid of D.
- If O, then no K. This gets rid of B.

At this point it's very likely that the answer is C, but we have one more rule to test. It's important to stay disciplined and test this final rule, to be 100% sure.

If O, then P and if P, then O. This doesn't get rid of C, so that's our answer.

QUESTION 20

If Barbara does not select any fish of species P, then it could be true that she selects fish of species

(A) J and of species K
(B) J and of species M
(C) K and of species M
(D) K and of species N
(E) L and of species O

Generally speaking, we'd make a new diagram for a question that starts with the word "if." But here, all we have to do is look at the contrapositive of our web of rules (since that's where the negative P lives.) If our friend Barb doesn't pick any fish of type P, then she can't pick any fish of type O either. That, in turn, means she can't pick any Ms or Ns. That's all it's gonna take to answer the question.

A) Sure, there's nothing wrong with Js and Ks in this scenario. This is probably the answer.
B) Nope, Ms are out.
C) Nope, Ms are out.
D) Nope, Ns are out.
E) Nope, Os are out.

Too easy. Our answer is A.

QUESTION 21

If Barbara selects fish of as many species as possible, then she cannot select any fish of which one of the following species?

(A) K
(B) L
(C) M
(D) N
(E) P

Which type of fish causes the most problems? Look at the webs. If Barb takes type M, then she can't have N or K. If she takes type N, she can't have M or K. That's a tie. Oh, there it is: If she takes type K, then she can't have any Os, Ms, or Ns. We haven't looked at the answer choices yet, but if K is listed, that's going to be our answer.

Sure enough, our answer is A.

QUESTION 23

If Barbara selects at least one fish for her aquarium, then which one of the following lists the minimum and maximum possible numbers, respectively, of different species of fish that Barbara selects?

(A) 1, 4
(B) 1, 5
(C) 1, 6
(D) 2, 5
(E) 2, 6

This question asks us about the minimums and maximums. The minimum is pretty clearly one, since J and L, each wild cards, don't require any other types of fish to be selected. So the answer must be A, B, or C.

The maximum is five, because J and L are wildcards and can go together with the combination of M, O, and P (or N, O, and P).

So our answer is B.

QUESTION 22

Which one of the following statements must be false?

(A) Barbara selects exactly four fish, at least one of which is a J.
(B) Barbara selects exactly four fish, at least one of which is an L.
(C) Barbara selects exactly three fish, at least one of which is an M.
(D) Barbara selects exactly three fish, at least one of which is an O.
(E) Barbara selects exactly three fish, at least one of which is a P.

No way to predict this one; we'll just have to tackle the answer choices. We're looking for a scenario that will not work.

A) Why would this be a problem? Starting with J gives us a lot of flexibility. Let's move past this answer, hoping that one of the other choices looks like an obvious problem.
B) L is also a wild card, and now we can be 100% sure that the answer is neither A nor B, since these answers are logically equivalent. (There's no difference between J and L, so there's no difference between A and B. That makes them both wrong.)
C) This won't work. If Barbara picks an M, then she has to also pick at least two Os and a P. That's a minimum of four fish any time she takes an M. This is our answer.
D) This would work if Barbara picked exactly two Os and one P.
E) Same thing: this would work if Barbara picked exactly two Os and one P.

Our answer is C, because it definitely won't work.

It's not the easiest game, but it's not the hardest one either. We won this fight in the early rounds, when we were putting our rule web together. Once we had that, there was no way we could lose.

GROUP 5, GAME 2 FROM PREPTEST 39, DECEMBER 2002

GROUP 5, GAME 2
EXTRA PRACTICE

Barbara is shopping at a pet store to select fish for her new aquarium from among the following species: J, K, L, M, N, O, and P. For each of the seven species, the store has several fish available. Barbara makes her selection in a manner consistent with the following conditions:

If she selects one or more K, then she does not select any O.
If she selects one or more M, then she does not select any N.
If she selects one or more M, then she selects at least one O.
If she selects one or more N, then she selects at least one O.
If she selects one or more O, then she selects at least one P.
If she selects one or more P, then she selects at least one O.
If she selects any O at all, then she selects at least two O.

19. Which one of the following could be a complete and accurate list of the fish Barbara selects for her aquarium?

(A) three J, one K, two M
(B) one J, one K, one M, three O
(C) one J, one M, two O, one P
(D) one J, one N, one O, two P
(E) one M, one N, two O, one P

20. If Barbara does not select any fish of species P, then it could be true that she selects fish of species

(A) J and of species K
(B) J and of species M
(C) K and of species M
(D) K and of species N
(E) L and of species O

21. If Barbara selects fish of as many species as possible, then she cannot select any fish of which one of the following species?

(A) K
(B) L
(C) M
(D) N
(E) P

22. Which one of the following statements must be false?

(A) Barbara selects exactly four fish, at least one of which is a J.
(B) Barbara selects exactly four fish, at least one of which is an L.
(C) Barbara selects exactly three fish, at least one of which is an M.
(D) Barbara selects exactly three fish, at least one of which is an O.
(E) Barbara selects exactly three fish, at least one of which is a P.

23. If Barbara selects at least one fish for her aquarium, then which one of the following lists the minimum and maximum possible numbers, respectively, of different species of fish that Barbara selects?

(A) 1, 4
(B) 1, 5
(C) 1, 6
(D) 2, 5
(E) 2, 6

GROUP 5, GAME 2
EXTRA PRACTICE

Barbara is shopping at a pet store to select fish for her new aquarium from among the following species: J, K, L, M, N, O, and P. For each of the seven species, the store has several fish available. Barbara makes her selection in a manner consistent with the following conditions:

If she selects one or more K, then she does not select any O.
If she selects one or more M, then she does not select any N.
If she selects one or more M, then she selects at least one O.
If she selects one or more N, then she selects at least one O.
If she selects one or more O, then she selects at least one P.
If she selects one or more P, then she selects at least one O.
If she selects any O at all, then she selects at least two O.

19. Which one of the following could be a complete and accurate list of the fish Barbara selects for her aquarium?

(A) three J, one K, two M
(B) one J, one K, one M, three O
(C) one J, one M, two O, one P
(D) one J, one N, one O, two P
(E) one M, one N, two O, one P

20. If Barbara does not select any fish of species P, then it could be true that she selects fish of species

(A) J and of species K
(B) J and of species M
(C) K and of species M
(D) K and of species N
(E) L and of species O

21. If Barbara selects fish of as many species as possible, then she cannot select any fish of which one of the following species?

(A) K
(B) L
(C) M
(D) N
(E) P

22. Which one of the following statements must be false?

(A) Barbara selects exactly four fish, at least one of which is a J.
(B) Barbara selects exactly four fish, at least one of which is an L.
(C) Barbara selects exactly three fish, at least one of which is an M.
(D) Barbara selects exactly three fish, at least one of which is an O.
(E) Barbara selects exactly three fish, at least one of which is a P.

23. If Barbara selects at least one fish for her aquarium, then which one of the following lists the minimum and maximum possible numbers, respectively, of different species of fish that Barbara selects?

(A) 1, 4
(B) 1, 5
(C) 1, 6
(D) 2, 5
(E) 2, 6

GROUP 5, GAME 3

A farmer harvests eight separate fields—G, H, J, K, L, M, P, and T. Each field is harvested exactly once, and no two fields are harvested simultaneously. Once the harvesting of a field begins, no other fields are harvested until the harvesting of that field is complete. The farmer harvests the fields in an order consistent with the following conditions:

Both P and G are harvested at some time before K.
Both H and L are harvested at some time before J.
K is harvested at some time before M but after L.
T is harvested at some time before M.

7. Which one of the following could be true?

(A) J is the first field harvested.
(B) K is the second field harvested.
(C) M is the sixth field harvested.
(D) G is the seventh field harvested.
(E) T is the eighth field harvested.

8. If M is the seventh field harvested, then any one of the following could be the fifth field harvested EXCEPT:

(A) H
(B) J
(C) K
(D) L
(E) P

9. Which one of the following CANNOT be the field that is harvested fifth?

(A) G
(B) J
(C) M
(D) P
(E) T

10. If J is the third field harvested, then which one of the following must be true?

(A) L is the first field harvested.
(B) H is the second field harvested.
(C) T is the fourth field harvested.
(D) K is the seventh field harvested.
(E) M is the eighth field harvested.

11. If H is the sixth field harvested, then which one of the following must be true?

(A) G is harvested at some time before T.
(B) H is harvested at some time before K.
(C) J is harvested at some time before M.
(D) K is harvested at some time before J.
(E) T is harvested at some time before K.

12. If L is the fifth field harvested, then which one of the following could be true?

(A) J is harvested at some time before G.
(B) J is harvested at some time before T.
(C) K is harvested at some time before T.
(D) M is harvested at some time before H.
(E) M is harvested at some time before J.

EXPLANATION

As you've seen by now, we won't always take all the rules in the order they're given. Sometimes we skip around, in order to make connections. Here, we'll start with the first rule and the third rule, since they both mention K. Check it out:

G H J K L M P T ___ ___ ___ ___ ___ ___ ___ ___

P
G ... K ... M
L

That's an awful nice base to build from. Now that we've got an L in there, let's use that to patch in rule 2:

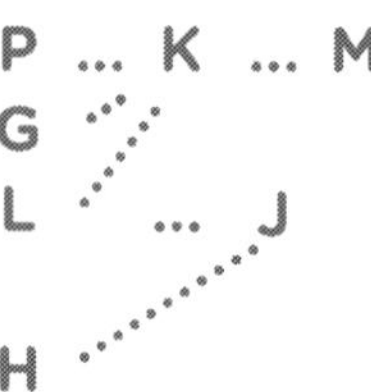

Finally, we'll tack on rule 4:

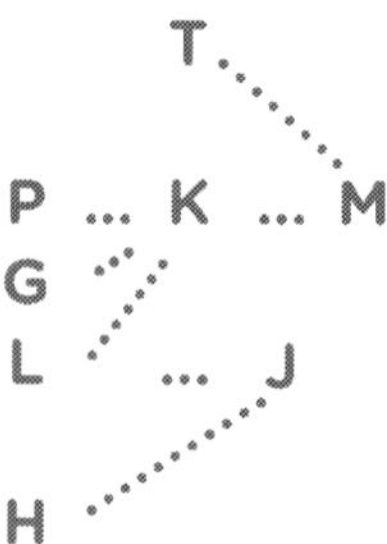

Eight players and they all link together in a single neat web. Piece of cake. Before we destroy the questions, we might peek at the first and last spots, since those are the ones that tend to get restricted. Here, the first spot actually has quite a few candidates. Nobody has to go before T, P, G, L, or H, so any of them can go first. That's not helpful. But the last spot is quite restricted; only M and J are eligible. Let's go ahead and make a note of that, like this:

The reason this last bit is important is that at least one of the questions is almost certain to say something like "if M goes sixth, which one of the following blah blah blah," in which case we would *immediately* know that J must go last (since only M and J can go last.) Once you get the hang of this principle, you're going to be shocked and delighted that the LSAT keeps testing it, since it's so goddamned simple.

Time for the questions; this should be fun. There's no list question, so we'll skip #7 and hunt down the "if" questions first.

QUESTION 8

If M is the seventh field harvested, then any one of the following could be the fifth field harvested EXCEPT:

(A) H
(B) J
(C) K
(D) L
(E) P

Told you they'd test this! If M goes seventh, then J has to go last. If J has to go last, then J can't go fifth.

Our answer is B, with zero work required.

QUESTION 10

If J is the third field harvested, then which one of the following must be true?

(A) L is the first field harvested.
(B) H is the second field harvested.
(C) T is the fourth field harvested.
(D) K is the seventh field harvested.
(E) M is the eighth field harvested.

Aaaaaaaaaaaand sure enough, there it is again! If J is third, then M has to go last. **Which makes E our answer.**

Once again, there's no work required. Dear LSAC: Please keep including this on the test, so we can keep racking up free points with minimal effort. Thanks!

QUESTION 11

If H is the sixth field harvested, then which one of the following must be true?

(A) G is harvested at some time before T.
(B) H is harvested at some time before K.
(C) J is harvested at some time before M.
(D) K is harvested at some time before J.
(E) T is harvested at some time before K.

Finally we're going to have to do some actual work. If H is sixth, the only thing we know for sure is that J has to go seventh or eighth. Like this:

Beyond that, nothing much happens. Let's dive into the answer choices, looking for something that we know for sure.

A) Why would this have to be true?
B) This must be false, not must be true.
C) No, we're pretty sure J can go last.
D) Yes, this has to be true because K has to go before M. (There's no way for K, J, and M to all go in the last two spots.) This will be our answer, but let's glance at E to be sure.
E) Nah, there's no reason to think this has to be true.

Our answer is D.

QUESTION 12

If L is the fifth field harvested, then which one of the following could be true?

(A) J is harvested at some time before G.
(B) J is harvested at some time before T.
(C) K is harvested at some time before T.
(D) M is harvested at some time before H.
(E) M is harvested at some time before J.

If L is fifth, then K, M, and J have to fill the last three spots, with K before M as always. So, like this:

That leaves T, P, G, and H for the first four spots. None of those players have any relationship to each other, so they can go in any order, like this:

No big deal. We're looking for something that could be true, which means the four wrong answers all must be false. Let's go.

A) Nope, J is going somewhere near the end and G is going near the beginning.
B) Same thing as above. J goes late while T goes early.
C) Nope. K goes late, T goes early.
D) Nope. M goes late, H goes early.
E) Yes, this is possible. The last three spots can be KJM or JKM, both of which would put M after J.

Our answer is E.

QUESTION 7

Which one of the following could be true?

(A) J is the first field harvested.
(B) K is the second field harvested.
(C) M is the sixth field harvested.
(D) G is the seventh field harvested.
(E) T is the eighth field harvested.

It's a Could Be True, which once again means that the four wrong answers will all be conclusively false.

A) This is false, since J has to go after both L and H.
B) This is false, since K goes after P, G, and L.
C) This seems like a possibility.
D) This is false, since G goes before both K and M.
E) This is false, since T goes before M.

Our answer is C, even though we made no effort to prove it.

The answer simply can't be A, B, D, or E, allowing us to comfortably choose C.

QUESTION 9

Which one of the following CANNOT be the field that is harvested fifth?

(A) G
(B) J
(C) M
(D) P
(E) T

Test each of these answers if you absolutely must, but when you get good at this type of game you can probably predict the answer just by glancing at the web of rules. M is the correct answer; M can't be fifth because it has five players (T, P, K, G, and L) that must precede it.

Our answer is C.

Extremely easy game here. You can learn to crush this type; everyone can. Keep practicing and using the tools we've learned here!

GROUP 5, GAME 3
EXTRA PRACTICE

A farmer harvests eight separate fields—G, H, J, K, L, M, P, and T. Each field is harvested exactly once, and no two fields are harvested simultaneously. Once the harvesting of a field begins, no other fields are harvested until the harvesting of that field is complete. The farmer harvests the fields in an order consistent with the following conditions:

> Both P and G are harvested at some time before K.
> Both H and L are harvested at some time before J.
> K is harvested at some time before M but after L.
> T is harvested at some time before M.

7. Which one of the following could be true?

(A) J is the first field harvested.
(B) K is the second field harvested.
(C) M is the sixth field harvested.
(D) G is the seventh field harvested.
(E) T is the eighth field harvested.

8. If M is the seventh field harvested, then any one of the following could be the fifth field harvested EXCEPT:

(A) H
(B) J
(C) K
(D) L
(E) P

9. Which one of the following CANNOT be the field that is harvested fifth?

(A) G
(B) J
(C) M
(D) P
(E) T

10. If J is the third field harvested, then which one of the following must be true?

(A) L is the first field harvested.
(B) H is the second field harvested.
(C) T is the fourth field harvested.
(D) K is the seventh field harvested.
(E) M is the eighth field harvested.

11. If H is the sixth field harvested, then which one of the following must be true?

(A) G is harvested at some time before T.
(B) H is harvested at some time before K.
(C) J is harvested at some time before M.
(D) K is harvested at some time before J.
(E) T is harvested at some time before K.

12. If L is the fifth field harvested, then which one of the following could be true?

(A) J is harvested at some time before G.
(B) J is harvested at some time before T.
(C) K is harvested at some time before T.
(D) M is harvested at some time before H.
(E) M is harvested at some time before J.

GROUP 5, GAME 3
EXTRA PRACTICE

A farmer harvests eight separate fields—G, H, J, K, L, M, P, and T. Each field is harvested exactly once, and no two fields are harvested simultaneously. Once the harvesting of a field begins, no other fields are harvested until the harvesting of that field is complete. The farmer harvests the fields in an order consistent with the following conditions:

Both P and G are harvested at some time before K.
Both H and L are harvested at some time before J.
K is harvested at some time before M but after L.
T is harvested at some time before M.

7. Which one of the following could be true?

(A) J is the first field harvested.
(B) K is the second field harvested.
(C) M is the sixth field harvested.
(D) G is the seventh field harvested.
(E) T is the eighth field harvested.

8. If M is the seventh field harvested, then any one of the following could be the fifth field harvested EXCEPT:

   (A) H
   (B) J
   (C) K
   (D) L
   (E) P

9. Which one of the following CANNOT be the field that is harvested fifth?

   (A) G
   (B) J
   (C) M
   (D) P
   (E) T

10. If J is the third field harvested, then which one of the following must be true?

    (A) L is the first field harvested.
    (B) H is the second field harvested.
    (C) T is the fourth field harvested.
    (D) K is the seventh field harvested.
    (E) M is the eighth field harvested.

11. If H is the sixth field harvested, then which one of the following must be true?

    (A) G is harvested at some time before T.
    (B) H is harvested at some time before K.
    (C) J is harvested at some time before M.
    (D) K is harvested at some time before J.
    (E) T is harvested at some time before K.

12. If L is the fifth field harvested, then which one of the following could be true?

    (A) J is harvested at some time before G.
    (B) J is harvested at some time before T.
    (C) K is harvested at some time before T.
    (D) M is harvested at some time before H.
    (E) M is harvested at some time before J.

GROUP 5, GAME 4

During a certain week, an animal shelter places exactly six dogs—a greyhound, a husky, a keeshond, a Labrador retriever, a poodle, and a schnauzer—with new owners. Two are placed on Monday, two on Tuesday, and the remaining two on Wednesday, consistent with the following conditions:

The Labrador retriever is placed on the same day as the poodle.
The greyhound is not placed on the same day as the husky.
If the keeshond is placed on Monday, the greyhound is placed on Tuesday.
If the schnauzer is placed on Wednesday, the husky is placed on Tuesday.

7. Which one of the following could be a complete and accurate matching of dogs to the days on which they are placed?

(A) Monday: greyhound, Labrador retriever Tuesday: husky, poodle Wednesday: keeshond, schnauzer
(B) Monday: greyhound, keeshond Tuesday: Labrador retriever, poodle Wednesday: husky, schnauzer
(C) Monday: keeshond, schnauzer Tuesday: greyhound, husky Wednesday: Labrador retriever, poodle
(D) Monday: Labrador retriever, poodle Tuesday: greyhound, keeshond Wednesday: husky, schnauzer
(E) Monday: Labrador retriever, poodle Tuesday: husky, keeshond Wednesday: greyhound, schnauzer

8. Which one of the following must be true?

(A) The keeshond is not placed on the same day as the greyhound.
(B) The keeshond is not placed on the same day as the schnauzer.
(C) The schnauzer is not placed on the same day as the husky.
(D) The greyhound is placed on the same day as the schnauzer.
(E) The husky is placed on the same day as the keeshond.

9. If the poodle is placed on Tuesday, then which one of the following could be true?

(A) The greyhound is placed on Monday.
(B) The keeshond is placed on Monday.
(C) The Labrador retriever is placed on Monday.
(D) The husky is placed on Tuesday.
(E) The schnauzer is placed on Wednesday.

10. If the greyhound is placed on the same day as the keeshond, then which one of the following must be true?

(A) The husky is placed on Monday.
(B) The Labrador retriever is placed on Monday.
(C) The keeshond is placed on Tuesday.
(D) The poodle is not placed on Wednesday.
(E) The schnauzer is not placed on Wednesday.

11. If the husky is placed the day before the schnauzer, then which one of the following CANNOT be true?

(A) The husky is placed on Monday.
(B) The keeshond is placed on Monday.
(C) The greyhound is placed on Tuesday.
(D) The poodle is placed on Tuesday.
(E) The poodle is placed on Wednesday.

12. If the greyhound is placed the day before the poodle, then which one of the following CANNOT be placed on Tuesday?

(A) the husky
(B) the keeshond
(C) the Labrador retriever
(D) the poodle
(E) the schnauzer

EXPLANATION

Our setup here is fairly straightforward; we have six dogs and six spots, two on each of Monday, Tuesday, and Wednesday. Since Monday, Tuesday, and Wednesday have an inherent order it's a no-brainer to use M, T, and W as the base of our diagram. Like this:

It's worth pointing out one potential pitfall here: See how "Labrador retriever" is two words, and in some cases those two words are printed across two lines? This opens up the possibility of listing the dogs as "GHKLRPS," which is of course wrong, since "Labrador retriever" is only one dog. This sort of thing appears constantly on the LSAT, so keep an eye out.

Now let's tackle the rules. If L and P have to occupy the same day, that looks like this:

If G and H *can't* occupy the same day, that looks like this:

From these two facts, we can immediately infer that K and S can't occupy the same day (because if they did, and if L and P had to be together on another day, then G and H would be forced together). So we might as well add this to our diagram. There wasn't an explicit rule, but there's certainly an implicit rule that looks like this:

That's an awful nice inference; it's not rocket science, but it's something that very few test-takers will notice. It's the kind of observation that tends to make games extremely easy.

The next rule is conditional, so we'll use the if-then arrow on it. Like this:

$$K_M \rightarrow G_T$$

But wait a minute... if K is on Monday and that forces G to be on Tuesday, then doesn't LP have to go on Wednesday? And since G and H hate each other, don't we know everything? Yes, yes, we do. If K is on Monday, it looks *exactly* like this:

K	G	L
H	S	P
M	T	W

If it doesn't look exactly like that, then K can't be on Monday. We haven't even looked at the last rule yet, and already we're making progress. The last rule is another conditional rule, like this:

$$S_W \rightarrow H_T$$

And just like the previous rule, this rule would, when in effect, trigger a whole avalanche of inferences. If S is on Wednesday and H is on Tuesday, then LP has to go on Monday. And since G and H hate each other, once again we know everything. Like this:

L	H	S
P	K	G
M	T	W

Sweeeeeeeeeeeeet. If it doesn't look exactly like that, then S can't be on Wednesday.

We're killing it. Let's tackle the questions.

QUESTION 7

Which one of the following could be a complete and accurate matching of dogs to the days on which they are placed?

(A) Monday: greyhound, Labrador retriever Tuesday: husky, poodle Wednesday: keeshond, schnauzer
(B) Monday: greyhound, keeshond Tuesday: Labrador retriever, poodle Wednesday: husky, schnauzer
(C) Monday: keeshond, schnauzer Tuesday: greyhound, husky Wednesday: Labrador retriever, poodle
(D) Monday: Labrador retriever, poodle Tuesday: greyhound, keeshond Wednesday: husky, schnauzer
(E) Monday: Labrador retriever, poodle Tuesday: husky, keeshond Wednesday: greyhound, schnauzer

Process of elimination.

- L and P must go together. This gets rid of A.
- G and H can't go together. This gets rid of C.
- If K is on Monday, then G is on Tuesday. This gets rid of B.
- If S is on Wednesday, then H is on Tuesday. This gets rid of D.

Having tested all the rules, the only remaining answer is E.

QUESTION 9

If the poodle is placed on Tuesday, then which one of the following could be true?

(A) The greyhound is placed on Monday.
(B) The keeshond is placed on Monday.
(C) The Labrador retriever is placed on Monday.
(D) The husky is placed on Tuesday.
(E) The schnauzer is placed on Wednesday.

If P is on Tuesday, then we know a lot. Not only does L have to go on Tuesday with P, but K can't be on Monday and S can't be on Wednesday, because the two conditional rules each put LP on a day other than Tuesday. So we know this, for starters:

M	T	W
	L	
	P	
~~K~~		~~S~~

There's only one day left for each of K and S. Once we place those, G and H can flip-flop in the remaining two spots. Like:

M	T	W
S	L	K
G/H	P	H/G

Great, let's answer the question. We're looking for something that could be true, which means we can probably eliminate four wrong answers that must be false.

A) This could be true in our diagram, so it must be the answer. But let's eliminate B-E just to be sure.
B) This is false; K is on Wednesday.
C) This is false; L is on Tuesday.
D) This is false, H can be either Monday or Wednesday, but not Tuesday.
E) This is false, S is on Monday.

Our answer is A.

QUESTION 10

If the greyhound is placed on the same day as the keeshond, then which one of the following must be true?

(A) The husky is placed on Monday.
(B) The Labrador retriever is placed on Monday.
(C) The keeshond is placed on Tuesday.
(D) The poodle is not placed on Wednesday.
(E) The schnauzer is not placed on Wednesday.

If G is with K, then K can't be Monday and S can't be Wednesday, because neither of those conditions led to G being with K. Placing GK on either Tuesday or Wednesday, we get these two scenarios:

S	G	L
H	K	P

(L	S)	G
(P ,	H)	K

Looking for a Must Be True...

A) No, H can be either Monday or Tuesday.
B) No, L can be any day.
C) No, K can be either Tuesday or Wednesday.
D) No, P can be any day.
E) Here we go. Yep, S can be either Monday or Tuesday, but not Wednesday.

Our answer is E.

QUESTION 11

If the husky is placed the day before the schnauzer, then which one of the following CANNOT be true?

(A) The husky is placed on Monday.
(B) The keeshond is placed on Monday.
(C) The greyhound is placed on Tuesday.
(D) The poodle is placed on Tuesday.
(E) The poodle is placed on Wednesday.

We've already seen two scenarios where H is placed the day before S. Once again, those are:

K	G	L
H	S	P
M	T	W

L	H	S
P	K	G
M	T	W

So we might not have to do any more work here. Let's use those two scenarios to try to eliminate four answer choices that *can* be true.

A) This can be true, according to the scenarios above.
B) This can be true, according to the scenarios above.
C) This can be true, according to the scenarios above.
D) This didn't happen in either of the scenarios above, so if we can get rid of E then this is our answer.
E) This happened in one of the scenarios above.

Our answer is D because we know that A, B, C, and E are all possible.

QUESTION 12

If the greyhound is placed the day before the poodle, then which one of the following CANNOT be placed on Tuesday?

(A) the husky
(B) the keeshond
(C) the Labrador retriever
(D) the poodle
(E) the schnauzer

We've seen three different ways that G can be placed on the day before P. Those look like this:

M	T	W
K	G	L
H	S	P

M	T	W
S	L	K
G	P	H

M	T	W
S	G	L
H	K	P

In those three scenarios, the dogs eligible to be placed on Tuesday are G, S, L, P, and K. So the answer *must* be H.

Sure enough, H is listed, so our answer is A.

QUESTION 8

Which one of the following must be true?

(A) The keeshond is not placed on the same day as the greyhound.
(B) The keeshond is not placed on the same day as the schnauzer.
(C) The schnauzer is not placed on the same day as the husky.
(D) The greyhound is placed on the same day as the schnauzer.
(E) The husky is placed on the same day as the keeshond.

Circling back to Question 8, we're confronted with a Must Be True. Let's dive right in.

A) No, we've seen K with G on a couple of occasions already.
B) Oh, yeah, this definitely has to be true. We made this inference before we even started the game. If we hadn't, we might need to do this question by process of elimination. Let's make sure we can get rid of C-E.
C) No, we've seen S with H a couple times.
D) We've seen G end up with S on several occasions, but they're not together in *every* instance. So this is out.
E) This also happens a lot, but it doesn't *always* happen.

Our answer is B, and we inferred it before the game even started.

We also confirmed that A, C, D, and E don't have to be true, so we're 200% confident choosing B here.

GROUP 5, GAME 4
EXTRA PRACTICE

During a certain week, an animal shelter places exactly six dogs—a greyhound, a husky, a keeshond, a Labrador retriever, a poodle, and a schnauzer—with new owners. Two are placed on Monday, two on Tuesday, and the remaining two on Wednesday, consistent with the following conditions:

The Labrador retriever is placed on the same day as the poodle.
The greyhound is not placed on the same day as the husky.
If the keeshond is placed on Monday, the greyhound is placed on Tuesday.
If the schnauzer is placed on Wednesday, the husky is placed on Tuesday.

7. Which one of the following could be a complete and accurate matching of dogs to the days on which they are placed?

(A) Monday: greyhound, Labrador retriever Tuesday: husky, poodle Wednesday: keeshond, schnauzer
(B) Monday: greyhound, keeshond Tuesday: Labrador retriever, poodle Wednesday: husky, schnauzer
(C) Monday: keeshond, schnauzer Tuesday: greyhound, husky Wednesday: Labrador retriever, poodle
(D) Monday: Labrador retriever, poodle Tuesday: greyhound, keeshond Wednesday: husky, schnauzer
(E) Monday: Labrador retriever, poodle Tuesday: husky, keeshond Wednesday: greyhound, schnauzer

8. Which one of the following must be true?

(A) The keeshond is not placed on the same day as the greyhound.
(B) The keeshond is not placed on the same day as the schnauzer.
(C) The schnauzer is not placed on the same day as the husky.
(D) The greyhound is placed on the same day as the schnauzer.
(E) The husky is placed on the same day as the keeshond.

9. If the poodle is placed on Tuesday, then which one of the following could be true?

(A) The greyhound is placed on Monday.
(B) The keeshond is placed on Monday.
(C) The Labrador retriever is placed on Monday.
(D) The husky is placed on Tuesday.
(E) The schnauzer is placed on Wednesday.

10. If the greyhound is placed on the same day as the keeshond, then which one of the following must be true?

(A) The husky is placed on Monday.
(B) The Labrador retriever is placed on Monday.
(C) The keeshond is placed on Tuesday.
(D) The poodle is not placed on Wednesday.
(E) The schnauzer is not placed on Wednesday.

11. If the husky is placed the day before the schnauzer, then which one of the following CANNOT be true?

(A) The husky is placed on Monday.
(B) The keeshond is placed on Monday.
(C) The greyhound is placed on Tuesday.
(D) The poodle is placed on Tuesday.
(E) The poodle is placed on Wednesday.

12. If the greyhound is placed the day before the poodle, then which one of the following CANNOT be placed on Tuesday?

(A) the husky
(B) the keeshond
(C) the Labrador retriever
(D) the poodle
(E) the schnauzer

GROUP 5, GAME 4
EXTRA PRACTICE

During a certain week, an animal shelter places exactly six dogs—a greyhound, a husky, a keeshond, a Labrador retriever, a poodle, and a schnauzer—with new owners. Two are placed on Monday, two on Tuesday, and the remaining two on Wednesday, consistent with the following conditions:

The Labrador retriever is placed on the same day as the poodle.
The greyhound is not placed on the same day as the husky.
If the keeshond is placed on Monday, the greyhound is placed on Tuesday.
If the schnauzer is placed on Wednesday, the husky is placed on Tuesday.

7. Which one of the following could be a complete and accurate matching of dogs to the days on which they are placed?

(A) Monday: greyhound, Labrador retriever Tuesday: husky, poodle Wednesday: keeshond, schnauzer
(B) Monday: greyhound, keeshond Tuesday: Labrador retriever, poodle Wednesday: husky, schnauzer
(C) Monday: keeshond, schnauzer Tuesday: greyhound, husky Wednesday: Labrador retriever, poodle
(D) Monday: Labrador retriever, poodle Tuesday: greyhound, keeshond Wednesday: husky, schnauzer
(E) Monday: Labrador retriever, poodle Tuesday: husky, keeshond Wednesday: greyhound, schnauzer

8. Which one of the following must be true?

(A) The keeshond is not placed on the same day as the greyhound.
(B) The keeshond is not placed on the same day as the schnauzer.
(C) The schnauzer is not placed on the same day as the husky.
(D) The greyhound is placed on the same day as the schnauzer.
(E) The husky is placed on the same day as the keeshond.

9. If the poodle is placed on Tuesday, then which one of the following could be true?

(A) The greyhound is placed on Monday.
(B) The keeshond is placed on Monday.
(C) The Labrador retriever is placed on Monday.
(D) The husky is placed on Tuesday.
(E) The schnauzer is placed on Wednesday.

10. If the greyhound is placed on the same day as the keeshond, then which one of the following must be true?

(A) The husky is placed on Monday.
(B) The Labrador retriever is placed on Monday.
(C) The keeshond is placed on Tuesday.
(D) The poodle is not placed on Wednesday.
(E) The schnauzer is not placed on Wednesday.

11. If the husky is placed the day before the schnauzer, then which one of the following CANNOT be true?

(A) The husky is placed on Monday.
(B) The keeshond is placed on Monday.
(C) The greyhound is placed on Tuesday.
(D) The poodle is placed on Tuesday.
(E) The poodle is placed on Wednesday.

12. If the greyhound is placed the day before the poodle, then which one of the following CANNOT be placed on Tuesday?

(A) the husky
(B) the keeshond
(C) the Labrador retriever
(D) the poodle
(E) the schnauzer

GROUP 5, GAME 5

Of the five Pohl children—Sara, Theo, Uma, Will, and Zoe—three are left-handed and two are right-handed. Each of the five children was born in a different one of seven calendar years, 1990 through 1996. The following conditions apply:

No two left-handed children were born in consecutive years.
No two right-handed children were born in consecutive years.
Sara, who is left-handed, was born before Uma.
Zoe was born before both Theo and Will.
A left-handed child was born in 1991.
Uma, who is right-handed, was born in 1993.

12. Which one of the following could be an accurate matching of each Pohl child with the year in which that child was born?

(A) Sara: 1990; Zoe: 1992; Uma: 1993; Will: 1994; and Theo: 1995
(B) Sara: 1991; Uma: 1993; Theo: 1994; Zoe: 1995; and Will: 1996
(C) Zoe: 1990; Sara: 1991; Uma: 1992; Theo: 1994; and Will: 1995
(D) Zoe: 1990; Sara: 1991; Uma: 1993; Theo: 1994; and Will: 1995
(E) Zoe: 1990; Sara: 1991; Uma: 1993; Theo: 1994; and Will: 1996

13. If Sara was born before Zoe was born, then which one of the following statements CANNOT be true?

(A) Will is left-handed.
(B) Zoe is left-handed.
(C) Theo was born after Will was born.
(D) Uma was born after Zoe was born.
(E) No child was born in 1990.

14. Which one of the following must be false?

(A) None of the children was born in 1990, nor was a child born in 1992.
(B) None of the children was born in 1992, nor was a child born in 1995.
(C) None of the children was born in 1994, nor was a child born in 1996.
(D) One of the children was born in 1990, and another in 1993.
(E) One of the children was born in 1993, and another in 1995.

15. If Theo was born after Will was born, then how many sequential orderings of the children, from firstborn to lastborn, are possible?

(A) one
(B) two
(C) three
(D) four
(E) five

16. If none of the children was born in 1995, then which one of the following statements must be true?

(A) Theo was born in 1994.
(B) Will was born in 1994.
(C) Will was born in 1996.
(D) Zoe was born in 1990.
(E) Zoe was born in 1994.

17. If Theo is right-handed, then each of the following statements must be false EXCEPT:

(A) Theo was born in 1996.
(B) Will was born in 1995.
(C) Uma was born exactly three years before Theo was born.
(D) Zoe was born exactly one year before Theo was born.
(E) Will is right-handed.

18. If Zoe was born before Uma was born, then which one of the following statements must be false?

(A) No child was born in 1992.
(B) No child was born in 1995.
(C) Theo is left-handed.
(D) Zoe is left-handed.
(E) Will is left-handed.

EXPLANATION

Whoa, what? Five kids in seven years, without any twins? Things have been busy in the Pohl household. Prodigious work by Mr.—and especially Mrs.—Pohl.

Anyway, consider this setup:

Two notes here: First, we've gone ahead and labeled the years from Year 0 to Year 6. We probably wouldn't bother writing the numbers if the list started with 1, but since it starts with 0 it seems safer to use labels. Second, we've added two Xs to our list of kids. These are the two miraculous years where the Pohls did *not* produce any spawn. (Maybe Mr. Pohl was on a submarine or something.) These Xs give us seven things for seven spots, which might be a bit easier to handle.

The first two rules are about the handedness of the kids, and look like this:

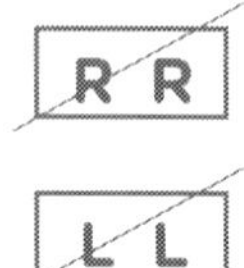

The third rule could look like this:

S U
L ... ___

And the fourth rule looks like this:

T
Z
W

The last two rules can be written directly into the diagram, like this:

			U			
	L		R			
0	1	2	3	4	5	6

Now, we get to make some inferences. Uma was mentioned in two separate rules, so let's start there. We know that S has to be before U, and we know that U was born in Year 3. So S has to be in year 0, 1, or 2. But S also has to be left-handed. And since Year 1 is a left-handed year, Years 0 and 2 can *not* be left-handed. This means there's only one spot for S: Year 1. Furthermore, since there's a left-handed kid in Year 1, and a right-handed kid in Year 3, Year 2 can't have any kid at all. That's one of our Xs.

Like this:

	S	X	U			
	L	X	R			
0	1	2	3	4	5	6
~~L~~		~~L~~		~~R~~		
		~~R~~				

This leaves us with two more left-handed children, and only three places (Years 4, 5, and 6) where they can possibly go. But since left-handed kids can't be born in consecutive years, they have to be born in Years 4 and 6. Let's write that in:

	S	X	U			
	L	X	R	L		L
0	1	2	3	4	5	6

And at that point, we've just about got it cracked. There's one more right-handed kid to place, and one more X. The only two years that don't have an X or a kid are Years 0 and 5. One of those years will have an X, and one will have an R. Let's go ahead and pencil out those two scenarios:

X	S	X	U			
X	L	X	R	L	R	L
0	1	2	3	4	5	6

	S	X	U		X	
R	L	X	R	L	X	L
0	1	2	3	4	5	6

Finally, we can consider the rule about Z, T, and W. In each of our two scenarios, we know exactly where Z goes, and T/W will flip-flop in the two remaining spots. Let's write those in:

X	S	X	U	Z	T/W	W/T
X	L	X	R	L	R	L

Z	S	X	U	T/W	X	W/T
R	L	X	R	L	X	L

Boom. As it turns out, there's not much flexibility in this game. There are only four total outcomes, and they fall neatly into two scenarios. Getting there was a decent amount of work, but that's *all* the work we're going to have to do for this game. With these two scenarios, we'll breeze through the questions without doing anything else. Watch.

QUESTION 12

Which one of the following could be an accurate matching of each Pohl child with the year in which that child was born?

(A) Sara: 1990; Zoe: 1992; Uma: 1993; Will: 1994; and Theo: 1995
(B) Sara: 1991; Uma: 1993; Theo: 1994; Zoe: 1995; and Will: 1996
(C) Zoe: 1990; Sara: 1991; Uma: 1992; Theo: 1994; and Will: 1995
(D) Zoe: 1990; Sara: 1991; Uma: 1993; Theo: 1994; and Will: 1995
(E) Zoe: 1990; Sara: 1991; Uma: 1993; Theo: 1994; and Will: 1996

Process of elimination.

- We made a nice inference that S has to go in Year 1 (1991, remember, not the first year), so let's test that first. This gets rid of A.
- U in Year 3. This gets rid of C.
- Z before T and W. This gets rid of B.
- Finally, let's look at the two blank spots. Our templates show that the two non-kid years have to be 0 and 2 or 2 and 5. This gets rid of D.

Our answer is E.

Notice that it precisely matches our second template, which makes it clear that we're on the right track.

QUESTION 13

If Sara was born before Zoe was born, then which one of the following statements CANNOT be true?

(A) Will is left-handed.
(B) Zoe is left-handed.
(C) Theo was born after Will was born.
(D) Uma was born after Zoe was born.
(E) No child was born in 1990.

If S is before Z, this puts us in our first template. Let's look for something that must be false in that template:

A) No, this can be true in Template 1.
B) This must be true in Template 1.
C) This can be true in Template 1.
D) This must be false in Template 1, so it will be our answer.
E) This must be true in Template 1.

Our answer is D, because it's the only one that cannot be true in Template 1.

QUESTION 14

Which one of the following must be false?

(A) None of the children was born in 1990, nor was a child born in 1992.
(B) None of the children was born in 1992, nor was a child born in 1995.
(C) None of the children was born in 1994, nor was a child born in 1996.
(D) One of the children was born in 1990, and another in 1993.
(E) One of the children was born in 1993, and another in 1995.

There's no point doing the "if" questions first on a game that we've dominated with templates and have basically mapped out every last possibility. There won't be any new diagrams to build to use down the line—we already made all of them. So let's use our templates to find something that must be false in both of them.

A) This can be true in Template 1.
B) This can be true in Template 2.
C) This can't be true in either template, so it's got to be the answer.
D) This can be true in Template 2.
E) This can be true in Template 1.

Our answer is C, because it's the only one that must be false in both templates.

QUESTION 15

If Theo was born after Will was born, then how many sequential orderings of the children, from firstborn to lastborn, are possible?

(A) one
(B) two
(C) three
(D) four
(E) five

Theo can be born after Will in both templates, and if it happened in either template, we would know the sequence of the five children precisely.

The sequences are different in the two templates, so our answer here is two, or B.

I almost feel bad for this question because we are so thoroughly destroying it. Not really though. It was asking for it.

QUESTION 16

If none of the children was born in 1995, then which one of the following statements must be true?

(A) Theo was born in 1994.
(B) Will was born in 1994.
(C) Will was born in 1996.
(D) Zoe was born in 1990.
(E) Zoe was born in 1994.

If no kids are both in 1995, this puts us in Template 2. Let's look for something that has to be true in this template.

A) No, Theo can be born in Year 4 or Year 6 in Template 2.
B) No, Will can also be born in Year 4 or Year 6 in Template 2.
C) Nope, see above.
D) Yes, this has to be true in Template 2.
E) No, this must be false in Template 2.

Our answer is D.

QUESTION 17

If Theo is right-handed, then each of the following statements must be false EXCEPT:

(A) Theo was born in 1996.
(B) Will was born in 1995.
(C) Uma was born exactly three years before Theo was born.
(D) Zoe was born exactly one year before Theo was born.
(E) Will is right-handed.

The only way Theo can be right-handed is in Year 5 in Template 1. We're looking for something that could be true in that specific scenario.

A) Nope. The only way for Theo to be right-handed is to be born in 1995.
B) No, if Theo is right-handed then he is born in 1995, nobody else.
C) No, U is 2 years before T in this scenario.
D) Yes, this not only could be true but *must* be true in order for T to be right-handed.
E) No, if T is right-handed then W is left-handed.

Our answer is D (for domination, which is totally what we're doing to this poor question).

QUESTION 18

If Zoe was born before Uma was born, then which one of the following statements must be false?

(A) No child was born in 1992.
(B) No child was born in 1995.
(C) Theo is left-handed.
(D) Zoe is left-handed.
(E) Will is left-handed.

If Z is before U, then we're in Template 2. Which one of the answers has to be false in this scenario?

A) This must be *true* in Template 2.
B) This also must be true in Template 2.
C) This must be true in Template 2 as well.
D) This is false in Template 2, so it's going to be our answer.
E) This must be true in Template 2.

Our answer is D, because it's the only one that must be false in Template 2.

GROUP 5, GAME 5
EXTRA PRACTICE

Of the five Pohl children—Sara, Theo, Uma, Will, and Zoe—three are left-handed and two are right-handed. Each of the five children was born in a different one of seven calendar years, 1990 through 1996. The following conditions apply:

No two left-handed children were born in consecutive years.
No two right-handed children were born in consecutive years.
Sara, who is left-handed, was born before Uma.
Zoe was born before both Theo and Will.
A left-handed child was born in 1991.
Uma, who is right-handed, was born in 1993.

12. Which one of the following could be an accurate matching of each Pohl child with the year in which that child was born?

(A) Sara: 1990; Zoe: 1992; Uma: 1993; Will: 1994; and Theo: 1995
(B) Sara: 1991; Uma: 1993; Theo: 1994; Zoe: 1995; and Will: 1996
(C) Zoe: 1990; Sara: 1991; Uma: 1992; Theo: 1994; and Will: 1995
(D) Zoe: 1990; Sara: 1991; Uma: 1993; Theo: 1994; and Will: 1995
(E) Zoe: 1990; Sara: 1991; Uma: 1993; Theo: 1994; and Will: 1996

13. If Sara was born before Zoe was born, then which one of the following statements CANNOT be true?

(A) Will is left-handed.
(B) Zoe is left-handed.
(C) Theo was born after Will was born.
(D) Uma was born after Zoe was born.
(E) No child was born in 1990.

14. Which one of the following must be false?

(A) None of the children was born in 1990, nor was a child born in 1992.
(B) None of the children was born in 1992, nor was a child born in 1995.
(C) None of the children was born in 1994, nor was a child born in 1996.
(D) One of the children was born in 1990, and another in 1993.
(E) One of the children was born in 1993, and another in 1995.

15. If Theo was born after Will was born, then how many sequential orderings of the children, from firstborn to lastborn, are possible?

(A) one
(B) two
(C) three
(D) four
(E) five

16. If none of the children was born in 1995, then which one of the following statements must be true?

(A) Theo was born in 1994.
(B) Will was born in 1994.
(C) Will was born in 1996.
(D) Zoe was born in 1990.
(E) Zoe was born in 1994.

17. If Theo is right-handed, then each of the following statements must be false EXCEPT:

(A) Theo was born in 1996.
(B) Will was born in 1995.
(C) Uma was born exactly three years before Theo was born.
(D) Zoe was born exactly one year before Theo was born.
(E) Will is right-handed.

18. If Zoe was born before Uma was born, then which one of the following statements must be false?

(A) No child was born in 1992.
(B) No child was born in 1995.
(C) Theo is left-handed.
(D) Zoe is left-handed.
(E) Will is left-handed.

GROUP 5, GAME 5
EXTRA PRACTICE

Of the five Pohl children—Sara, Theo, Uma, Will, and Zoe—three are left-handed and two are right-handed. Each of the five children was born in a different one of seven calendar years, 1990 through 1996. The following conditions apply:

No two left-handed children were born in consecutive years.
No two right-handed children were born in consecutive years.
Sara, who is left-handed, was born before Uma.
Zoe was born before both Theo and Will.
A left-handed child was born in 1991.
Uma, who is right-handed, was born in 1993.

12. Which one of the following could be an accurate matching of each Pohl child with the year in which that child was born?

(A) Sara: 1990; Zoe: 1992; Uma: 1993; Will: 1994; and Theo: 1995
(B) Sara: 1991; Uma: 1993; Theo: 1994; Zoe: 1995; and Will: 1996
(C) Zoe: 1990; Sara: 1991; Uma: 1992; Theo: 1994; and Will: 1995
(D) Zoe: 1990; Sara: 1991; Uma: 1993; Theo: 1994; and Will: 1995
(E) Zoe: 1990; Sara: 1991; Uma: 1993; Theo: 1994; and Will: 1996

13. If Sara was born before Zoe was born, then which one of the following statements CANNOT be true?

(A) Will is left-handed.
(B) Zoe is left-handed.
(C) Theo was born after Will was born.
(D) Uma was born after Zoe was born.
(E) No child was born in 1990.

14. Which one of the following must be false?

(A) None of the children was born in 1990, nor was a child born in 1992.
(B) None of the children was born in 1992, nor was a child born in 1995.
(C) None of the children was born in 1994, nor was a child born in 1996.
(D) One of the children was born in 1990, and another in 1993.
(E) One of the children was born in 1993, and another in 1995.

15. If Theo was born after Will was born, then how many sequential orderings of the children, from firstborn to lastborn, are possible?

(A) one
(B) two
(C) three
(D) four
(E) five

16. If none of the children was born in 1995, then which one of the following statements must be true?

(A) Theo was born in 1994.
(B) Will was born in 1994.
(C) Will was born in 1996.
(D) Zoe was born in 1990.
(E) Zoe was born in 1994.

17. If Theo is right-handed, then each of the following statements must be false EXCEPT:

(A) Theo was born in 1996.
(B) Will was born in 1995.
(C) Uma was born exactly three years before Theo was born.
(D) Zoe was born exactly one year before Theo was born.
(E) Will is right-handed.

18. If Zoe was born before Uma was born, then which one of the following statements must be false?

(A) No child was born in 1992.
(B) No child was born in 1995.
(C) Theo is left-handed.
(D) Zoe is left-handed.
(E) Will is left-handed.

GROUP 5, GAME 6

Each of exactly six lunch trucks sells a different one of six kinds of food: falafel, hot dogs, ice cream, pitas, salad, or tacos. Each truck serves one or more of exactly three office buildings: X, Y, or Z. The following conditions apply:

The falafel truck, the hot dog truck, and exactly one other truck each serve Y.
The falafel truck serves exactly two of the office buildings.
The ice cream truck serves more of the office buildings than the salad truck.
The taco truck does not serve Y.
The falafel truck does not serve any office building that the pita truck serves.
The taco truck serves two office buildings that are also served by the ice cream truck.

18. Which one of the following could be a complete and accurate list of each of the office buildings that the falafel truck serves?

(A) X
(B) X, Z
(C) X, Y, Z
(D) Y, Z
(E) Z

19. For which one of the following pairs of trucks must it be the case that at least one of the office buildings is served by both of the trucks?

(A) the hot dog truck and the pita truck
(B) the hot dog truck and the taco truck
(C) the ice cream truck and the pita truck
(D) the ice cream truck and the salad truck
(E) the salad truck and the taco truck

20. If the ice cream truck serves fewer of the office buildings than the hot dog truck, then which one of the following is a pair of lunch trucks that must serve exactly the same buildings as each other?

(A) the falafel truck and the hot dog truck
(B) the falafel truck and the salad truck
(C) the ice cream truck and the pita truck
(D) the ice cream truck and the salad truck
(E) the ice cream truck and the taco truck

21. Which one of the following could be a complete and accurate list of the lunch trucks, each of which serves all three of the office buildings?

(A) the hot dog truck, the ice cream truck
(B) the hot dog truck, the salad truck
(C) the ice cream truck, the taco truck
(D) the hot dog truck, the ice cream truck, the pita truck
(E) the ice cream truck, the pita truck, the salad truck

22. Which one of the following lunch trucks CANNOT serve both X and Z?

(A) the hot dog truck
(B) the ice cream truck
(C) the pita truck
(D) the salad truck
(E) the taco truck

EXPLANATION

Last game! Sweet. We've come a long way. There's nothing you need to know about the LSAT logic games that hasn't been covered in the 30 games in this book. Practice them until you've mastered them. If you can master these 30, then you've mastered the LSAT logic games.

Seriously, that is 100% true. You already bought this book so I'm not trying to sell you on this concept—you just need to believe it so that you will put in the practice time to get the score you deserve.

This is a fairly basic grouping game. Using Rule 1 as our guide, let's kick it off like this:

```
F H I P S T
                    ___
                     H
               ___  ___  ___
                     F
               ___  ___  ___
                X    Y³   Z
```

Six trucks, FHIPST, each of which visits one or more buildings. The first rule says that F, H, and exactly one other truck visit building Y. We've written the F and H right into the diagram, and added one more blank spot to building Y. We've also added a superscript "3" to building Y to make it ultra-clear that we've got exactly *one* more spot, no more and no less, that needs to be filled.

The next three rules can be added to the diagram like this:

```
F² H I P S T
                    ___
                     H
               ___  ___  ___
   I²,³ > S¹,²       F
               ___  ___  ___
                X    Y³   Z
                     T̸
```

Note that the ice cream truck can visit exactly two buildings if the salad truck only visits one; on the other hand, if the salad truck visits two buildings, then ice cream will have to visit all three.

The next rule leads to a nice inference. If F and P hate each other, but F has to visit exactly two buildings, then that means P must visit exactly one building. And since F already visits building Y, P can't go there.

That leaves building X and Z. F must visit one of those buildings, and P must visit the other. Like this:

P/F (crossed out)

X	Y^3	Z
	H	
F/P	F	P/F
	~~T~~ ~~P~~	

The next rule also leads to a nice inference. If T and I have to go together exactly twice, then they both have to visit both building X and building Z, because there's not room for them to go together in building Y (and T can never go to Y). We can write them in, like this:

X	Y^3	Z
T		T
I	H	I
F/P	F	P/F
	~~T~~ ~~P~~	

At this point, the only thing left to do is consider the third spot in the Y group. It can't be T, and can't be P; the only remaining players are I and S. Either one will work, so let's write that in:

X	Y^3	Z
T	I/S	T
I	H	I
F/P	F	P/F

That ought to take care of it. Let's tackle the questions.

QUESTION 20

If the ice cream truck serves fewer of the office buildings than the hot dog truck, then which one of the following is a pair of lunch trucks that must serve exactly the same buildings as each other?

(A) the falafel truck and the hot dog truck
(B) the falafel truck and the salad truck
(C) the ice cream truck and the pita truck
(D) the ice cream truck and the salad truck
(E) the ice cream truck and the taco truck

There's no list question, so we'll start with the game's lone "if" question. If the hot dog truck visits more buildings than the ice cream truck, then the hot dog truck must visit all three buildings, and ice cream can only visit two. That means the salad truck has to be the last truck that visits building Y. Like this:

X	Y³	Z
H		H
T	S	T
I	H	I
F/P	F	P/F

That will be all for the salad truck, since salad has to visit fewer buildings than ice cream (as it should be). We're asked to identify a pair of trucks that have to have exactly the same list of buildings. Let's see.

A) No, we don't know exactly where all the Fs are, so this can't be the answer.
B) Same explanation as A. We also know that F goes twice, while in this scenario S only goes once.
C) No, P only goes once, while I goes twice.
D) No, the salad truck visits building Y and I does not.
E) Yes. Both I and T visit buildings X and Z, and neither can visit building Y. So they have the exact same list.

Our answer is E.

QUESTION 18

Which one of the following could be a complete and accurate list of each of the office buildings that the falafel truck serves?

(A) X
(B) X, Z
(C) X, Y, Z
(D) Y, Z
(E) Z

In our starting diagram, we can see that the falafel truck has to visit building Y, along with *either* building X or Z and not both (because the falafel truck visits exactly two buildings.) This question is asking us which one "could be a complete and accurate list," so the answer must be either XY or YZ.

That makes D our answer.

Note that the answer would have been C if the question had asked "which one of the following *is* a complete and accurate list of all the buildings the falafel truck can visit." It's a subtle distinction, so make sure you can tell the difference. If not, hit me up at nathan@foxlsat.com. Operators are standing by. (Just kidding, I don't have operators. But I am happy to help.)

QUESTION 19

For which one of the following pairs of trucks must it be the case that at least one of the office buildings is served by both of the trucks?

(A) the hot dog truck and the pita truck
(B) the hot dog truck and the taco truck
(C) the ice cream truck and the pita truck
(D) the ice cream truck and the salad truck
(E) the salad truck and the taco truck

This question asks us for a pair of trucks that can't avoid visiting at least one building in common. Let's see:

A) No, H and P don't have to go together.
B) No, H and T don't have to go together either.
C) Yes. The ice cream truck has to visit both X and Z, and P must go to one of these two buildings. So we don't know exactly *which* building has an overlap between I and P, but we do know that there's an overlap. This will be our answer.
D) No, I and S don't have to overlap.
E) No, S and T don't have to overlap.

Our answer is C, because there's no way that I and P can 100% avoid each other.

QUESTION 21

Which one of the following could be a complete and accurate list of the lunch trucks, each of which serves all three of the office buildings?

(A) the hot dog truck, the ice cream truck
(B) the hot dog truck, the salad truck
(C) the ice cream truck, the taco truck
(D) the hot dog truck, the ice cream truck, the pita truck
(E) the ice cream truck, the pita truck, the salad truck

Let's start by thinking about which trucks *can't* visit all three buildings:

- F can't visit all three because it must visit exactly two.
- P can't visit all three because it hates F.
- S can't visit all three buildings because it has to visit less buildings than I.
- T can't visit all three buildings because it can't visit building Y.

So we're left with I and H. Either of these trucks can visit all three buildings. So if I, H is one of the answers, that's the one.

Sure enough, our answer is A.

QUESTION 22

Which one of the following lunch trucks CANNOT serve both X and Z?

(A) the hot dog truck
(B) the ice cream truck
(C) the pita truck
(D) the salad truck
(E) the taco truck

Last question! Congratulations for making it this far. By now, you've surely begun to realize that the LSAT's logic games are very learnable, if you put in the time and effort. I'm proud of you!

We're asked for a truck that can't serve both X and Z. The answer could be either F or P, since they both have to visit one, and not both, of these two buildings.

Since F isn't listed, our answer is C.

GROUP 5, GAME 6
EXTRA PRACTICE

Each of exactly six lunch trucks sells a different one of six kinds of food: falafel, hot dogs, ice cream, pitas, salad, or tacos. Each truck serves one or more of exactly three office buildings: X, Y, or Z. The following conditions apply:

The falafel truck, the hot dog truck, and exactly one other truck each serve Y.
The falafel truck serves exactly two of the office buildings.
The ice cream truck serves more of the office buildings than the salad truck.
The taco truck does not serve Y.
The falafel truck does not serve any office building that the pita truck serves.
The taco truck serves two office buildings that are also served by the ice cream truck.

18. Which one of the following could be a complete and accurate list of each of the office buildings that the falafel truck serves?

(A) X
(B) X, Z
(C) X, Y, Z
(D) Y, Z
(E) Z

19. For which one of the following pairs of trucks must it be the case that at least one of the office buildings is served by both of the trucks?

(A) the hot dog truck and the pita truck
(B) the hot dog truck and the taco truck
(C) the ice cream truck and the pita truck
(D) the ice cream truck and the salad truck
(E) the salad truck and the taco truck

20. If the ice cream truck serves fewer of the office buildings than the hot dog truck, then which one of the following is a pair of lunch trucks that must serve exactly the same buildings as each other?

(A) the falafel truck and the hot dog truck
(B) the falafel truck and the salad truck
(C) the ice cream truck and the pita truck
(D) the ice cream truck and the salad truck
(E) the ice cream truck and the taco truck

21. Which one of the following could be a complete and accurate list of the lunch trucks, each of which serves all three of the office buildings?

(A) the hot dog truck, the ice cream truck
(B) the hot dog truck, the salad truck
(C) the ice cream truck, the taco truck
(D) the hot dog truck, the ice cream truck, the pita truck
(E) the ice cream truck, the pita truck, the salad truck

22. Which one of the following lunch trucks CANNOT serve both X and Z?

(A) the hot dog truck
(B) the ice cream truck
(C) the pita truck
(D) the salad truck
(E) the taco truck

GROUP 5, GAME 6
EXTRA PRACTICE

Each of exactly six lunch trucks sells a different one of six kinds of food: falafel, hot dogs, ice cream, pitas, salad, or tacos. Each truck serves one or more of exactly three office buildings: X, Y, or Z. The following conditions apply:

The falafel truck, the hot dog truck, and exactly one other truck each serve Y.
The falafel truck serves exactly two of the office buildings.
The ice cream truck serves more of the office buildings than the salad truck.
The taco truck does not serve Y.
The falafel truck does not serve any office building that the pita truck serves.
The taco truck serves two office buildings that are also served by the ice cream truck.

18. Which one of the following could be a complete and accurate list of each of the office buildings that the falafel truck serves?

(A) X
(B) X, Z
(C) X, Y, Z
(D) Y, Z
(E) Z

19. For which one of the following pairs of trucks must it be the case that at least one of the office buildings is served by both of the trucks?

(A) the hot dog truck and the pita truck
(B) the hot dog truck and the taco truck
(C) the ice cream truck and the pita truck
(D) the ice cream truck and the salad truck
(E) the salad truck and the taco truck

20. If the ice cream truck serves fewer of the office buildings than the hot dog truck, then which one of the following is a pair of lunch trucks that must serve exactly the same buildings as each other?

(A) the falafel truck and the hot dog truck
(B) the falafel truck and the salad truck
(C) the ice cream truck and the pita truck
(D) the ice cream truck and the salad truck
(E) the ice cream truck and the taco truck

21. Which one of the following could be a complete and accurate list of the lunch trucks, each of which serves all three of the office buildings?

(A) the hot dog truck, the ice cream truck
(B) the hot dog truck, the salad truck
(C) the ice cream truck, the taco truck
(D) the hot dog truck, the ice cream truck, the pita truck
(E) the ice cream truck, the pita truck, the salad truck

22. Which one of the following lunch trucks CANNOT serve both X and Z?

(A) the hot dog truck
(B) the ice cream truck
(C) the pita truck
(D) the salad truck
(E) the taco truck

ACKNOWLEDGEMENTS

This book, comprised entirely of logic games, was far more difficult to produce than my previous five volumes and would not exist if it weren't for the help of a talented, international team. The reader, having come this far, might like a peek behind the curtain:

Ben Olson, my Washington, D.C. co-host on The Thinking LSAT Podcast (available on iTunes!), gave me the motivation to get started as well as the "groups" template on which to hang the book. I wrote a large chunk while traveling, and I distinctly remember writing a few of the initial explanations at an oceanside bar in Rincon, Puerto Rico, while drinking a pina colada. I typed on my Mac and sketched out the diagrams on whatever paper I had handy. More than once, this turned out to be a cocktail napkin. Ben's initial comments on this book were highly influential on the shape of the finished product, and on motivating me to get it done even while boozing by the beach.

Eric Uhlich, my amazing designer in Vancouver, deciphered my photographs of chicken scratches on cocktail napkins and turned them into the clear digital diagrams you see here. I can't imagine what this task must feel like for someone with no LSAT training (let alone interest). This book is clean, precise, and easy to use because of him.

Once we had a rough draft, I distributed the book to my current LSAT classes, online students, and the Thinking LSAT Podcast community. I'm grateful for the detailed feedback these early readers provided; the book benefitted immensely from your help. Countless people emailed me with notes and comments, created their own competing diagrams, scanned their feedback into PDFs, even handed me pages marked up with red pen and sticky notes. Overwhelmed, I didn't do much with this feedback for a few weeks. (Fine, months. I'm very lazy.) But this book wouldn't be the same without all of their generous time and help.

Ally Mushka, my apprentice LSAT tutor (also in Vancouver), took on this herculean task. She carefully considered each comment and distilled it down into a single list of edits. I dread this sort of detail-wrangling, but Ally did it with cheer. She also edited my explanations for content, making sure that I was not only getting the answers right, but for the right reasons. (I'm frequently wrong; thank god my team is there to save me.)

Mike Krolak, my college buddy and part-time roommate in Los Angeles, put the finishing touches on the book, and is wonderful at toning down my bullshit without killing my voice entirely. If you laughed while reading this book, but weren't too horribly offended, Mike was responsible for that.

You, dear reader, are the reason this book exists. Thank you for working so hard, and for trusting me with such an important step in your education and career.

Nathan Fox
Los Angeles, CA

NATHAN FOX

I took the official LSAT in February 2007 and scored 179. A month later, I was teaching an LSAT class in San Francisco for a well-known test prep company. I wasn't remotely qualified. Sure, I had a high score, but I had zero teaching experience and no intention of teaching permanently. I was only there to pick up some quick cash, and also, I was shitting my pants. I've always been an extremely nervous public speaker. I'd had about two weeks of training (which did not include meeting a single fellow employee in the flesh). I faced a room full of students paying a combined course fee of $30,000, and this sea of faces expected me to help them conquer the most important test of their lives. So the first words out of my mouth were these: "I'm contractually obligated *not* to tell you that you're my very first LSAT class... but um... yeah... you are."

Then the miracle happened, the one that would change my life forever: *They laughed.*

With that, I was hooked. Somehow I got great teaching evaluations from that first class, and got a raise. Then I got more terrific teaching evaluations, and got another raise. Then, about a year later, my employer told me I had maxed out; they just couldn't pay a teacher more than they were paying me. So I did some quick math, figured out how much they were making off my classes, and, having still never met another fellow employee face to face, I quit. I started Fox LSAT in the summer of 2009, between my first and second years of law school. And I've never looked back.

Nine years later, I have the greatest job in the world and feel like I'm finally learning to *teach* the LSAT. I've always been able to get the questions right. This shit just comes naturally to me. But I'm extremely grateful to my students for their patience as I've struggled to actually *explain* these things.

I welcome your feedback on this book. Please email nathan@foxlsat.com, or call or text 415-518-0630; that's my personal cell phone. And yes, I really will respond. I have the greatest gig in the world, and I wouldn't have it if it weren't for people like you, helping me get a little bit better every day.

Made in the USA
Coppell, TX
07 May 2022